Innovation Management and the Law

In economic theory and in management studies, innovation is widely regarded as the motor of economic activities and as being the primary source of renewal in the economic system. This view emphasizes how innovation work is organized in specialized teams inside the firm, or, alternatively, located to start-ups and similar small ventures that are strongly incentivized to innovate to survive. Rather than assuming that innovation work is a mere product of incentives provided by the market system, propelled by the individual and collective skills of the innovation team participants and the resources that they mobilize in their work, this volume examines how a market for innovation ideas is being constructed on the basis of policy making and legislative activities. *Innovation Management and the Law* examines how the idea of value creation is understood to be a matter of innovation activities and how such innovation activities are premised on legal rights that create not only incentives, corporations, and markets, but also more widely signal to market actors what kind of activities are consistent with policy makers' economic and social welfare objectives. The volume thus adds to the innovation management literature by introducing a comprehensive analysis of the patent system, illustrating that the patent system is itself an institution and that it should be examined in such terms when studying how innovations are generated on the basis of team production activities and legal rights that are enforceable. It will be of interest to researchers, academics, professionals, and advanced students in the fields of management, economic theory, and law.

Alexander Styhre is Chair of Management and Organization in the Department of Business Administration of the School of Business, Economics and Law at the University of Gothenburg, Sweden.

Routledge Studies in Management, Organizations and Society

This series presents innovative work grounded in new realities, addressing issues crucial to an understanding of the contemporary world. This is the world of organized societies, where boundaries between formal and informal, public and private, local and global organizations have been displaced or have vanished, along with other nineteenth century dichotomies and oppositions. Management, apart from becoming a specialized profession for a growing number of people, is an everyday activity for most members of modern societies.

Similarly, at the level of enquiry, culture and technology, and literature and economics, can no longer be conceived as isolated intellectual fields; conventional canons and established mainstreams are contested. *Management, Organizations and Society* addresses these contemporary dynamics of transformation in a manner that transcends disciplinary boundaries, with books that will appeal to researchers, students and practitioners alike.

Recent titles in this series include:

Organizations and Industry 4.0
Management Solutions Beyond Technology
Vojko Potočan, Kornélia Lazányi and Zlatko Nedelko

Social Impact, Organisations and Society
The Contemporary Role of Corporate Social Responsibility
Edited by Katarzyna Bachnik, Magdalena Kaźmierczak, Magdalena Rojek-Nowosielska, Magdalena Stefańska and Justyna Szumniak-Samolej

Innovation Management and the Law
An Institutional Approach
Alexander Styhre

For more information about this series, please visit: www.routledge.com/Routledge-Handbooks-in-Religion/book-series

Innovation Management and the Law

An Institutional Approach

Alexander Styhre

Routledge
Taylor & Francis Group
NEW YORK AND LONDON

First published 2025
by Routledge
605 Third Avenue, New York, NY 10158

and by Routledge
4 Park Square, Milton Park, Abingdon, Oxon, OX14 4RN

Routledge is an imprint of the Taylor & Francis Group, an informa business

ISBN: 978-1-032-60593-7 (hbk)
ISBN: 978-1-032-60692-7 (pbk)
ISBN: 978-1-003-46022-0 (ebk)

DOI: 10.4324/9781003460220

Typeset in ITC Galliard Pro
by Apex CoVantage, LLC

Contents

Preface

In economic theory, legal issues are conventionally regarded as either extra-disciplinary affairs (i.e., a question for legal scholars and other legal specialists to handle), or rendered fairly marginal as they are understood as what comes at the very of end of various commercial and business-related activities to be handled and sorted out. This negligence is perhaps justifiable in the former case as disciplinary specialization is widely understood as the pathway to a happy and successful career and life in the academy; in the latter case, it is merely a matter of professional ignorance as it is apparent that legality is at the very heart of commercial and business-related activities, not some kind of administrative afterthought. Therefore, the tendency in, e.g., business schools to entirely circumvent the question of legality and the role of laws and regulations, and to pass on the responsibility to examine these issues to law departments and law schools is both deplorable and in a sense an act of irresponsibility.

There is little value in having everyone striving to become legal experts, but to confuse elementary legal terms such as patents with economic terms such as innovations (as in the "patents-as-proxies-for-innovative-capacities" study design) is not entirely sustainable either. This volume presents an analytical framework wherein innovation work—the work to produce innovations individually, in a team-based production activity inside an organization, or in collaborative efforts between organizations—is being couched in a legal theory framework, legal institutionalism, so that the very idea of the patent and the patent system become both intelligible and analytically useful. That is, it is free for any scholar to use registered patents as any proxy for whatever they wish it would be, but such analytical models need to be faithful to the idea that the patent system is in fact developed on the basis of specific interests and policy goals in mind, and that these institutional conditions need to be understood by relevant actors so they are able to see both how the patent system operates in a real-world economy setting and what its shortcomings and limitations are. Therefore, to equate, e.g., patents and innovations as if a registered patent would be the antecedent of an innovation, is not only empirically incorrect but also inconsistent with legal theory. Some innovations are patented and some are not, and some patents results in an innovation materializing, whereas most patents on file do not; to reach this understanding of the cause and effects of the patent system, attention needs to be paid not only to details but also to a broader and more comprehensive view that locates the patent system in both an historical context (which shows that the patent system changes whenever there is sufficient political traction in the advocacy of legal reforms) and in a "synchronic" perspective, wherein patents are only one possible way to protect the work invested in developing innovations provided by the sovereign and legislative state. In the end, this exercise in reading and reviewing legal texts provides a more integrated view of how innovations are in fact the product (rather than the cause) of the legal system, which includes also the legal device of the patent qua intellectual property right.

This book is thus written with the ambition to make management studies scholars, economists, and economic sociologists a bit more concerned with the legality of the claims made regarding what an innovation is and what it is not. This does not suggest that there are no management studies scholars, economists, and economic sociologists who are informed about these conditions (they do exist, as a matter of fact), but that in general, it would be helpful if scholars in these disciplines would cease regarding legal questions as being dull and uneventful, and rather recognize them as the very basis for the advanced economic system that generates unprecedented levels of economic and social welfare on a day-to-day basis, at least for the last decades and century.

*****

A substantial part of this work was written during a sabbatical at Centre de Sociologie de l'Innovation, Mines Paris Tech (École des Mines) in Paris, October to December 2022. I would like to express my gratitude to the institute's director and especially Professor Fabian Mniesa for providing me with this chance to work at the Center for a period of time.

In June 2023, I was informed that I had been fortunate to be selected for the three-year Torsten Söderberg Research Professorship for the 2023–2026 period, and the completion of this work in the period July 2023 to February 2024 has been part of the research activities associated with this research grant. I am grateful for the Söderberg Foundation and their generous support for scholarly research work.

I would like to thank the commissioning editor Brianna Ascher at Routledge/Taylor & Frances for contracting this book. At my home department, the School of Business, Economics, and Law, University of Gothenburg, I would like to thank all of the colleagues whom I collaborate with in a number of research programs. This group includes Björn Remneland-Wikhamn, Sara Brorström, Kajsa Lindberg, Fredrik Lavén, and Sandra Samuelsson. Finally, I would like to thank Sara and my family for being supportive in every possible way.

1 Introduction

The legal basis of markets

Preamble: The November 2022 Theranos case verdict, the FTX bankruptcy, and the question of how to determine economic value

November 2022 was not a particularly good month for what Gittelman (2016: 1581) refers to as the "Silicon Valley model of entrepreneurship." On Friday, November 11, the cryptocurrency platform trade company FTX applied for a Chapter 11 bankruptcy reorganization (Bloomberg News, 2022. For an overview of cryptocurrency trade and its policy implications, see, e.g., Omarova, 2019, 2020). The following Friday, on November 18, Elizabeth Holmes, the once highly praised and esteemed entrepreneur and founder of the blood-testing technology Theranos was sentenced to an 11-year prison term by a court in San José, California (Paul, 2022). While John Carreyrou (2018) has accounted for the ghastly case of Theranos and Holmes's unusual but for long periods widely acclaimed entrepreneurial activities and business practices, the FTX case was now for the first time disclosed to a broader public. Just like in the Theranos case, wherein Holmes operated on the basis of braggadocio, legal threats to silence skeptics, and an aggressive management style to advance her interests and to pursue her career as some kind of female Steve Jobs figure,[1] what the investigators

1 As has been noted by several commentators, the Silicon Valley entrepreneurship model is heavily gendered, with male entrepreneurs, venture capital investors, and legal counsellors being overwhelmingly overrepresented (Snellman and Solal, 2023). For instance, "89 percent of VCs [venture capital investors] and 96 percent of senior partners in VC firms are male," Shapin (2020: 340) writes. There was thus a great deal of anticipation regarding the first female "super-entrepreneur" entering the scene, a condition that presumably contributed to the Theranos hype. The fact that Holmes was female does not justify that Theranos put not only the business goals and the money invested at peril but also the patients' health. "There have been other examples of Silicon Valley companies that rose meteorically, but none has put patients' health at risk," Eric Topol (2018: 308), executive vice-president of the Scripps Research Institute in La Jolla, California, writes in a commentary. Also Pollman (2019b: 206) remarks that "the blood-testing scandal" at Theranos "[h]armed not only investors and employees but also innocent third-party patients." "Holmes described the MiniLab [the trade name of the Theranos blood-testing device]

DOI: 10.4324/9781003460220-1

of FTX's business activities encountered was not exactly pretty. As the UK-based newspaper *The Guardian* reports, "In a stinging court filing posted on Thursday, John Ray III, the new boss of the bankrupt crypto exchange FTX, said the company had suffered an 'unprecedented and complete failure of corporate controls'" (Rushe, 2022a). "Ray has overseen some of the biggest bankruptcies ever, including the collapse of the energy giant Enron, and has 40 years of experience in restructuring companies. He said he had never seen anything as bad as FTX," *The Guardian* reporter continues (Rushe, 2022a). While being shrouded in secrecy during most of November 2022, the immediate period following the FTX bankruptcy filing, documents obtained by the *Financial Times* suggest FTX currently has $1 billion of liquid—i.e., easily sellable—assets, whereas the liabilities amount to $9 billion. It is expected that FTX has "more than one million creditors" (Rushe, 2022a).[2]

---

as 'the most important thing humanity has ever built,'" Topol (2018: 36) adds, but this statement was basically vacuous, a fact that Topol (2018: 308) is concerned with: "How did a company rise to a valuation of $9 billion in a network of so many influential people, even as people were endangered?" "In my view," Topol (2018: 308) continues, "letting this technology loose (despite grand claims) without a single publication by independent scientists, never mind replication, was a recipe for jeopardy. Had the medical community and regulators held the company accountable, this could have been pre-empted."

Given these concerns regarding patients' safety being jeopardized, it is ironic that the downfall of Theranos was not due to the reported violations of clinical laboratory regulations (which are associated with "virtually no whistleblower protection" [Rogal, 2021: 1675]), but on the basis of Theranos executives "defrauding investors," in contrast to clinical laboratory regulations violations being an area of law "that offers relatively strong whistleblower protection" (Rogal, 2021: 1675). You may put thousands of patients' safety and welfare at peril with impunity, but if you mislead investors, you are worse off, according to American state and federal law as it is written and enforced, Rogal (2021) shows.

In the end, the Theranos scandal was a most embarrassing case for anyone who acclaimed the new blood-testing technology *in blanco*, but who eventually carried no responsibilities for the $9 billion lost and the non-pecuniary reputational harm done to the Silicon Valley entrepreneurship system, nor the potential harm done to patients, which is most difficult to estimate *ex post* facto.

2 In her account of the emerging fintech industry, wherein the minting and trade of cryptocurrencies are included, the institutional embedding of the finance industry cannot be ignored. On the micro-level, Omarova (2019: 739) writes, "finance often appears primarily, if not purely, transactional: a matter of individualized private exchange among market actors." On the macro-level, however, modern finance is a matter "not only of great public importance but also of great public involvement" (Omarova, 2019: 739). Consequently, the analysis of fintech and its systematic consequences demands that legislators and regulatory agency officials recognize that "specific fintech applications affect the public's capacity to maintain the stability of the macro-environment" (Omarova, 2019: 755). For instance, the use of new cryptotechnology "enables private firms to synthesize tradable financial assets effectively out of thin air," thus being the culmination of a decades-long process of "virtualization of financial claims," which will "finally render financial markets *entirely* self-referential," Omarova (2019: 791) writes. As established fintech applications are exhibiting signs of "skewing the balance further in favor of private actors' unrestrained freedom to generate and over-generate financial risk" (Omarova, 2019: 742), such "hyper-fast, hyper-expansive financial markets" will require "a hyper-fast and hyper-capacious public actor of 'last resort,'" Omarova (2019: 780) proposes. Omarova (2019: 775) refers to the case of Bitcoin as a financial claim that is created without any "relation to the production of any actual goods or services in the nonfinancial economy." As a factual matter, the supply of Bitcoin "grows simply as a result of trading and transacting *in Bitcoin*"—it is, "an entirely self-referential and self-reproducing secondary-market phenomenon" (Omarova, 2019: 775). Consequently, the sheer scale and complexity of the financial market "effectively 'liberated' from

When the case was examined in court for the first time, the court was told that FTX's customers "were largely based offshore" in the Cayman and Virgin Islands, which accounted for "a third of customers" (Rushe, 2022b). The next two biggest customer bases were China and the UK (Rushe, 2022b). Whether these clients can acquire their wealth invested in cryptocurrencies remains unclear, but John Ray III said he had "substantial concerns" about the company's "financial statements," and that a "substantial portion" of assets held by FTX may be "missing or stolen" (Rushe, 2022a). Ray's declaration, made prior to the court hearing, was also echoed in the statement made by James Bromley, co-head of the restructuring practice at law firm Sullivan & Cromwell, in the court and before judge John Dorsey: "A 'substantial amount' of FTX Group's assets 'have either been stolen or are missing,'" Bromley said. "FTX was in the control of inexperienced and unsophisticated individuals, and some or all of them were compromised individuals." This use of the not entirely flattering adjectives "inexperienced" and "unsophisticated" presumably pertains to the "business practices" that John Ray III regarded as "unprecedented":

> "In the Bahamas, I understand that corporate funds of the FTX Group were used to purchase homes and other personal items for employees and advisors. I understand that there does not appear to be documentation for certain of these transactions as loans, and that certain real estate was recorded in the personal name of these employees and advisors on the records of the Bahamas," Ray wrote.
>
> (Rushe, 2022a)[3]

By the end of November 2022, two weeks after the bankruptcy was publicly announced, Sam Bankman-Fried, the former CEO and founder of FTX, the *wunderkind* who was—not entirely unlike Elizabeth Holmes—declared to be some "cryptocurrency genius" who would pave the way for new business

---

exogenously imposed constraints on its growth" are plausibly making financial markets "inherently more volatile and unstable," and consequently, both far more dependent on "public support and requiring far greater quantities of such support," Omarova (2019: 792) concludes. The FTX bankruptcy and the following court case are first-hand empirical evidence of the need for such "public support" in the event of specific financial claims failing to serve as intended.

3 These two empirical cases of failed business ventures may be indicative of a deeper challenge for the Silicon Valley model addressed by some scholars and the Silicon Valley actors they encounter in their fieldwork. As Bill Gurley, a general partner of venture capital firm Benchmark, said, "There's a systematic problem in Silicon Valley: the venture capitalist board members are finding [it] harder and harder to speak up and hold entrepreneurs responsible for financial performance" (cited in Pollman, 2019b: 206). Gurley lamented that Silicon Valley board rooms have today "mostly become applauding audiences of clapping hands," Pollman (2019b: 206) writes. "Recent examples of severe information problems and even fraud among the private company unicorns are not difficult to find," De Fontenay (2017: 499) writes, referring explicitly to the type of concerns that John Ray III raised regarding the FTX bankruptcy.

models and new ways of thinking of economic value, participated in the *New York Times*' DealBook Summit. According to Bankman-Fried's statement, it was apparent that his lawyers thought it was a good idea to have him clarify a few points after being widely criticized for being unhelpful in handling the new situation, including his Twitter (now X) message to a reporter, saying "F*** regulators, they make everything worse," which unsurprisingly acquired much attention (Rushe, 2022a). Unfortunately, Bankman-Fried's participation in the DealBook Summit did not seem to stem the tide, and at the same conference, the BlackRock CEO Larry Fink said that FTX's collapse was "the result of not just mismanagement, but bad behavior" (cited in Helmore, 2022). The CEO of the world's largest private investment fund also hinted that BlackRock, which had about $24 million invested in FTX, "may have been given misleading information" (cited in Helmore, 2022). Treasury secretary Janet Yellen said in turn that the FTX collapse was a " 'Lehman moment' for the crypto industry," and described cryptocurrencies as "very risky assets" (cited in Helmore, 2022).

On November 2, 2023, less than a year after the legal case was opened, Sam Bankman-Fried was "found guilty on all counts of defrauding his customers" in Manhattan federal court. Carl Tobias, the chair of the University of Richmond law school, made a statement on the evening of the same day that "he was not surprised the jury returned a verdict so quickly": "It was a compelling case that prosecutors assembled and put on," Tobias said. "I don't think anything that Bankman-Fried said undermined their case or gave the jury much pause. They came in with a strong verdict" (cited in Bekiempis, 2023). On March 28, 2024, Sam Bankman-Fried was sentenced to 25 years in prison by the New York Court. His lawyer "reiterated a pledge to appeal the sentence the same day" (Robins-Early, 2024).

Both the Theranos case, which ended with disgrace, the loss of billions of US dollars—that could have been invested in other productive innovation management activities—and lengthy prison terms (Rogal, 2021), and the FTX case, which included considerable financial capital losses and a loss in faith in cryptocurrencies as a robust storage of economic value, beg the question of what economic value is, at the end of the day, and beyond and above all the technical terms that can be invoked to vindicate such a term and its use. In both cases, billions of value were being accounted for, largely in terms of expectations regarding future revenues (as in the case of Theranos), or on the basis of the presumption that faith in the cryptomarket would remain imperturbable over business cycles, thus making also unorthodox IOUs a safe storage of economic wealth (as in the case of FTX), but then suddenly these values simply were no more. Like the Cheshire cat, they disappeared, but unlike in Lewis Carroll's story, it is not a smile that remains when the cat and the economic value have disappeared, but only a long series of legal investigations and painful court appearances.

The legal constitution of market and market entities: an empirical illustration

It is apparent that there is some kind of accounting-based idea regarding economic value, but such a construct is derived from within a theoretical and legal-political framework that at this point has already made a considerable number of assumptions regarding what value is. In more epistemic terms, would it be possible to define economic value outside of such a more narrow theoretical and legal-political framework? If such an analysis starts within an existing market, i.e., an economic theory of economic value is being sought for, it is apparent that the market system itself cannot serve as the basis for a proper answer to this question, or providing these services as value is a matter of marginal utility, and marginal utility is not possible to calculate outside of the specific context: "According to the orthodox [economic theory] view, which defines value subjectively by the principle of marginal utility, *real* value on the market does not exist," Reinecke (2010: 564) writes. That is, if markets that enable and facilitate transactions cannot support this pursuit to formulate a solid definition of economic value, then more specific empirical domains need to be explored. Then let us consider, say, the market for reproductive medicine services as that is an exemplary case of a recently established market wherein the marginal utility and price elasticity of the services acquired are remarkably high. To become a parent is not everyone's wish, nor is it a human right, but advances in the technoscientific biosciences have resulted in clinical applications that can help sub-fertile couples and single women become parents through in-vitro fertilization (see e.g., Styhre and Arman, 2016). Vertommen, Pavone, and Nahman (2022: 114) report that "according to recent studies," the global fertility market is estimated to become "a US$40 billion market by 2026." That is, the willingness to pay for in-vitro fertilization services to become parents is considerable, and to become a parent is largely a high marginal utility affair: either you become a parent or the in-vitro fertilization cycle fails. Anyway, when examining what Vertommen, Pavone, and Nahman (2022) refer to as *global fertility chains*, it is apparent that the human gametes such as oocytes (eggs) and sperm acquire their economic value within the specific legal and political framework that enables IVF clinics to operate, not the least because this business manages to transcend or to circumvent the regular meaning of work. Vertommen, Pavone, and Nahman (2022) argue:

> Under capitalist modes of accumulation, processes of ovulation, gestation, and parturition are not valued as labor, neither in their unpaid form as motherhood and "natural" pregnancy nor in their commodified form as commercial surrogacy or egg cell provision. In the surrogacy and egg-providing industries we have researched, where reproductive labor is

> one of the obvious sources of profit, we witnessed how fertility brokers still use the language of donation, gift-giving, or altruism to promote their services.
>
> (Vertommen, Pavone, and Nahman, 2022: 123–124)

Several other students of reproductive medicine, including the study of the trade of human gametes, account for this contradiction (e.g., Almeling, 2011) and show how something being almost invaluable or priceless for the childless couple is at the same time degraded to be non-economic in quality, i.e., to be either described in quasi-theological and saintly terms (in the case of female egg donors "giving the gift of life"), or, in sharp contrast, described in more lighthearted and humorous terms regarding male sperm donors ("making money never felt so good," one sperm bank announced in one of its advertisements, intended to recruit new donors). In this industry, economic value, social norms, national and international legislation, and transnational regulatory rules, and allegedly non-valuable biological entities (human gametes) are aligned in a manner that is, if nothing else, intellectually intriguing. Consider, for instance, how Israeli IVF clinics rely on Georgian women to supply oocytes to maintain their business activities:

> In Georgia, Israeli surrogacy agencies cooperate with a local fertility agency and with a medical clinic. Some Israeli surrogacy brokers contract professional couriers to ship the frozen sperm, egg cells, or embryos to their Georgian counterpart, while others save costs by personally delivering the reproductive materials, transported in carry-on cryopreservation tanks on a regular passenger flight.
>
> (Vertommen, Pavone, and Nahman, 2022: 122)

Fair enough, to have babies made, there need to be some supply-chain management activities in place, and Georgia is apparently a place as good as any to supply from, according to Israeli IVF clinic executives' assessment. The interesting thing is still how the providers of the human gametes are supplying biological material that only has an economic value within this idiosyncratic supply-chain framework. Vertommen, Pavone, and Nahman (2022: 128) write:

> [O]ocytes have almost no economic value upon extraction from a donor when they are framed as a gift or as "surplus" or "waste" material from fertility clinics. Yet, when sold as "Caucasian Ivy League eggs" by fertility agencies, or turned into patentable stem cell lines by biotech companies, their value increases.
>
> (Vertommen, Pavone, and Nahman, 2022: 128)

That is, there is an almost magical transformation of what the Georgian female donor supplies—her highly valued eggs, painful and uncomfortable as it is to extract them from the ovaries, another feature of the industry that several scholars pay attention to (Oberman, Wolf, and Zettler, 2010; Elster, 2010; Ikemoto, 2009)—and what is basically framed within a gift culture or barter economy system, otherwise being regarded as archaic (see e.g., Fontaine, 2014; Sahlins, 1972), whereas when arriving at the site of the IVF clinic, such human gametes suddenly acquire a considerable economic value for the IVF clinic.

The point to be made in this volume is that this transformation from "gift" (wherein sperm donors are barely deemed to make the sacrifices that are described by the quasi-theological vocabulary) to "economic asset"—a "process of assetization," for some scholars such as Birch (2017) and Golka (2023)—is no miracle work. This trade is of course embedded in a narrative that rests on a deontic vocabulary that addresses moral and ethical issues and beliefs, and a theological vocabulary that invokes goodness and gift-giving as social virtues to be honoured via participation in IVF industry activities, but what truly matters is the legislation and the regulatory rules that structure and shape, e.g., the commercial branches of reproductive medicine. That is, economic value can be construed on the basis of various economic and accounting-based theories (e.g., economic value is premised on the marginal utility derived from the access to specific resources), or on the basis of deontic and theological vocabularies (e.g., economic value derived from the sense of the moral righteousness of giving to charities, or on the basis of a sense of being part of a higher purpose), but such storytelling is only complementary and secondary to the legal rights that define and generate economic value.

In the two failed business venture cases of the Silicon Valley entrepreneurship model, the work conducted by Theranos and FTX and the enormous values they acquired and were associated with were ultimately grounded in the work conducted by the sovereign state wherein these business entities were domiciled. Without the legal framework that would recognize blood-testing technologies (via the patent system, examined in Chapters 3 and 4 in this volume), or the intricate technological system that generates cryptocurrencies and their trade, there would be no economic value to account for. That is, rather than turn to economic theory to define economic value—which would only generate a self-referential and recursive definition of economic value (Muniesa, 2022: 749)—it is analytically useful to turn to legal texts as the claim to economic value, and the assets that embody these values (say, in the currency system) ultimately are not an *economic* but a *legal* matter. This claim may appear to be counterintuitive, but economic affairs are of necessity grounded in legal rights, and legal rights are dependent on political power, which in turn is dependent on an allocation of power being consistent with social norms. That is, what at first sight appears to be a question of economic interests only is often on closer inspection premised on legal conditions and legal rights, which are not just emerging *ex nihilo*, but being created by intelligent men and women to assist what they regard as reasonable objectives, and what they believe is conducive to net economic and social welfare. This means that legal rights are at the core of any economic theory that is formulated on the basis of the work to understand or to explain why certain innovation projects are successful, while others fail.

To define economic value creation

Muniesa (2017: 445) addresses the issue of what the commonplace expression "value creation" denotes in a substantive meaning of the term. "Of the many ideas that control economic reasoning and the policies that go with it, that of 'value creation' is certainly a most intriguing one," Muniesa (2017: 445) writes. He (2017: 445) continues: "Something called 'value' is assumed to be 'created' and this essentially virtuous process is supposed to guide not only economic conduct but the orientation of the transformation of the world altogether." In this understanding of the expression, value creation is not simply a semantic term, used to denote how economic value can be generated through specific and often highly coordinated practices, but value creation serves as some assertorial claim that such value creation activities need to be honoured and respected, or else such benefits may be lost. At the same time as this expression is bestowed with a certain halo, as it purports to apprehend the very basis for economic welfare, it is a term that is "under pressure," Muniesa (2017: 447) proposes: value creation is "marked by a tension" between, on the one hand, a primary, strictly financial meaning that "refers quite straightforwardly to the idea of making money," and, on the other hand, "the properly demiurgic idea of the production of a substance—'value'—that augments the social world and whose virtuous character is undeniable" (Muniesa, 2017: 447). In the former case, value creation is a technical and analytical term, derived from a finance industry vocabulary, embedded in and engrained with the *métier* to manage a stock of financial assets; in the latter case, the expression has teleological overtones inasmuch as the creation of value is advocated as the sole legitimate purpose of human societies.

Ortiz's (2014) study of French asset-based securities (ABS) traders illustrates how finance theory is both based on an epistemic vocabulary (i.e., terms that pertain to what is knowable) and a deontic vocabulary (i.e., terms that pertain to what is morally and ethically correct or desirable), and how these two vocabularies are entangled in ways that make it difficult to separate them whenever that would be useful or necessary (as during and after financial crises, when the costs to restore the faith in financial markets via so-called *ex post* resolution systems are allocated between, e.g., market actors and tax-payers; see, e.g., Levitin, 2011). Ortiz accounts for an anecdote from his fieldwork as the assistant of one financial trader:

> In the last month of my internship, Marie [a finance trading manager] introduced me to several employees of the company whom I could interview. While writing an e-mail message to them, she asked me to tell her the subject of my research. When I said I was studying "the definition of *value*," she frowned and corrected me while continuing to write: "We will say that you are doing research on the creation of value."
>
> (Ortiz, 2014: 46)

This may appear to be a minor drift in how terms are examined from a semantic perspective, but Ortiz (2014) argues that the "definition of value" and the "creation of value" denotes two entirely different views of the traders' work in the traders' minds: "In this widespread usage, creating value for one's clients or for one's company meant generating monetary profits for them. Given the remuneration system, it also meant potentially increasing one's own revenues," Ortiz (2014: 46) writes. In addition, Ortiz (2014: 46) continues, the expression "creation of value" has "a moral and political content linked to its genealogy in liberal doctrines":

> In that context, saying, as I did clumsily, that value was "defined," I missed the ontology on which its moral and political content rests, which implies that the value talked about really exists and can be created by the financial industry. The concept of value creation operates thus as an anchor for the techniques of valuation and investment, and for the justification of their distributive effects.
>
> (Ortiz, 2014: 46)

In this view, the finance theory framework that includes concepts, methods, and calculative practices is not only "tools of the trade" (Beunza and Stark, 2004) that carries significant epistemic authority, but it is also associated with moral and ethical beliefs that are closely bound up with this epistemological (or even ontological) understanding of financial trade as having the undeniable "virtuous character" that Muniesa (2017: 447) speaks of as the basis for the authority of financial institutions and finance market actors more widely. However, while this bundling and braiding of epistemological and deontic vocabularies may help creating professional role confidence (Cech, Rubineau, Silbey, and Seron, 2011) for financial traders, who are constantly reminded of the abstract and "speculative" nature of their work (basically being the work to trade and allocate calculated risks; see, e.g.,

Lépinay, 2011; de Goede, 2005), Ortiz (2014) is still concerned that financial traders can preserve a secrecy in their trade even though it generates externalities and that, in the long-term perspective, result in a democratic deficit—outcomes that no changes in the semantic meanings of key analytical terms can remedy:

> Instead of free citizens acting in open arenas obtaining material justice and equality, as is stated in liberal theory, we observe employees following bureaucratic procedures within institutions, access to which is extremely limited to a small minority, while the rest of the population has little or no agency in the process, and global inequalities remain the result.
>
> (Ortiz, 2014: 47)

This tension is of relevance for what Muniesa (2017: 445) refers to as the "three fundamental concepts of our liberal economic order": "innovation, finance and democracy." Although innovation and finance are largely bundled into a complex that is difficult to disentangle—innovation in finance is commonplace, and innovation in all business areas is determined by financial resources to fund the development work—how this complex or assemblage relates to the political system of democracy is less clear at first glance. Under all conditions, the first two terms relate to economic affairs, and thus to the domain of economic welfare, wherein the concept of democracy is an entirely different question, introducing social norms and social welfare as relevant parameters when examining what value creation would mean in substantive and practical terms. As will be argued in this volume, the connections between economic affairs (e.g., innovation and finance) and political issues are mediated and bridged by legal activities and legislation, and more specifically what is here referred to as a legal institutionalism framework.

To illustrate the issue at hand, mainstream neoclassical economic theory and its conventional wisdom regarding the role of markets and market creation are examined. William Baumol (2002) speaks of the "free market" as an "innovation machine," which indicates that he regards what he portrays as "the growth miracle" of the period, say, since 1800 until today, as being a matter of capitalist markets operating at their very best capacity. Such a description may be relevant and even true on an aggregated level *ex post*, when all of the mechanisms and devices that enable and support innovations to be developed and economic growth to be registered and accounted for are in place, but it is still a most vague assertion that "capitalist markets" make all of this happen, as neither "capitalism" nor "markets" are fixed things, but terms that denote complex socio-economic and political-legal conditions, and processes that generate a variety of outcomes, whereof, e.g., innovations and economic growth are of particular interest here. When delving into the details that are part of this declared growth miracle, it is evident that the market is not the primus motor of such accomplishments. This does not mean that markets and market-making do not matter—in fact, they do—but the assertion that such markets would singlehandedly accomplish anything miraculous is not a plausible proposition as markets cannot be assumed to be the antecedent of economic growth, i.e., what exists prior to the various activities that eventually generated such economic growth being accounted for and praised.

The question of market competition and the role of innovation

The question then is what the true primus motor of innovative output and economic growth would be if the market system is an implausible candidate. Richard Nelson (2022), a renowned economist with innovation management as his specialty, has recently accounted for the fallacy to believe that markets are the antecedents of a variety of economic benefits and accomplishments being recognized. Rather than speaking directly of the market, Nelson addresses the derivative concept of *competition*, which is held in esteem by proponents of neoclassical economic theory as the very basis for human accomplishments as competition is treated as what provides incentives to self-discipline human agents, and to make them perform at the very top of their capacity. "Virtually all advocates of private enterprise and markets recognize the importance of competition in spurring and constraining for-profit firms to keep prices in line with costs and pressuring them to try to meet user demands," Nelson (2022: 596) writes. Nelson (2022: 604) does not share this belief in the foundational role of competition, but instead argues that there is an "[o]versimplified understanding of how our economies actually are structured and how they work." More specifically, Nelson (2022) argues that the role of the state, ideally represented by democratic entities such as the government, parliaments, and the legislative bodies and regulatory agencies that they oversee, is largely undervalued and underappreciated in terms of the importance among many scholars, and among economists in particular. Nelson refers to the concept of innovation as an illustrative case of how the role of the government is marginalized in most scholarly accounts:

> [W]hile most people tend to think of innovation as something that is done by private profit-seeking firms and entrepreneurs, the institutions supporting and orienting innovation include universities, governmental agencies and laboratories, scientific and technical societies, foundations, the roles and importance of which vary greatly across different fields and industries where innovation is going on.
>
> (Nelson, 2022: 600)

In fact, this specific domain of practice in the economic system does not differ from how other domains are organized and monitored. However, Nelson (2022: 603–604) writes:

> there is little explicit recognition that only a small portion of the economy is organized and governed through market structures that look like the textbook model, or that virtually all economic activities are associated in some degree with one or more of the conditions that cause unadulterated market organization to be infeasible or socially problematic.

That is, many scholars and other analysts prefer to maintain their favoured theoretical idea regarding how the economy operates, rather than examine how it operates in practice in a real-world economy. That is why highly abstract and in many cases intuitively questionable ideas regarding "rational" and even "self-regulating" markets have been associated with a certain authority over the last five decades. This view of the market is a centerpiece in the neoclassical economic theory model that describes the economy in both analytical and normative terms. Following the 2008 financial crisis, and not the least the growth of, e.g., synthetic cryptocurrencies and other digitally generated market devices, ranging from so-called smart contract (Cong and He, 2019; Young, 2018) to fintech mortgage lending activities (Berg, Fuster, and Puri, 2022; DiMaggio and Yao, 2021; Tantri, 2021), this post–World War II theory doctrine is gradually losing its authority and relevance (Chwieroth and Walter, 2022; Gorton, 2018; Wolfson and Epstein, 2013; Reinhart and Rogoff, 2009). Instead of regarding the market as some kind of first and indisputable ground for economic practices, and the structural features they generate in the market context, the analysis is shifting back to the role of the state, and more specifically its legislative capacities and practices.

"Economic theories of the firm often proceed in an institutional and legal vacuum, downplaying the role of law and state institutions," Pargendler (2021: 726) writes. Economists have largely considered their own discipline as being sufficiently conceptually contentful to be able to address all of the intricacies of an advanced economic system, and without any input from adjacent disciplines such as political science, legal studies, psychology, or sociology. Fourcade, Ollion, and Algan (2015: 92) account for the insularity of the discipline of economics, and show that when measuring so-called "within-field citations," economics "[s]tands out markedly," with 81% of within-field citations in 1997, whereas other disciplines such as sociology (with 52% within-field citations), anthropology (at 53%), and political science (at 53%) were less insular in their scholarly orientation. In particular, in this context, the negligence regarding legal scholarship has arguably resulted in economic theory being underdeveloped in terms of the capacity to recognize the role played by the legislative and regulatory state. As a consequence, economic theory has failed to account for "the importance of states" that serve to provide "fertile conditions for economic growth through the creation and maintenance of institutions, including adequate legal and regulatory frameworks, counter-cyclical demand stimulation, reliable information diffusion, a skilled and healthy workforce, and new technology development," in Hamm, King, and Stuckler's (2012: 301) summary statement.

At the same time, research has been conducted in the discipline of economics that recognizes the role of the patent system (which is a creation of the sovereign state in collaboration with transnational governance organizations, TGOs) in supporting innovation work activities and innovation output, and that in turn contributes to economic growth and economic welfare (see, e.g., Moser, 2016). Kogan, Papanikolaou, Seru, and Stoffman (2017) examine the firm-level consequences of innovation investment and output and economic growth, and find a positive relationship. As an empirical condition, after 1980, there is "a rapid acceleration" of the number of patents granted in the US. Such changes in patenting activity may be explained by both the pace of technological innovation and/or by changes in "the legal environment" (Kogan, Papanikolaou, Seru, and Stoffman, 2017: 703). At the same time, researchers have observed a "secular increase in the ratio of R&D to patents," i.e., companies receive a marginally lower return on the funds committed to innovation work, being the antecedent of patents applied for and registered (Kogan, Papanikolaou, Seru, and Stoffman, 2017: 703). Some explanations for this secular increase of the R&D/patent ratio have been considered in several structural models used, including a decline in the productivity in the research sector and a decline in the patenting rate due to increased costs of patenting (Kogan, Papanikolaou, Seru, and Stoffman, 2017: 703).

To examine how patenting activity may predict corporate performance over time, Kogan, Papanikolaou, Seru, and Stoffman (2017: 666) combine a novel data set that includes patent grants over the period 1926 to 2010 and stock market data. Stock market data have the advantage that "set prices are forward-looking," and hence provide the analysts with "an estimate of the private value to the patentholder" being based on *ex ante* information. Importantly, such a "private value" does not necessarily "coincide with the scientific value of the patent" (which is typically assessed by the counting of forward patent citations). This means, for instance, that a patent may represent only "a minor scientific advance," yet the patent may be very effective in restricting competition, and thus generate "large private rents" (Kogan, Papanikolaou, Seru, and Stoffman, 2017: 666). Based on this study design, Kogan, Papanikolaou, Seru, and Stoffman (2017: 667) find that the patent-level estimates of economic value "are strongly positively related to forward citations." This correlation is also robust to a number of "patent- and firm-level controls" (Kogan, Papanikolaou, Seru, and Stoffman, 2017: 667). This means in practical terms that one additional patent citation is associated with "an increase of 0.1% to 3.2% in the economic value of a patent" (Kogan, Papanikolaou, Seru, and Stoffman, 2017: 667). That is, firms that innovate acquire a higher market valuation than companies that do not innovate:

> Firms that experience a one standard deviation increase in their innovation output experience higher growth of 2.5% to 4.6% over a period of five years. Conversely, firms that fail to innovate in an industry that experiences a one standard deviation increase in its innovative output experience lower growth of 2.7% to 5.1% over the same horizon.
>
> (Kogan, Papanikolaou, Seru, and Stoffman, 2017: 667)

The estimates thus suggest that "differences in innovative outcomes can account for a substantial fraction of *ex post* differences in firm growth rates" (Kogan, Papanikolaou, Seru, and Stoffman, 2017: 700). Furthermore, and equally important, in addition to firm growth, Kogan, Papanikolaou, Seru, and Stoffman (2017: 667) find similar effects on "revenue-based total factor productivity (TFPR)" in the economy. This means that the aggregated rate of innovative output is associated with "significant resource reallocation and growth," which is indicative of how economic resources are put to use in an efficient manner if the "innovation and patenting" activity can be upheld.

Given such evidence that the patent system does matter for innovative activities and output, in this volume, the legal device of the patent will be examined as a specific form of legal coding (with Pistor's, 2019, key term) that serves as a central mechanism in generating the outcomes that Baumol (2002) describes as being miraculous. The point being made here is that in the production of what the pragmatist analytical philosopher Wilfrid Sellars (1956) refers to as rational empirical knowledge, there is no need for introducing theological or mysticism concepts such as miracles to explain how innovations are produced, or on what basis economic growth is generated. Rather than staring into the skies to find an answer to what may be regarded as existential or cosmological questions, it is better to look into law journals and legal scholarship studies, as they examine the mechanisms and devices that both propel and stabilize economic activities and the economic growth they generate.

The moderate economic theory view of market efficiency

Most mainstream economists and other scholars who are informed about economic affairs are skeptical regarding an economic theory that defines rationality backwards on the basis of daring conjectures and propositions regarding original markets that bestow the gift of rationality on the market actors who eventually populate these allegedly spontaneous orders. Says economist and institutionalist and the Bank of Sweden's Nobel Memorial Prize laureate Douglass North:

> It is necessary to dismantle the rationality assumption underlying economic theory in order to approach constructively the nature of human learning. History demonstrates that ideas, ideologies, myths, dogmas, and prejudices matter; and an understanding of the way they evolve is necessary for further progress in developing a framework to understand societal change.
>
> (Douglass North, cited in Burk, 2016: 428, footnote 27)

In a similar vein, Robert C. Merton, another stellar economist and the Bank of Sweden's Nobel Memorial Prize laureate, shares such beliefs:

> [I] believe that financial models based on frictionless markets and complete information are often inadequate to capture the complexity of rationality in action. For example, in the modern tradition of finance, financial economic organizations are regarded as existing primarily because of the functions they serve and are, therefore, endogenous to the theory. Yet, derived rational behavior in a perfect-market setting rarely provides explicit and important roles for either financial institutions, complicated financial instruments and contracts, or regulatory constraints, despite their observed abundance in the real financial world.
>
> (Merton, 1987: 484)

Rather than defining rationality as what is generated within the market practices that are reproduced when transacting, rationality needs to be defined as not only instrumental and calculative practices, but to also include and recognize social norms and beliefs, as suggested by Burk (2016). Unlike calculative practices, premised on the capacity to access reliable data that mirror actual conditions, or are otherwise useful, social norms and beliefs are never fully complete or absolutely true, and yet they are the scripts upon which human beings and, of specific interest here, market actors operate:

> We live in a society in which . . . justifying myths are frequent, ubiquitous, and pervasive: hard work pays off in the end, all men are created equal, free enterprise leads to prosperity, honesty is the best policy, and untold similar cultural tropes are generally and reflexively assumed in social action. . . . Most such assumptions are probably wrong at some level, and many seem demonstrably false. Certainly very few such assumptions are likely to be empirically verified.
>
> (Burk, 2016: 427–428)

To be rational and reasonable is not to put on display some superior and extraordinary calculative practices to be able to perform at the top of the game chosen to be included in, but to be able to navigate in an economic landscape wherein all kinds of rationalities, norms, and beliefs co-exist and jointly contribute to an economic reality and economic welfare that benefits, if not all, at least most of society's members.

If the economic theory standard explanation for how markets emerge (they are already in place, plain and simple) and how they operate (they are always perfectly information-efficient) is discounted, what would then be the more plausible theory when examining the market system and the market economy? A legal institutionalism theory of market making and market regulation has the capacity to explain how markets are established, and how they are preserved and rendered operational over time and the business cycle, including episodes of market turbulence, or even economic crises. Such a theory is primarily introduced and examined in Chapter 2 of this volume, but in this chapter, some of the issues that need to be addressed prior to this literature review are discussed.

Prices are set by the market, which in turn are made by market makers, i.e., the legislative state and its agencies and partners

In a legal scholarship tradition, the free-market view of the market has the causality backwards: rather than markets being the antecedent of any social activity and being generated *sui generis*, markets are the creations of the legislative state and the transnational governance organizations that the state recognizes. Legal scholars are concerned with the proposition that the market pre-dates legislative activities for two reasons: first, because it is a highly venturesome conjecture whose substance needs to be verified, not only asserted as some elementary axiomatic first principle, or on the basis of some loose thought-experiment wherein markets are the placeholder construct that enables other economic devices and mechanisms (say, competition, interest rates, prices) to be orderly introduced and structured within in an analytical framework. Second, legal scholars, who consider the legislature as the expression of political will, and thus of political power, are skeptical regarding the idea of the market as being some non-moral or non-political entity as it is commonly portrayed in elementary economic theory (Judge, 2021: 204).

Boyd (2020) addresses how free-market theorists have developed what they refer to as price theory to circumvent any kind of politicized theory of the market. In the price theory framework, market prices are assumed to accurately reflect all available public information, and as public information is continuously processed and evaluated by a significant number of market actors, price theory is based on the assumption that this continuous assessment of data and information would result in informational-efficient markets, i.e., market prices reflect the underlying public information stock so that, e.g., the possibility of arbitrage would be excluded. Although this is an interesting conjecture, free-market theorists simply accept this dictum prior to the evidence of its accuracy being provided, and this in turn results in an overoptimistic, and in many cases factually deceptive, image of market prices:

> [W]hile prices play an important epistemic role in coordinating economic activity . . . such a view misses the fundamental ways in which prices (and the price system) are political. While this matters more in some markets, and with some prices, than in others, once we recognize that prices are not simply economic signals, we can begin to see a broader set of possibilities regarding the use of markets to achieve various ends and we can recognize (yet again) that there is no pre-political set of criteria for deciding how to harness the power of competition and direct it toward public ends.
>
> (Boyd, 2020: 747)

As prices define what rents (revenues minus production and distribution costs) market actors can generate, it is important that market prices are understood not only as being partially determined by public information, but also by the legislative practices that both establish markets in the first place and thereafter render them operable through a variety of legislations and legal devices. Godechot (2019: 89) says that the "rent is neither the product of labour productivity nor that of capital." Rather, it is the "result of complex mechanisms that limit competition: regulations, property rights, oligopolistic concentration, fixed costs or transaction costs" (Godechot, 2019: 89). The presence of such regulations, property rights, oligopolistic concentration, fixed costs, or transaction costs in the market system cannot simply be construed as "public information," as stipulated by price theory, but these are the outcomes from legislative and regulatory activities that both precede markets and are introduced as markets are in operation. Tingle (2023) emphasizes that market inefficiencies can be caused by a variety of conditions:

> Inefficiencies in market processes can be produced by externalities, informational asymmetries, strategic behavior, laziness, irrationality, and the risk that market actors bring competing moral priorities such as distributional equity or deontological justice to their decisions.
>
> (Tingle, 2023: 685)

Premised on these conditions, markets are not defined by their degree of efficiency or to what extent they are regulated. Tingle (2023) argues:

> Markets aren't defined by the presence or absence of either government or private parties; they are defined by the presence of certain kinds of

> activities. The most important of these activities are experimentation, cooperation, competition, and bargaining.
>
> (Tingle, 2023: 703)

Furthermore, such activities are not introduced to optimize the "efficiency" of markets only, as free-market theorists argue: legislation and market rules are introduced through a variety of political interests that pertain to, e.g., economic and social welfare, economic equality issues, long-term sustainability concerns, and more general social norms that pertain to justice and fairness. That is, efficiency in market operations is not a bad thing, or what is being dismissed as irrelevant, or being lower prioritized than any other policy goal than political entities such as governments and parliaments have to consider, but it is by no means the parameter that defines what legislation and regulatory rules to implement or to enforce. Rather than making "market efficiency" as such a policy goal, efficiency is at best what may be generated through transparent and understandable laws and regulations that create the stability needed to promote a market system and, on the aggregated level, a market economy. To confuse legislative capacities and efficiency is to fail to see the causality between such terms and to fail to recognize the broader institutional context wherein they are introduced and operate.

Free-market theorists are thus guilty of confusing an epistemic and a political view of the market price system, Boyd (2020: 823) argues: "[The] conception of the price system, as activated in various applications of mechanism design, contains within it a deeply conservative posture of anti-politics that stops short of any serious investigation into the political economy of market design." This shunning of the political constitution of the market system, and the advocacy of the price system as an infallible information processing device on the basis of an epistemic theory of the relationship between information and prices, is unsustainable and analytically delimiting. Boyd (2020: 756) says: "[P]rices are not simply things that emerge from markets; rather, it is the specific ways of price making that allow different markets to emerge." That is, by implication, prices are "not simply pieces of information," but are also "objects of struggle"—an insight that one can find in Max Weber's "understanding of markets and prices," as well as in the work of "the institutional economists and legal realists" (Boyd, 2020: 823).

Boyd (2020) continues to assert that a legal institutionalism view of market holds the greatest potential for explaining how markets are established and how they change and develop over time:

> By looking at the larger institutional and political environment in which decisions about market design are made, it becomes clear that there can

never be any pre-political set of criteria for determining how to design markets and, in the process, how to shape and format competition.

(Boyd, 2020: 823)

Expressed in other terms, free-market theory (which by and large reflects the conventional view of markets in neoclassical economic theory, at least until the finance market collapse of 2008), has tried to erase what Mehrpouya and Salles-Djelic (2019: 15) refer to as *homo juridicus* (the individual seen as the purveyor of rights) and *homo politicus* (the individual seen as the locus of voice and political claim-making), and to introduce some hyper-rational *homo oeconomicus* figure, portrayed as an economic actor bestowed with the capacity to operate freely without either legislation (and more specifically, with the exception of the elementary legal right to own property) or politics. Not only is this theoretical model implausible, it also fails to account for much of the work conducted by market actors such as corporations, including lobbying (Coen, Katsaitis, and Vannoni, 2021; Drutman, 2015) and political campaign donation activities (Claessens, Feijen, and Laeven, 2008; De Figueiredo and Edwards, 2007), apparently having a value for such market actors:

> [O]nce we recognize that market devices and the various ways of price making in different markets are objects of conscious design and struggle, it is relatively easy to see how questions of market power and anti-competitive conduct are intimately connected with the microstructures of price formation.
>
> (Boyd, 2020: 823)

In summary, if the market is understood as a human-made accomplishment, not some transcendental space pre-dating human interests and needs being expressed and acted on the basis of, and as being fundamentally shaped by politics and social norms, expressed as legislation and regulatory rules, then the question becomes how detailed such legal and regulatory rules should be, and to what extent the self-organizing qualities of the market (after elementary legislation such as property rights, etc. have been implemented) should be relied on. The legal institutionalism framework (discussed in detail in Chapter 2) does not reject that market actors reveal considerable capacities for contracting and transacting without any intervention of the state or the judiciary, but still advocate the proposition that such day-to-day contracting and transaction always occur in the shadow of the legislative and law-enforcing state. Furthermore, as efficiency in market operation is recognized as a legitimate goal in market making and market regulation, then there needs to be a balancing between mandatory and the supplementary rules that pertain to market activities. Expressed differently, just because the legislative state plays a key role as market maker and market regulator, it does not follow that private ordering is of necessity ineffective: on the contrary, private ordering is a key component of the market system, also in the legal institutionalism framework.

The policy question: balancing state legislation and private ordering in the market system

Private ordering is "self-regulation voluntarily undertaken by private parties," Elkin-Koren (2005: 376) writes. Private ordering theory holds that in the commercial context, "contracting parties, under certain conditions," develop their own norms of honesty and take action "to penalize opportunism in others" (Kadens, 2019: 533). If such conditions are the case, then market transactions are accomplished through legal devices, market rules widely recognized, and social norms that are self-perpetuating as market actors believe such rules and beliefs help them manage their day-to-day business activities. These activities can then be managed without any interventions from the state. "Because the community generates its own rules, unenforced by government, legitimacy derives from consensus agreement on the rules themselves," Schwarcz (2002: 327) writes. Mainstream economic theory may overstate the regularity of these conditions, but such a theory is accurate inasmuch as most economic activities are managed through private ordering principles and devices. Furthermore, economic theory may also overstate how private ordering devices are exclusively market-based, while in fact there is a variety of sources where private ordering devices originate, Schwarcz (2002: 319) proposes:

> Private ordering can be viewed as part of a broad spectrum within which rulemaking is classified by the amount of governmental participation involved. At one end of the spectrum are rules of law originated and put into force by sovereign governments. At the other end are rules that are adopted entirely by private actors. . . . [F]irst, rules originated and put into force by sovereign governments; second, rules originated by private actors but put into force by sovereign governments; third, rules originated and put into force by private actors pursuant to governmental delegation; and fourth, rules adopted by private actors without government sanction or enforcement.
>
> (Schwarcz, 2002: 324)

In some cases, private ordering rules may appear to be market-based as governments often delegate the authority to "make specific regulatory determinations to private actors," or "sanctions and enforces privately made rules,"

Schwarcz (2002: 319) remarks. Under these conditions, the role of the government may be considered to be marginal, but in fact, the legislative state acts as the principal for the private ordering rules work being conducted by, e.g., private actors. Furthermore, several scholars remark, many private ordering devices such as contracts are "relatively open ended, vague, or of dubious legal enforceability," simply because these widely described contractual terms "allow parties the flexibility they need to get the job done" (Mayer and Argyres, 2004: 406). Such vaguely formulated contracts—both legal scholars and economists recognize the analytical term *incomplete contracts* (Nyarko, 2021; Aghion and Bolton, 1992; Ayres and Gertner, 1989)—would for the most part not be operable in an economic system wherein the legislative state would refrain from intervening into business affairs: the very use of, e.g., incomplete contracts is premised on the contracting parties being backed by a legislative and law-enforcing sovereign state, further assisted by transnational governance organizations, and international law and its court system. In this view, the private ordering model provides many possibilities for reducing transaction costs, but such benefits are at the same time premised on the presence of the legislative state, even when it is not actively involved.

Under all conditions, as state legislation and private ordering practices are preferably kept in a delicate balance to support efficiency interests, and the political ambition to only have the state intervene in business affairs when necessary, the question is then how to justify what has been referred to as "paternalist legislation," i.e., legal rules that interfere with the interest of a subject (e.g., a market actor), as such an interference may be inconsistent with other legal principles or rules, or policy goals (Kronman, 1983). For instance, to avoid violating social norms and legal rules that pertain to the dignity of human beings, an open market for human organs is prohibited by national and international law, even as there is presumably a considerable demand for human organs (such as human hearts, livers, and kidneys). Such legislation thus makes it illegal for anyone to sell one's own organs (Cherry, 2005; Sharp, 2003; Lock, 2002), and such legislation is therefore a case of paternalist legislation that delimits the individual's capacity to autonomously manage one's economic and other resources, which some commentators may regard as an inadequate use of legislative capacities as it violates elementary liberties.

In some countries such as Sweden, it is illegal to purchase sexual services (being widely regarded as a law against prostitution), which is yet another case of a paternalist law that restrains both the provider and buyer of such services on the basis of the belief that they violate the dignity of human beings and that the need to protect particularly vulnerable groups against exploitation is the higher prioritized policy goal than to vindicate individual rights. However, critics recognize that paternalist legislation may have a role to play if, and only if, the absence of such legislation would generate more externalities than it would if the legislation is being implemented and enforced.

Critics of paternalist legislation also argue that paternalist legislation should be associated with solid law enforcement activities and ambitions, or else the state is at risk to use legislation to merely signal to its citizens that certain social norms being expressed by the law are valued, but otherwise does not enforce the legislation as it is written and intended to operate. This in turn tends to hollow out the meaning and authority of law, as some laws remain enforceable, some laws merely serve to signal the perceived value of social norms or to express policy goals, and some laws are essentially communicative in nature, making the substantive meaning of law confusing for the public. In that case, the public may be given the impression that abiding by the law would be some kind of choice to be made, rather than being a mandatory citizenry duty and obligation. In the case of the Swedish prostitution law, which makes it illegal to buy—but not, importantly, to sell sexual services—the law signals that the would-be seller of sexual services (e.g., women being involuntarily involved in trafficking activities) needs the protection of the state, has been persistently criticized for resulting in only limited law enforcement activities and actual court cases, i.e., few sexual services buyers have appeared in a court of law, which would make the law functional and complete (Levy and Jakobsson, 2014). To repeat, if the state passes paternalist legislation but without resolutely enforcing it, citizens may think of the legal system as some kind of norm-enforcing or even political signaling system that can be used freely and at low cost to accomplish a variety of goals that are not necessarily legal in nature. If that is the case, the authority and legitimacy of the legislature and the judiciary is at risk to be watered down, as laws are passed on the basis of political beliefs and moral sentiments, rather than on the basis of the intention to act as robust legislative reforms supportive of either policy or principle goals.

In legal theory terms, the concept of "legal paternalism" is premised on the proposition that "[a]ny legal rule that prohibits an action on the ground that it would be contrary to the actor's own welfare is paternalistic" (Kronman, 1983: 763). In many cases, the introduction of paternalist legislation need to be justified, and under such conditions, the justifications are premised on the introduction of terms from a deontic vocabulary that pertains to moral rights and duties (Kronman, 1983: 764). The legal theory literature also discriminates between "hard" and "soft" paternalism—"hard paternalism generally involves measurable instruments," Glaeser (2006: 151) proposes—and between *ex ante* and *ex post* paternalism (Klick and Mitchell, 2006), described accordingly:

> *Ex ante* paternalism reduces the incentive to search for information, carefully evaluate decision options, or develop good decision-making

> strategies. *Ex post* paternalism reduces the risk of thoughtless action, because the government will insulate the decision maker from the consequences of the thoughtless choice. Thus, *ex post* paternalism operates as a form of social insurance for irrational behavior.
>
> (Klick and Mitchell, 2006: 1636)

Under all conditions and regardless of what taxonomies are introduced to structure the analysis of paternalist legislation, the conventional wisdom is that in a democratic state that is premised on the legislators' accountability vis-à-vis the citizens, "[t]he paternalist should bear the burden of demonstrating that the benefits of a paternalistic intervention will likely outweigh the costs," Klick and Mitchell (2006: 1661) write. Kronman (1983: 764–765) adds that

> [b]y acknowledging that it is ever morally permissible to prevent a person from acting solely because he himself will be harmed by the action, one embraces paternalism (in however limited a form) and has an obligation to explain why such interference is permissible in some instances but not in others.

These admonitions and concerns regarding the moral authority of paternalist legislation should still not be mistaken for evidence against its legislative value. As Clark (1989: 1718) notices, antipaternalists frequently claim that it "is unlikely that regulators know better than the regulated what is in their interests." Clark (1989: 1719) dismisses this claim on the basis that this proposition is based on the assumption that "no information asymmetry exists," i.e., citizens know better than the legislators do as they costlessly can access and process available information, which is an implausible condition in several "real-world contexts." On the contrary, in a wide variety of contexts, what Clark (1989: 1726) refers to as "paternalistic elitism" has "decisive relative advantages" over, e.g., private ordering devices. The legislators still have to set "the optimal mix" between legislation (whereof some are paternalist) and private ordering practices, so that certain policy goals are to be accomplished (Clark, 1989: 1726).

In many cases, legal scholars in favour of the presence of some paternalist legislation are critical of the "either/or" logic of economic theory reasoning, wherein social actors are stipulated to have the capacity to adhere to only one set of market rules at a time. In practice, human beings reveal a considerable ability to operate within rules and instructions that are incomplete or ambiguous, and that therefore demand deliberations and discussions on how to handle certain issues and decisions. Godi (2019) speaks of how "administrative regulators" have the capacity to act competently within rules that are "neither paternalistic nor libertarian," but that reveal a "mixed framing":

> To regulate efficiently and effectively, agencies often don't have to paternalistically settle those debates and burn political capital. Instead, in many circumstances, agencies should acknowledge the limits of human cognition isolated by behavioral economists, while adopting an approach that stays clear of both paternalism and libertarianism.
>
> (Godi, 2019: 2039)

That is, the demands for theoretical consistency that, e.g., economists impose on themselves are not necessarily replicated in regulatory affairs, wherein administrative regulations have the capacity to navigate in a legal-regulatory system that may be far from perfect, yet provides guidelines and cues regarding how the policy makers and legislators want certain affairs to be handled. In this view, paternalist legislation such as the intellectual property rights systems examined in Chapters 3 and 4 is both legitimate and has a role to play, at the same time as legislators need to provide evidence that the benefits of the legislation outweigh its costs, externalities, and unintended consequences.

The legal devices: intellectual property rights, patents, and the basis for economic venturing and enterprising

In order to appreciate legal theory, it is important to become acquainted with not only legal theory concepts but also underlying legal theory principles and norms that guide and direct legal actors in their professional practices. At the very bottom of any claim to legality is the recognition of the sovereign state having the authority to pass legislation and to enforce its legislation via, e.g., the court system in its jurisdiction. That is, Lifshitz and Finkelstein (2017: 524) write, "legal interpretation, as expressed in judicial opinions, involves the use of government authority and the power of enforcement." Already at this stage, there is a political component in legal theory that is often absent, understated, or buried in economic theory, which to a higher extent assumes that private ordering practices such as contracting are used, and that for most the part is understood in voluntaristic terms, even as the sovereign state stands as the final warrant for, e.g., contractual devices honoured by business partners. Furthermore, following from this political view of the legislation as being essentially mandatory—to follow the law is not some choice to be made, but is part of what it means to be a citizen in a state, or to otherwise be legally recognized by the state (as in the case of the incorporated business ventures)—legal agents (say, judges in the court of law) are not primarily concerned with the plaintiff's, or the defendant's, or anyone else's view of the law, or legal affairs for that matter, as they are concerned with preserving the authority of the law, and to make sure that it is being honoured, at least until some new legislative reform is being passed by the legislator (in most cases some democratically elected parliament, or its comparable legislative bodies in nondemocratic jurisdictions). "[C]ourts do not limit themselves to evidence of parties' thinking; they take into account what a fair meaning would be, or what parties owe each other in light of background legal norms," Bagchi (2019: 37) says. LoPucki (1997: 480) writes that the "principal functions" of legal scholarship are "to describe institutions, to explain their existence, and to recommend changes." This scholarly pursuit in turn demands a "systems view" of how law operates in practice, i.e., law cannot be understood *au pied de la lettre*: "[t]he fallacy in the traditional approach to law" is to regard it as "a purely conceptual system," LoPucki (1997: 508) says:

> As nearly every law student realizes by the end of the first year, bright judges are not significantly constrained by conceptual law. The judge who realizes that a strategist is manipulating the system can always find sufficient flexibility in rules of law or in equitable doctrine to deny the system-unintended result.
>
> (LoPucki, 1997: 507)

In the end, it is important to study law *in situ*, i.e., as a social practice that considers a large number of conditions that matters for the case to be determined; "the type of systems analysis described [here] is heavily dependent on empiricism," LoPucki (1997: 522) summarizes her argument.

Based on this proposition, Reyes (2021) pays attention to how patent law, the specific piece of legislation that this volume deals with, can be considered a "legal technology"—and more specifically as "a technology within a technology"—within enterprising activities being protected by the legal right to own property or intellectual assets. As patent law confers rights to the patentee as that individual or corporation discloses its newly formulated knowledge, patents are legally understood as contracts that prescribe certain rights and liabilities, Reyes (2021) argues:

> [L]aw is a social technology—it is created, used, and applied within a broader social context. Contracts, as a sub-system of law, therefore, represent a technology within a technology—they offer a tool for privately ordering the rules applicable to a specific social context, the transaction between the parties.
>
> (Reyes, 2021: 983)

More specifically, Rock (2021: 393) argues that economists tend to misconstrue such contracts, as part of the wider "technology" of legislative affairs, as comparably free-standing legal devices, and consequently they underrate how legal devices are also open to interpretations and assessments whose outcomes cannot be known *ex ante*, but are only determined *ex post* through the work of legal agents bestowed with the authority to rule in legal cases. This is a fairly subtle argument wherein legality on the one hand is confirmed and vindicated, while on the other hand, such legality is portrayed as a "technology," i.e., assumed to be reliable, but far from infallible. This condition, and the claims derived from observations of the condition, calls for a more detailed engagement with the concept of legality as such.

Innovation ideas, innovation management, and economic welfare on the basis of intellectual property protection

To examine how economic value is generated on the basis of innovations, and how innovations are in turn being embedded in a legal system that protects intellectual property, demands an analytical model that is based on widely accepted definitions. In this volume, the concepts of ***innovation ideas***, ***innovation***, and the ***economic and legal systems*** are terms that are used in a consistent manner. An ***innovation idea*** is premised on the literature on policy ideas (Campbell and Pedersen, 2015; Kogut and Muir, 2011) and economic ideas (Berman and Pagnucco, 2010; Blyth, 2002), examined in the social sciences literature. As policy-making studies scholars have demonstrated, policy ideas are not just appearing *ex nihilo*, but are rather constructed on the basis of a variety of resources being present, or more recently introduced in the policy-making process: "Without theories of how economic, political, and social worlds work—theories that vary among groups and over time—it will not often be clear that what policy options will help advance one's interests, and thus what actions one should take," Berman and Pagnucco (2010: 366) write. "These theories," they continue, "are not absolute truths, but can be contingent, evolving, and the product of larger worldviews." Blyth (2002: 11) argues that what he refers to as "economic ideas" are the elementary units of analysis in the policy-making process: "Economic ideas provide agents with an interpretative framework, which describes and accounts for the workings of the economy by defining its constitutive elements and 'proper' (and therefore 'improper') interrelations," Blyth (2002: 11) says. Economic ideas have the benefit of both providing a "scientific" (or what purports to be a scientific) account and a normative account of a condition, and which when combined render a specific economic idea both trustworthy and as a plausible candidate when making policy decisions. The scientific part of the economic idea is premised on the use of what Brandom (2019: 667) refers to as an *alethic* vocabulary, which makes substantive claims regarding *how things are*, i.e., have some epistemic content, whereas the normative claim is premised on the use of a *deontic* vocabulary, which expresses what is *the morally correct decision to* *make*, or at least asserts that the spokesperson supports the decision to be made, regardless of its limitations.

Furthermore, which is important for the legal institutionalism framework that is examined in Chapter 2, Blyth (2002: 11) argues that such economic ideas become, when widely endorsed, the "blueprints of new institutions." In the end, economic ideas allow agents to "[r]educe uncertainty, propose a particular solution to a moment of crisis, and empower agents to resolve that crisis by constructing new institutions in line with these new ideas," Blyth (2002: 11) says. Rodrik, Subramanian, and Trebbi (2004: 158) list a number of concepts being included in economic ideas, such as "incentives," "competition," "hard-budget constraints," "sound money," "fiscal sustainability," and "property rights," as being exemplary of terms that are used in market regulation policy. At the same time, *pace* Blyth (2002: 11), Rodrik, Subramanian, and Trebbi (2004: 158) suggest that these economic ideas "do not map directly into institutional forms"; there is a certain discontinuity between economic ideas and the institutional forms they generate when being translated into policy goals. That is, economic ideas cannot serve exactly as "blueprints" as that image expresses an overoptimistic belief regarding a continuity and consistency in the policy-making process. Instead, economic ideas act as "tools for making active interventions" within, e.g., markets (Pinzur, 2021: 918). Economic ideas are the stuff that policy makers draw on, but any deviation between economic ideas as formulated in books and their active role in, e.g., regulating markets needs to be recognized. Several anecdotes indicate that economic advisors and pundits have a hard time accepting such deviations, as in the case of economists lambasting either policy makers and market actors for failing to implement allegedly correct economic theories in actual market-regulating practices, thus being an analytical strategy that is inconsistent with good analytical consciousness as it both rests on *ad hominem* arguments and blames the agent rather than the underlying theory for failures.[4] Anyway, for more seasoned analysts, it is apparent that economic ideas serve to guide policy makers and other decision makers, who occasionally find themselves in the dark regarding their

4 For instance, and in anecdotal terms, Milton Friedman, in his role as a member of the President's Economic Policy Advisory Board (PEPAB), advised the Reagan Administration on how to push down inflation and to enable price stability on the basis of Friedman's monetarist theory, but when the cure did not seem to help the patient, the American economy, both Friedman and Beryl Sprinkel, the Undersecretary for Monetary Affairs in Reagan Administration, also committed to the monetarist doctrine, insisted that "[i]t was a temporary phenomenon and shouldn't be factored into efforts to manage the money supply." In response to arguments that the "unprecedented volatility of interest rates pointed towards the failure of monetarism," both Friedman and Sprinkel insisted that "the problem lay not with the theory but with those implementing it—in other words, the Federal Reserve" (Best, 2022: 566–567). To save the highly controversial theory, blame was conveniently shifted to the regulators rather than resulting in some thoughtful revision of the underlying theory itself.

capacity to handle difficult economic conditions (see e.g., Best, 2022), but the claim that such ideas are faithfully mirrored in the policies passed and implement is disputed.

In this volume, the concept of *innovation ideas* is used (and in Chapter 4 in particular) as a term that denotes an intellectual idea that describes an innovation in technical, scientific, and/or practical terms, and that explains how the innovation idea would be possible to materialize in a practical context. Expressed differently, the innovation idea is based on two components that are consistent with how patent law is formulated and put to use in patent offices: it includes a *technical idea*, but it also provides instructions for *how the idea is to be materialized*, and it explains in what way this materialization makes a contribution to "the state of the arts" (in the patent law vocabulary). This two-tiered concept of innovation ideas is consistent with the analytical model that Budish, Roin, and Williams (2015) use. Budish, Roin, and Williams (2015: 2049) conceptualize R&D as "consisting of two stages": *invention* and *commercialization*. By invention, Budish, Roin, and Williams (2015: 2049) mean "developing the basic idea for a product to the point where it is patentable." Examples include the work conducted to produce a new chemical compound, to build a prototype, and to provide similar evidence of the "advances in the prior art," in the patent law vocabulary. By commercialization, Budish, Roin, and Williams (2015: 2049) mean all activities that are involved in "bringing an invented product to market." Such activities include, e.g., getting FDA approval for a new chemical compound, to produce a prototyped "good at efficient scale," etc. In many cases (but not necessarily in every case) there is a "commercialization lag" in R&D projects, defined as "the amount of time between invention and commercialization" (Budish, Roin, and Williams, 2015: 2049): invention comes first, and commercialization may follow. As has been stated, for a significant proportion of all patents on file, the commercialization stage may never arrive as the patent is merely on file to provide intellectual property rights for the invention (Moore, 2005). The concept of the innovation idea denotes and accommodates both the invention and commercialization stages. Similar to the linguist Ferdinand de Saussure's (1959) concept of the *sign* as what denotes both the signifier (e.g., the word "tree") and the signified (the idea of the tree as a biological species and a living entity, in turn related to a *referent*—an actual tree), the innovation idea denotes both the invention as the abstract idea or advancement "in the prior arts" and the commercialization activities that the invention would generate if taken farther than to merely be a formal description of an invention. To recognize this dual expression of the innovation idea has the benefit that the patent system and its recognition of legal rights and protection *in the absence* of any meaningful materialization or commercialization of the innovation idea being patented is accepted out of hand: a patent contains an *idea* and a *promise* or *assertion*, and these two components need to be included to generate a patent system that is operable and that is justified in legal terms.

The research question formulated

Some economists such as Pagano (2014) are concerned with how patent law and its interpretation and enforcement result in faltering competition, which in turn result in lower incentives to invest resources in innovative activities, and monopsony in labour markets that push down labour compensation, and thus further reduce the demand that in turn limits competition. Furthermore, increased economic concentration, widely observed in the US in particular (Covarrubias, Gutiérrez, and Philippon, 2020; Philippon, 2019; Grullon, Larkin, and Michaely, 2019; Autor et al., 2017), and more limited entrepreneurial activities in the US economy (Decker, Haltiwanger, Jarmin, and Miranda, 2014, 2017), undermine market competition, which in turn is stipulated to result in a loss of economic and social welfare in neoclassical economic theory. If economic concentration has resulted in soaring and, as in the US, unprecedented levels of economic inequality and a marked decline in enterprising activities, such conditions cannot be fully explained by the introduction of sweeping ad hoc hypotheses, such as references to globalization processes or technology shifts. The explanation for such conditions are most plausibly to be found in legislative practices in both specific jurisdictions (say, in the US) or in transnational legislative entities such as the European Union, but also in how, e.g., TGOs enforce what is referred to as "soft law," market rules that have not yet achieved the status of legislation but that nonetheless are perceived and acted upon as if that was the case (i.e., soft law is a primary case of legal fiction). Although many branches of legislative activities affect economic welfare (e.g., international trade laws, jurisdiction-specific antitrust legislation, etc.), this specific volume will examine patent legislation as a case of what has been referred to as legal institutionalism, an analytical framework that regards the legislation as constitutive of the institutional environment wherein the corporation acts to both generate an output and to make a profit that ensures its long-term survival (or, as in the case of start-ups, relying on a different governance model than incumbent companies do, focused in the work to develop assets and capacities that are valued by some incumbent company or by venture capital investors willing to invest in the business venture). To provide such an analysis, the two principal objectives of this volume are to:

1. Examine the institutional theory and legal institutionalism literature to provide a comprehensive case in favour of an analytical model wherein legislation creates the basis for the market economy that generates value ("value creation," in Muniesa's [2017] formulation) and that serves to

preserve a healthy level of competition even if certain market actors become highly successful in introducing innovations that change market conditions. In this legal institutionalism view, markets *per se* cannot be assumed to generate economic welfare as there is limited empirical support for markets being self-regulating, nor of the price function having the stabilizing role that its proponents believe (if that would be the case, a whole range of market practices such as speculation, stock repurchase announcements, and finance industry instabilities would not be observed as market regularities). This means that only the legislative state in collaboration with its defined market regulating agencies and transnational legislative organizations have the capacity to both generate markets (via its legislative function) and to preserve market competition and functionality (via a combination of market regulation activities and extraordinary financial operations, such as finance institution bailouts during episodes of failing financial markets).

2. Review the recent literature on patent law and patenting legislation to show that in addition to markets not being infallible and exclusively premised on the use of private ordering devices such as contracts, patents—another important market device being legally coded—are also loosely coupled descriptions of ideas and what legal scholars calls "prophecies" regarding how these ideas can be materialized if the patentee would develop the idea further. This analysis is of great importance for the analytical framework that includes institutional theory and legal institutionalism, and being widely used in management studies, not the least in innovation management studies. If patent legislation is premised on the belief that granting a patent to any ideas as soon as it is being disclosed by a patent-granting office (e.g., the United States Patent and Trademark Office, USPTO), and that this patent is conducive to growing economic welfare as new ideas are made public, then a patent is primarily assertorial in nature: a patent provides an account that includes the promise that if, and only if, the patent is further developed to the point where it can materialize, then economic welfare may increase. This essentially assertorial claim stands in sharp contrast to the belief that patents can be taken as a proxy for innovative capacities and realizations. In this view, a patent is unambiguously related to a would-be innovation that exists not only in its conception but also in its materialization. As a sizeable legal theory literature indicates, there are only weak arguments in favour of such a study design as many patents, and not the least those patents granted to companies, and large companies in particular, are granted on the basis of such prophecies. This means that patent legislation still plays a key role in advanced economies as it introduces legality as a factual matter, and rather than merely being based on social norms that pertain to honour or honesty as in the case of private ordering, the legal device of the patent

introduces a third part—the sovereign state—in the relationship between market actors. The literature review indicates that the patent legislation may be far from perfect, but it nonetheless plays a key role as potential patent infringement always occurs in the shadow of the legislative state, having several legal mechanisms and devices ready to use to preserve the market competition that is assumed to support economic welfare in more predictable ways than any other governance mechanism known to date would be able to.

These two objectives widely correspond with the content of the second and third chapters, and the fourth and fifth chapters of this volume, respectively. The sixth and final chapter summarizes the arguments made and points at some empirical studies that support the view that patents and other legal devices that protect intellectual work conducted, and thus supporting enterprising more widely, do play a key role in market-making activities, but only within the broader analytical framework of legal institutionalism. Legal institutionalism is therefore a highly valuable and analytically attractive theoretical perspective that should be more widely applied in management studies, and not the least in innovation management studies, a scholarly discipline that all too easily glosses over the important question of what a patent right in fact denotes, not only in the court of law if a dispute regarding the potential infringement on a property right is to be handled, but also in the broader perspective on day-to-day work in organizations. In making these remarks on the basis of the literature being reviewed, this volume makes a contribution in formulating an institutional theory of the legal embedding of innovation. Such an institutional theory of innovation is significant as innovative capacities are commonly reduced to be considered as a matter of individual intellectual capacities and the ability to coordinate and align "some of the best minds" to materialize innovative ideas. Such activities and skills indubitably do matter, and are in many cases firm-specific competences within the team-production activities that are the corporate entity's *raison d'être*, but only *after* such innovative ideas can be subject to legal protection. Therefore, in order to understand how innovation occurs, or, less assuring, to examine why innovative activities seem to be in decline, it is important to start with the legislation and to only thereafter turn to the market for explanations, not the other way around. This is potentially a controversial idea as generations of economists and scholars pledging allegiance to other disciplines have been trained to think of the market as the origin of all things economic, while in fact this doctrine is based on the category mistake to confuse the price function of the market with the legislative activities that generate both prices and markets in the first place. Among the many things the author of this volume hopes to accomplish, is to correct this analytical inconsistency so that category mistakes are avoided counts among them.

Summary and conclusion

Economic growth and the economic welfare derived therefrom—if economic values are distributed in a substantive sense of the term—are the key concerns for a variety of scholarly communities and experts, and for economists in particular. Economists need, like any epistemic community, to develop a shared theoretical framework to unify and preserve the discipline over time and geographical distances, and one of the key features of the neoclassical economic theory model is the commitment to the idea of the market as the superior, for some even unsurpassable, device for the processing of public information and the allocation of economic resources on the basis of such information processing. Other scholarly disciplines and epistemic communities, including management studies scholars, legal scholars, economic sociologists, and political scientists, commonly share the belief that efficient markets have several welfare-generating benefits, but only insofar as such markets are established in the first place. Some schools of economic theory have representatives who disregard such claims as the very idea of markets being created on the basis of a combination of policy, law, regulatory rules, and private ordering devices such as contracting fall to the side of, or even contradict, their stated beliefs. As markets are occasionally assumed to be "naturally occurring" in elementary economic theory, it is by default markets that act as the *explanans* for politics, law, and managerial practices, rather than the other way around, i.e., markets being constructed and preserved on the basis of such social resources and practices to incentivize individuals to engage in enterprising activities and venturing. For mainstream management studies scholars, legal scholars, economic sociologists, and political scientists, it is a fallacy to believe that complex socio-legal mechanisms would occur naturally, thus being a form of wishful thinking to avoid having to deal with how the, e.g., sovereign state and TGOs enact policies and pass legislation that in turn generate the markets that some economists take for granted. In this account, the market is the *explanandum*, which needs to be explained to formulate a robust economic theory on the origin of markets, market pricing, etc., and in this case it is the legal-political practices being the antecedents of market making that is the *explanans* for why market exists. This does not in any way mean that management studies scholars, legal scholars, economic sociologists, and political scientists deny the value of having functional and operational markets if increased economic and social welfare is a desideratum, but such benefits, repeatedly emphasized by card-carrying economists, do not render a logically inconsistent proposition or, at worst, a mythological explanation of market creation and market governance more plausible or practically useful.

2 Legal institutionalism and the question of legal coding

Introduction

Adam Smith is commonly portrayed as a form of patron saint for economics (see, e.g., Liu, 2022), but in fact it would be more adequate to let the French legal theorist and philosopher Charles-Louis de Secondat Montesquieu be honoured this way. Writing before Smith and perhaps also being inhibited by the fact that his most widely used work, *L'espirit des Loix*, gives an impression of being primarily about legal theory rather than economic affairs, Montesquieu made clear that the rule of law makes the difference between the liberal (and modern) state and the state stuck in what today is referred to as a crony capitalism condition. However, at *le temps* of Montesquieu, there were not yet any full-fledged capitalist economic systems to actively criticize, nor to promote, but at this stage, there were still theories about economic wealth and the economic welfare that could be derived from such economic wealth. Therefore, similar to his Scottish contemporary David Hume, who was equally critical of an economic system dominated by the interventions of a rent-seeking monarchy, Montesquieu argued that "as a general rule," a nation that operates under monarchical rule, more work is done to "conserve" than to "accumulate" wealth ("on travaille plus à conserver qu'à acquérir"), than in a liberal economy, wherein the opposite is the case ("dans une nation libre, on travaille plus a acquérir qu'à conserver") (Montesquieu, 1788a: 127).

This condition is not coincidental as the liberal economy is governed by the rule of law, whereas the monarchy-governed economy relies on other mechanisms. Montesquieu (1788a: 141) thus asserts that "commercial cities" (or states, the city writ large) are ruled by the law, not by judges: "[d]ans une ville commerçate, il y a moins de juges, et plus de loix" (Montesquieu, 1788a: 141). That is, the more precise legal rules, the less influence of judges (and, by implication, rent-seeking monarchs meddling with legal matters): when judges are in charge, judgment become arbitrary; when the rule of law is the case, the law gives a judge a fixed rule ("Lorsque le juge presume, les

DOI: 10.4324/9781003460220-2

jugement deviennent arbitraries; lorsque la loi presume, elle donne au juge une régle fixe" (Montesquieu, 1788b: 25).

Furthermore, the laws that govern the economy and, by implication, the welfare of the society and its people are not easily determined, but need to be balanced to include and address all of the interests and objectives that the law is intended to regulate. Just as in "good politics" and in "good morality," legislation is always of necessity located between two endpoints on a continuum: "L'espirit de moderation doit être celui du legislateur; le bien politique, comme le bien moral, se trouve toujours entre deux limites" (Montesquieu, 1788b: 1). Expressed in other terms, legislative activities are of necessity political in nature as they need to serve not only one interest, or one purpose, but many interests and many purposes, each being expressed on the basis of idiosyncratic conditions that the legislators by no means can anticipate in all their details, but would still consider that the law enacted would be capable of providing adequate rules for courts applying the law to specific cases. Not the least for the economic system of late-modern competitive capitalism, characterized by great diversity and a dynamic capacity to price and transact all sorts of goods and services, demands that legal rules are enacted and enforced.

"Capitalism is fundamentally a legal ordering: the bargains at the heart of capitalism are products of law," Grewal (2014: 652) writes. This is an elementary proposition in the legal institutionalism literature, that the economic system is both constituted by law and subject to detailed legal regulation, while the legal system is of necessity incomplete, and thus contains loophole and possibilities for legal arbitrage, the active work to navigate between legal systems to maximize rents and economic returns. However, this general proposition needs to be examined in more detail to substantiate the claim that legal affairs such as legal reforms and new law enforcement affect transactions, business practices, and venturing "on the ground." Such evidence also needs to be complemented by theoretical propositions that both justify the current legislation and that promote or, alternatively, prevent legal reforms that would unintendedly impose additional costs on economic agents in the marketplace. Taken together, legislation and legal matters are the most potent and pervasive governance devices that policy makers access and can make use of, but this also means that policy makers should be concerned with using legal reforms at a too frequent rate as there are commonly unintended consequences of also a purposeful use of legislative activities. For instance, economists tend to advocate policy changes over legal changes (Listokin and Murphy, 2019: 379); policy decisions are made in democratic entities such as parliaments, and can therefore be amended or modified when needed, whereas legal reforms take time to establish and are also costly to modify if they are assessed to be unsuccessful in accomplishing their stated goals, or otherwise causing unintended consequences, including not the least the harm caused if economic actors may lose some of their faith in the value of having laws at all (see, e.g., Fennell and McAdams, 2016; Liscow, 2014).

This chapter first examines the concept of law as such to provide the theoretical platform for the concept of legal institutionalism. Thereafter, institutional theory perspectives on how corporate entities respond to and handle legislation and legal reforms are addressed. Thereafter, in the third section, the concept of legal institutionalism is examined. The fourth and final section examines the empirical studies conducted on the basis of a legal institutionalism theory framework, including studies of the growth of the securities market, and the credit formation process centered on chartered banks, monitored by regulatory agencies but otherwise granted the authority to supply finance capital in contemporary society.

The concept of law and its role in regulating social and economic affairs

As an elementary analytical proposition, the advanced democratic society is being regulated and managed on the basis of the rule of law, not the rule of men. There is always room for policy making and legislative reforms being shaped by specific interests (otherwise, the business lobbying industry would not be as prominent and vocal as it is), but that fact does not *per se* undermine the original proposition. Cohen (1935: 836) makes a reference to a seminal definition of law in the legal scholarship literature as being "a rule of civil conduct, prescribed by the supreme power in a State, commanding what is right, and prohibiting what is wrong." Such elementary definitions often call for more questions to be asked than they provide answers, as in this case regarding how to draw the line between right and wrong, and what the concept of "rule" denotes *de jure* and *de facto*. Still, laws are defined to be what are passed by the sovereign state and that serve to provide both practical but also moral and normative guidelines for what are commended or tolerated practices or behaviours. Under all conditions, in a legal institutionalism perspective, legal rights, rules, etc. are not primarily determined through linguistic analysis of syntax and semantics (which of course does not mean that syntax and semantics are irrelevant for legal matters), as the operative value of law is to be found in its context of application and the wider institutional setting wherein the law is implemented and enforced.

On basis of this elementary proposition, many complementary qualities of law need to be specified. One such quality is that rights, as they are both understood in legislative and law-enforcing circles and communities, as well as in lay communities (the proverbial "man on the street"), are "the fruits of law, and of the law alone," as stated by Jeremy Bentham (cited in De Araujo,

2009: 366): "There are no rights without law—no rights contrary to the law—no rights anterior to the law," Bentham continues. Furthermore, the rule of law that has the capacity to bestow such rights on its subjects is constituted on the basis of a comparably limited number of legal principles, mechanisms, and devices that are applied to handle a considerably more complex practical terrain. Berle (1963) argues:

> The basic law setting up the structure of the American economic republic rests on a small group of constitutional rules and federal statutes which have attained a measure of constitutional stature. These are amplified and carried out by law, partly statutory, partly administrative, and partly unwritten.
>
> (Berle, 1963: 100)

A third feature is that even if legislation purports to mirror underlying values, beliefs, norms, and morals that are timeless and decontextualized, i.e., are premised on the claim to a certain degree of universality, law is of necessity always the product of the specific society that passes the law. "Law, despite its 'a-historical' appearance and like all social activities, is a product of the play of power and contradictory perceptions that cut across society," Fontaine (2014: 129) writes. That is, what some legal scholars refer to as "truth in law" (e.g., Cole and Bertenthal, 2017: 352), i.e., the capacity to establish a legal view of a practical matter (say, in a patent infringement dispute) on the basis of the material acquired and being regarded as being of relevance for the case at hand, such legal truths differ from scientific truths that deal with either epistemological or ontological truths (or combinations thereof, as in e.g., astrophysics or organic chemistry). An additional feature that pertains to the concept of "truth in law" is that legislators are commonly not singlehandedly concerned with efficiency as it is defined in, e.g., economic theory and in law and economics scholarship, which regard law as what should normatively express economic theory propositions so that such propositions can become true by implication, even if they were not so when they were first developed through normative beliefs. On the contrary, legislators consider a broader view of societal interests and concerns (e.g., regarding the creation of innovation ideas, as in the case of patent law), and even though efficiency is a desideratum also for legislators who consider public interest as part of their work, such complex *ex post* measures cannot be developed and rendered operational prior to a whole set of other legal issues being handled. That is, if efficiency is the case after the fact, e.g., when new legislation is introduced, that is a good thing, but the very idea of and preference for efficiency *per se* cannot *ex ante* determine what legislation that should be passed, even if law and economics scholars claim that they have the capacity to determine how such desirable outcomes are accomplished. In Brown's (2014: 183) formulation, "[t]here are unrecognized risks inherent to greater process efficiency; it may do criminal justice more harm than good." Based on such premises, it is inadequate to criticize legislation on the basis of specific case conditions as it is often possible to identify corners of society that law does not regulate in detail, but that nonetheless can for the most part be regulated on the basis of the various legal mechanisms and devices that are available in the total ensemble of legal devices.

The expressive quality of law

One feature of law is that in order to preserve the authority of law and the legislators that enact new legislation, there cannot be a too high degree of divergence between prevalent social norms and legal rules. Totalitarian societies such as Russia pass laws (both prior to and during Russia's invasion in Ukraine in February 2022) that are merely supportive of the interests of a small and well-protected group of the apex of the Russian kleptocracy, but in democratic societies that seek to preserve the long-term viability of the social order and economic welfare (see e.g., Funke, Schularick, and Trebesch, 2023), laws cannot deviate too far from what citizens regard as being reasonable legal rules. This connection between and mutual constitution of social norms and legislation is referred to as the *expressive theory of law* (Cooter, 1998). As Sunstein (1996: 2026) notices, "[a]n appropriately framed law may influence social norms and push them in the right direction." In this way, new legislation may in fact further reinforce the law as it signals that the endorsement of a specific norm is now not only a matter of private beliefs, but is also a shared societal interest, now being protected by the force of law (Lane, Nosenzo, and Sonderegger, 2023). In addition, a new legislation may better justify and explain the reasons why certain social norms are beneficial (say, the social norm that shames the physical punishment of children, eventually to be outlawed in many countries, but being widespread by the middle of the twentieth century, and thereafter gradually disappearing as a child-rearing practice by the latter half of the century). As Sunstein (1996: 2047) says, unless a social norm is being widely endorsed and followed, it is little use in passing legislation that provides such norms with legal protection, as such norms will not be respected anyway, and such a piece of legislation would also come at the cost of the subject losing faith in the legal system and the legislators' capacity to govern public affairs in a competent manner.

If norms and laws have this kind of intimate connections in the expressive theory of law, the question is then what norms are and to what extent they are already congenial with legislative affairs. Posner (1996: 1699) portrays norms accordingly:

> A norm can be understood as a rule that distinguishes desirable and undesirable behavior and gives a third party the authority to punish a

> person who engages in the undesirable behavior. Thus, a norm constrains attempts by people to satisfy their preferences. In these ways, a norm is like a law, except that a private person sanctions the violator of a norm, whereas a state actor sanctions the violator of a law.
>
> (Posner, 1996: 1699)

Despite emphasizing the punitive and repressive qualities of social norms (norms can be equally permissive and enabling), Posner (1996) recognizes that social norms are already "lawlike" inasmuch as they are social devices that regulate social behaviours and practices, albeit on the basis of other means than law, i.e., norms and laws are different in degree rather than different in kind: "Norms and laws can be usefully distinguished according to their degree of centralization, that is, the extent to which the power to create and modify the rules is concentrated in the hands of a small number of people who can easily cooperate" (Posner, 1996: 1700). Katz (1996: 1749), drawing on information economics theory, adds that social norms are not only to be understood as conventions, widely endorsed rules for how practices should be conducted, or what beliefs are legitimate, but that norms also embody and at least partially express *information*:

> Norms and rules, whether publicly or privately created, embody and convey information. They cannot be followed unless information is transmitted regarding their substantive content; they cannot be enforced unless information is transmitted regarding who has obeyed them, who has violated them, and who is to impose any associated punishment or reward.
>
> (Katz, 1996: 1749)

If social norms contain or convey information that can be practically useful, then it follows from economic theory deductions that norms have an economic value that arguably can only be realized under the rule of specific legislation. Consequently, Katz (1996: 1747) proposes "[t]he proper role for state lawmaking is to correct for failures in what we might call the 'market for norms.'" Whether such a market construct is reasonable and practically useful, as there is a close alignment of prevalent social norms (that recursively may be shaped by new legislation, and that shape how new legislation is being passed), law, and market and market-making activities. Although these propositions are widely expressed *in blanco* at this stage, these connections do matter for patent law, which is examined in the coming chapters.

Law enforcement

LoPucki (1996: 3) specifies that policy makers *qua* legislators enforce law on the basis of essentially two mechanisms: incarceration and liability.

Incarceration is the penalty for a series of crimes that are grave to the extent that the convict needs to be isolated from society for some time to be rehabilitated, or as a personal sacrifice done to society for failing to follow its legislation and, by implication, the social norms society rest on to preserve and reproduce itself. Whether incarceration is an effective or suboptimal solution to the perceived problem of rehabilitation, and how to impose penalties on law violators, is a hotly debated topic in criminology research circles (Hinton, 2016; Wacquant, 2009; Beckett and Western, 2001), but is essentially a question beyond the scope of this volume. It remains clear, however, that some kind of penalty following law violations is consistent with social norms that pertain to fairness and justice, but to what degree and under what terms remain subject to discussion.

In the second case, liability, wherein the legal system "enforces liability through the entry and forcible collection of judgments for the payment of money" (LoPucki, 1996: 4), the questions to be answered are no less complex. For instance, in the case of patent right infringements, the violator of the legal rule may not be conscious of making any breaches of patent rights, and even if he or she was aware that such was the case, the work conducted may have caused minimal harm for the patent owner, or may have generated net economic value in and through the development work conducted. In this view, the patent infringement, when described in such terms, appears to have only limited consequences, but courts still consider what the wider consequences would be. The courts must therefore strike a balance between economic efficiency concerns (which, in this fictive case, the patent right may be harmed in most marginal terms) and the wider consequences for the faith and trust in the law that society needs to maintain and protect via, e.g., court ruling cases, especially on the Supreme Court level where "hard cases" (Dworkin, 1975) are determined and eventually bought back into legal practices, including how patent applications are written by patent lawyers and other legal counsellors.

These difficulties discussed in this case are indicative of how law in many cases is composed on loosely coupled components that individually contribute to the legal system, but that on their own would be incapable of apprehending and resolving the legal issues at hand. Legal scholars thus speak of the "incompleteness of law" as a legal condition that both legal professionals need to recognize, at the same time as they cannot announce too widely that such perceived incompleteness is the case, as that would potentially reduce the faith in the legal system that upholds its moral authority and that renders it operable. "Statutes, like contracts," Krawiec (2013: 83) writes, "can be more or less complete, but will inevitably have some gaps and ambiguities that courts or agencies must fill." Under these conditions, lawmakers may delegate "discretionary authority" to other "governmental branches for a variety of salutary reasons" (Krawiec, 2013: 83). Ricks (2011) expresses this idea in educational terms, relating to how law is taught in law schools at universities:

> Every law student learns the shibboleth that law is inherently open-textured and flexible. But its flexibility is not infinite; there are limits to plausible interpretation. The burden of persuasion here would seem to rest with those who for some reason doubt that legal constraints are binding in this area.
>
> (Ricks, 2011: 135)

This is an important point that Ricks (2011) makes: just because the legal system is incomplete and thus to some degree flexible under this description, it does not follow that such flexibilities are unlimited. On the contrary, legal scholars have persistently noticed that what is referred to as "judge-made law" on the basis of specific cases (and as opposed to statutory law) is in many cases necessary, but it is also problematic to the extent that it bestows the individual judge with too much authority and leeway regarding how legal rules are to be interpreted and enforced. Kahan and Kamar (2002: 695) emphasize, for instance, how corporate governance practice is premised on the fiduciary duties of care and loyalty that directors assume vis-à-vis the corporate entity that they are assigned to manage:

> An important element of a state's corporate legal structure is its judge-made law. It is judge-made law, rather than statutory law, that governs such fundamental issues as the fiduciary duties of directors, officers, and controlling shareholders in self-dealing transactions, the scope of corporate opportunities, the obligations of directors in dealing with control challenges, the prerequisites for a derivative suit, directors' disclosure obligations, and the scope of impermissible corporate waste.
>
> (Kahan and Kamar, 2002: 695)

Judge-made law is a necessary evil of the legal system as it drifts towards the "rule of men," being a condition that generates externalities and that casts a shadow of doubt over the legal system. On many occasions, the verdict is still that it is better to have a legal system that is incomplete and imperfectly designed and operating, rather than to rely on some other governance mechanism. However, in the legal institutionalism perspective, this means that laws and legislative activities are not infallible, but are rather premised on the intention to pass legislation and to render it operable in a domain of social practice so that it can generate favourable outcomes, and if less so than intended, to modify and reform either the law or the procedures through which law is enforced, so that intended outcomes can be achieved.

The institutional theory view of how corporations respond to legal reforms

Once markets have been established and rendered operational, new legislation and new regulatory rules are likely to be gradually implemented (as in the case of the finance industry, allegedly being the most closely monitored and regulated market in the contemporary era). When such new legislation and regulatory rules are implemented, they gradually establish what Shaffer (2009: 177) refers to as a *legal culture*, defined as "[t]he attitudes and behavior that people have and exhibit toward law and legal institutions within a domestic system." This legal culture is consistent with what proponents of institutional theory refer to as the "institutional theory view of law," or, as in this volume, "legal institutionalism." "For institutionalists, the law plays a role in shaping organizational behavior, not necessarily discourages the sanctioned behavior," Hirsh (2009: 248) says. Given these conditions, law and legislative practices are also understood in institutional terms, i.e., as Romano (2005: 1524) remarks, "[s]uccessful law reform in the national arena typically involves the recombination of old elements that have been advanced in policy circles for a number of years prior to adoption." In this view, legal reform can be examined on the basis of a garbage-can decision-making model (Cohen, March, and Olsen, 1972), wherein previous legislation, new policy ideas and objectives, certain conjectures and deliberations regarding the plausible outcomes and benefits of specific legal rule changes, and a variety of legal principles and doctrines are available and reassembled in ways that indicate that no legislation is exclusively conceived and constructed entirely *de novo*, but must always of necessity contain some elements that are already available. However, once a new law is formulated, passed in legislative assemblies, and implemented, this legislative process is subject to what Smith and Gai (2017), who study the governance of the hedge fund industry, refer to as "legal amnesia," i.e., detailed questions that pertain to legal affairs are easily forgotten as they essentially sink into the legal environment of the corporation, and thus become a specialism that legal experts and counsellors handle, to some extent out of sight of executive decision makers.

The legal environment of the corporation

Organizations respond to changes in their environment to ensure that their legitimacy is preserved, and to enable the long-time survival of the organization (Meyer and Rowan, 1977). The neoinstitutional theory literature identifies a number of mechanisms and devices that enable organizations to actively detect signals and to effectively respond to them. Selznick (1949: 10), an early institutional theorist, says that "no organization subsists in a vacuum. Large or small, it must pay some heed to the consequences of its own activities (and even existence) for other groups and forces in the community." Selznick (1948: 34, original emphasis omitted) introduces the concept of *cooptation* to denote the process of "[a]bsorbing new elements into the leadership or policy-determining structure of an organization as a means of averting threats to its stability or existence." Cooptation is thus a mechanism that renders organizations more receptive to changes in their environment. Furthermore, Selznick (1949: 10) distinguishes between *formal cooptation* and *informal cooptation*. In the former case, there is a need for an organization to "publically absorb new elements." Formal cooptation thus involves the establishment of "openly avowed and formally ordered relationships" (Selznick, 1949: 10). For instance, if a new regulation is implemented, an organization may need to formally adjust its practices to accommodate the new regulatory rules, thus being a case of formal cooptation. The case of informal cooptation, in contrast, occurs when "[t]here is a need of adjustment to the pressure of specific centers of power within the community" (Selznick, 1949: 259). If, say, a consumer protest campaign is initiated (see, e.g., Ingram, Vue, and Rao, 2010), the executive leadership may privately believe that the claims made by activists are illegitimate or unjustifiable, while it publicly needs to act as if they were in fact justifiable to avoid negative publicity, or to avoid appearing unreasonable regarding how to respond to opposing views on a factual matter, thus being a case of informal cooptation. Under all conditions, formal and informal cooptation result in organizations being responsive to and accommodating external pressures and/or changes in the milieu.

Based on this general proposition, that organizations respond to external changes, scholarly literature examines how organizations respond to external changes such as new legislation and new regulatory rules (Zhang, 2022; Skaggs, 2009). Knight, Dobbin, and Kalev (2022) examine how nondiscrimination legislation affects how corporations recruit managers from underrepresented communities. Unfortunately, the empirical material suggests that "[i]n the majority of establishments, lawsuits do not generate positive results." Instead, the study indicates that "[g]ains in managerial diversity are isolated to only the largest firms following lawsuit losses," and, among these firms, changes "accrue mostly in headquarters" (Knight, Dobbin, and Kalev, 2022: 186). Such evidence suggests that legislation is a blunt tool for promoting diversity in organizations. Furthermore, Dobbin and Kalev (2021: 288) found that "antibias training," at times included in new regulatory frameworks to support diversity, is ineffective: "A recent review of over 900 studies finds weak, and sometimes adverse, effects of training on attitudes." Dobbin and Kalev (2021: 288) write:

> In the average company, mandatory diversity training for managers led to a 10% decline in Black women managers and 4% to 5% declines in Asian

> American men and women managers. . . . Harassment training led to a 5% decline in white women managers. . . . No underrepresented group saw a positive effect in either study.
>
> (Dobbin and Kalev, 2021: 288)

These results indicate that both new legislation and regulatory rules may be ineffective in shaping diversity management practices. In fact, Dobbin, Schrage, and Kalev (2015: 1015) propose that what they refer to as "discretion control initiatives," being a broad category of activities that include "job tests for choosing workers, performance ratings for selecting promotion candidates, and grievance systems for stopping discriminatory managers," tend to spark "managerial rebellion and decrease diversity" (Dobbin, Schrage, and Kalev, 2015: 1015). The solution to this concern is, Dobbin, Schrage, and Kalev (2015: 1034) propose, to enable managers to preserve the agency to promote diversity at all levels in organizations and to hold them accountable for the outcomes:

> Reforms that engage managers in recruiting and training women and minorities for management posts promote diversity. Those designed to control managerial bias lead to resistance and tend to backfire. Reforms that increase hiring and promotion transparency advance diversity by expanding the applicant pool and eliciting accountability. Accountability to diversity managers or federal regulators, moreover, leads managers to be more attentive to the effects of reforms, rendering discretion-control and transparency reforms more effective.
>
> (Dobbin, Schrage, and Kalev, 2015: 1034)

This emphasis on agency and accountability is a significant result as it has implications for the role of new legislation and regulatory reform. However, rather than being incapable of shaping organizational activities, legislation that supports managerial agency is in fact conducive of changes in e.g., diversity management practices, but such legislation must express social norms that are recognized by the social actors that the legislation targets. As Kelly and Dobbin (1999: 485) notice, what they refer to as "legal ambiguity," i.e., the situation where the legislation calls for social activities to cope with a specific issue, but without specifying in detail what practices to implement, or what decisions to make, such new legislation tends to lead to "strong corporate responses." Lucas, Grimes, and Gehman (2022: 974) found that sustainability legislation that supports local norms (examined at the state level in the US) tends to generate more robust changes. Lucas, Grimes, and Gehman (2022: 979) refer to this condition as a " 'crowding-in' effect," wherein comparably "weak legislation" (i.e., legislation that does not prescribe specific practices) still incentivizes corporate actors to implement new sustainability practices. Traditionally, legislation has been understood to work best when "a strong, top-down, coercive force which might overcome the limitations of bottom-up governance" is part of the process (Lucas, Grimes, and Gehman, 2022: 979), but Lucas, Grimes, and Gehman (2022: 982) dispute the efficacy of such legislative processes and propose that "rather than coercing or compelling organizations to make binding commitments, our research suggests there is power in the proliferation of strong but voluntary alternatives." These research results thus indicate that formal and informal cooptation are accomplished, not primarily on the basis of coercive legislation that specifies in detail how organizations should act to handle challenges and issues defined by the new legislation, but on the contrary, when new legislation is comparably "weak," there are possibilities for conferring agency to managers and to make them accountable for their activities and the outcomes (Dobbin, Schrage, and Kalev, 2015).

This result is also indicative of how organizations are by no means passive recipients of new legal or regulatory information. On the contrary, organizations actively respond to new legal statutes and regulatory rules. Edelman, Fuller, and Mara-Drita (2001: 1592) use the term "the managerialization of law" to describe how legal counsellors, hired by organizations to implement new legislation, in fact "[r]hetorically refashion legal ideas that challenge traditional managerial prerogatives and suggests new ideas, which they claim are more innovative, more rational, and more progressive." That is, when legislation is broad inasmuch as it expresses a social norm, or a belief in a certain value (say, in the value of a more diverse and equal labour market; Skaggs, 2009), legal counsellors actively reframe the law in ways that make it "[a]ppear more consistent with traditional managerial prerogatives" (Edelman, Fuller, and Mara-Drita, 2001: 1592). Organizations thus actively contribute to turn *de jure* statutes into *de facto* legislation as new practices are established on the basis of the interpretation of the legislators' intentions, including the social norms that the law expresses (Kelly and Dobbin, 1999: 485).

The neoinstitutional literature indicates that in a domain of practice, the so-called expressive theory of law (Jolls, Sunstein, and Thaler, 1998), its capacity to simultaneously express an existing social norm and to reinforce the same social norm that the legislation supports, structure action. "According to the expressive theory of law, the expression of social values is an important function of the courts or, possibly, the most important function of the courts," Cooter (1998: 586) writes. Cooter (1998: 586) continues: "[l]aw can change the individual values of rational people. Internalizing a social norm is a moral commitment that attaches a psychological penalty to a forbidden act." In this analytical framework, new legislation, regulatory rules, or policy signal the legislators' or policy makers' commitment to social norms and, as indicated by the literature reviewed, legislation may be broad or even "weak" as long as it confers agency and accountability to actors being held responsible for implementing practices that are consistent with the new law or regulation.

An important quality of the expressive theory of law is that new legislation and policy may formally target, e.g., public sector organizations, while in fact there is evidence of what Zhang (2022) refers to as "regulatory spillover" inasmuch as social norms recognized by public sector organizations (e.g., public housing companies) become normatively binding also for private companies. Consistent with the literature on cooptation and the value of weak legislation derived from the expressive theory of law, regulatory spillover generates normative isomorphisms (DiMaggio and Powell, 1983) in industries and organizational fields. Say, a new policy that expresses a social norm regarding the dignity and integrity of students that targets public universities also applies normatively to private universities, and thus acts as if this social norm and its underlying policy also apply to this class of organizations. Over time, a piece of legislation may be incomplete yet authoritative inasmuch as it does not prescribe precise practices as long as it generates robust outcomes that are consistent with legislators and policy makers' intentions, but only if laws or policies express a social norm that is widely shared (Sutton and Dobbin, 1996).

The legal institutionalism framework

Deakin et al. (2017: 188) examine how legislation is central to the constitution and maintenance of the economic system of competitive capitalism, and how this legal system involves both the state, "broadly construed to refer to a realm of public ordering," and "private or customary arrangements," i.e., private ordering devices. In modern complex societies, such as the late modern society and its economic system of competitive capitalism, "there is a legislature that has the capacity to act proactively and in response to socio-economic changes," Deakin et al. (2017: 190) write. The analytical and theoretical framework of legal institutionalism examines how law, law-enforcing organizations, and regulatory agencies jointly create the politico-legal framework that structures and organizes economic activities on the basis of legal rights and other legal devices that confer certain types of authority to market actors and market regulators:

> In legal institutionalism . . . law is treated as more than custom: it is primarily constituted by the state. Once we consider the problems of enforcement in a complex legal system with many agents, and the motivational reasons why individuals might obey the law, then something like the state is required ultimately to ensure enforcement.
>
> (Deakin et al., 2017: 190)

For instance, when examining innovations, new technologies, services, or the bundling of such assets and practices into new entities that can be offered on the market, the legislative state offers a variety of legal devices that ensure the original innovator can claim the exclusive right to use a specific innovation idea. Such legal devices include intellectual property rights derived from patents, trade secrets, copyrights, or registered trademarks (Asay, 2017: 7). However, such a variety of intellectual property rights can only be provided by the legislative state or by the legislative state in collaboration with transnational governance organizations (that normally are dependent on sovereign states that enact jointly agreed rules in its political entities, bestowed with such rights).

Pistor (2020: 165) talks about innovation ideas as *intangibles* (thus being part of the same class of legal entities such as, e.g., financial assets such as corporate bonds or securities), and proposes that such intangibles are bound up and protected by the "coercive powers of the state." Intangible assets thus "come in the form of intellectual property rights, as financial assets, or as a combination of both" (Pistor, 2020: 165):

> [I]ntangibles are wealth producing assets that are coded in law; in the law of contracts and property with additional protections that come from trust, corporate, or bankruptcy law. . . . Understanding the contribution that law makes to the creation and distribution of these assets is therefore critical.
>
> (Pistor, 2020: 166)

In the ideal case, the market is populated by enterprising individuals who actively promote and realize their innovative ideas by, e.g., acquiring finance capital from capital owners with an appetite for investments associated with risks, but also with the promise of above-average returns. Such actors and the resources that they mobilize and have organized on the basis of, e.g., contracting, is nonetheless only secondary to the work conducted by the sovereign state to establish the legal rules that render such private ordering activities effective. When considering, e.g., innovation management activities, the various forms of intellectual property right protections provided by the state are elementary to how these activities are structured: "Without state backing, large-scale anonymous markets for trading promises to future payments would simply not exist," Pistor (2020: 166) says, and refers to how financial assets such as corporate bonds can be traded at large volumes on a day-to-day basis when being legally coded.

A key issue in the legal institutionalism framework is that information has a value for market actors, i.e., information is costly to assess, to acquire, and to share (Merton, 1987: 489). Consequently, information costs are a fact of life, and to protect actors who either develop new information (e.g., by formulating new innovation ideas, as in the case of the patent system) or have invested in collecting valuable information (in most cases, part of the work to develop a new innovation idea), intellectual property rights are protected by the state. The state has an interest in both promoting enterprising and innovative activities, and reducing the risks of opportunistic behaviour such as free-riding and rent-seeking, as such activities are at odds with social norms that value fairness inasmuch as the person who develops an innovation idea should also have a fair chance to materialize the innovation idea on the basis of, e.g., patent system protection. "[T]he value of information," Pistor (2020: 173) writes, "depends critically on the coercive threat of law enforcement and is only as good as this threat is." By implication, in a legal institutionalism perspective, law is not "exogenous to the process of wealth creation," but is rather "the cloth from which wealth is cut" (Pistor, 2020: 183).

One of the major implications from the legal institutional perspective, both part of an analytical perspective and a legal practice, is that the centrality of the rule of law and the active role of the sovereign state in what Pistor (2019: 130) refers to as "legal engineering" become part of the market activities (see, e g., Riles, 2011). This condition is indicated by not the least the growth of legal firms in the US, both in size and in numbers, Pistor (2019: 162) proposes:

> As late as 1984, the top fifty firms in the United States had on average 259 attorneys and an average of $3.4 million. By 2006, the average law firm employed 974 attorneys and was bringing in revenues just short of $40 million, a more than tenfold increase.
>
> (Pistor, 2019: 162)

As market actors such as corporations learn that legislation influences their capacities to make a return on the equity invested in, e.g., innovation management activities, they commit more resources to ensure that their intellectual property rights are enshrined, in many cases prior to the very innovation idea materializing in the conventional sense of the term, i.e., a new technology or artifact is being developed, or as in the form of a prototype or a proof of concept. This demand for legal counselling and an active interaction with the legal system that bestows, e.g., companies with various forms of intellectual property rights, is determined by the fact that law "is inherently incomplete," Pistor (2022: 345) says: "Law is by definition even more incomplete than are contracts. Where a contract seeks to specify the terms of a deal, a law must anticipate a multitude of deals now and in the future."

One of the consequences of this legal incompleteness proposition is that corporations and other market actors may participate in what Pistor (2022: 345) refers to as a *legal arbitrage*, i.e., to productively—from the corporate entity's point of view, but not necessarily for all actors—"find gaps in the scaffolding of laws and regulations and to exploit them for private gain." As law's incompleteness is a "fertile ground for legal arbitrage, that is, for compliance with the letter of the law even as end runs are devised around its spirit" (Pistor, 2022: 345), legislators and regulatory agencies that are given the authority to ensure that the law is being adhered to both as it is written and intended to operate and in an ongoing and ceaseless struggle to keep track of the various forms of legal arbitrage being observed and/or reported. In, e.g., finance markets, innovations are introduced at a high pace, at the same time as these innovations are often quickly adopted by all markets actors, Awrey (2013: 410) notices. As a corollary, Awrey (2013: 410) adds, drawing on the elementary economic theory proposition that an innovator may have an interest in exclusively using the new innovation to cover the development costs, and to acquire the financial capital needed to organize the next innovation project, "we might expect to observe relatively little innovation." In fact, the opposite situation is the case, and this observation is possibly best explained by the fact that a significant proportion of financial innovations are introduced to mitigate "the impact of various regulatory requirements" (Awrey, 2013: 410). For instance, following the 2008 finance industry collapse, caused by the presence of so-called toxic assets of the balance sheets on financial institutions, which generated systemic risks in the short-term repo market that financial institutions rely on to balance short-term debt and long-term asset holdings, which in turn resulted in more strict capital requirements for banks, the financial innovation of structured finance techniques are widely used to circumvent new capital requirement rules.[1] The growth of fintech firms in, e.g., the mortgage lending industry have been examined on the basis of such new regulatory requirements (Berg, Fuster, and Puri, 2022: 196). In the end, such legal arbitrage is an unintended consequence of purposeful action that policy makers and legislators at times tolerate (or even recognize as being a driver of new innovation), whereas in other cases it may be counteracted with new and more detailed legislation or regulatory control.

Another key feature of a variety of social systems (e.g., infrastructures, the legal system, and its subsystems such as the patent system) is that they are characterized by what Spears (2019: 347) refers to as their "disjunction,"

1 Financial innovation is also produced on the basis of other interests and perceived market opportunities. Awrey (2013: 410) lists at least two other reasons for innovating, with the first being a response to "the emergence of genuine demand within the marketplace" (as in the case of fintech-based mortgage lending, wherein the conventional mortgage lending industry actors fail to service a significant proportion of the households, e.g., low-net-worth households). The second reason is—examined in more detail in the next chapter—to create possibilities for above-average returns on the basis of the monopolistic intellectual property rights that grant exclusivity right to a patent holder. Still, the possibilities for legal arbitrage remain a strong incentive to innovate, not the least in the finance industry, which trades large volumes each trading day.

i.e., law itself "tends to be characterized by contradicting and ambiguous principles and concepts." To cope with this condition and to otherwise be able to operate in a milieu characterized by legal ambiguity and considerable information costs that pertain to the legal system's rules and principles, "[a] lot of legal change occurs without policing by a court or endorsement by a legislature," Pistor (2022: 346) proposes. That is, corporations seek the assistance of lawyers and legal counsellors to optimize their possibilities for complying with legal rules, at the same time as they can exploit the possibilities for generating rents, and in many cases legal devices such as contracts and social norms regarding secrecy are equally important for preserving the market system's efficiency as any new piece of legislation would be (Edelman and Suchman, 1997; Edelman, Fuller, and Mara-Drita, 2001). In other words, legal rights wield a considerable authority in the marketplace, but the disjunctive nature of the legal system provides possibilities for both legal arbitrage and private ordering activities. Legal institutionalism scholars do neither deny the existence of such market practices, nor do they necessarily deplore them, but what they insist on is that such private ordering activities (e.g., contracting between corporations, say, a supplier and a manufacturing company) of necessity occur in the shadow of the legislative state, and being shaped by the state's capacity to pass new legislation or regulatory rules to uphold or restore market efficiency and to achieve other policy goals.

Unintended consequences of the legal system

While legal institutionalism scholars are cognizant of the difficulties involved in creating a legal system that operates perfectly and that rules out all possibilities for legal arbitrage or any other source of unfairness that the legal system purports to eliminate by rationalist protagonists, and thus being largely agnostic regarding the moot question whether the current legal system is the best one possible or not, there are nonetheless cases of opportunistic behaviour that are intolerable as they undermine the authority of the legal system as externalities are generated. Pistor (2022: 346) calls attention to the fact that policy makers may both wish to support free market activities (an objective premised on the belief in leniently regulated markets being more efficient in terms of how they can allocate resources, and provide other economic benefits, widely covered in detail in elementary neoclassical economic theory), and to preserve tolerable levels of economic equality (addressed in terms of distributive justice), and how these dual objectives may at times diverge:

> [L]awmakers and adjudicators often support private interests that endorse free markets, free movement, and private autonomy, even when these

> principles are in tension with principles of distributive justice, when they threaten to destabilise the financial system or destroy the environment.
> (Pistor, 2022: 346)

By implication, if a legal system is essentially supportive of enterprising on the basis of leniently regulated markets, then there are possibly opportunities for what Pistor (2022: 344) refers to as "strategic private actors" to appropriate, to support private wealth creation, "one of, if not the most formidable collective resource, the legal system," and often "without taking into consideration how this might affect others or society as a whole." That is, the claim that something is "legally protected," and therefore commendable, or consistent with prevalent social norms, etc., is a fallacy as such strategic private actors largely use the term "legal" as a code word for accessing "the centralised means of coercion that allows them to uphold their claims against others," Pistor (2022: 344) claims. As indicated earlier, in the field of finance innovations, innovations may be developed for a variety of reasons, and one of them is plausibly to circumvent and to neutralize the undesirable (from the innovator's point of view) effects of, e.g., additional regulatory rules, defined by new legislation. This means that innovations may be legally sanctioned, but without being consistent with the legislator's intentions, nor with the social norms that pre-date the legislation that made the new innovation legally protected. For legal institutionalism scholars, the question of legality and, by implication, the moral authority of specific legal statutes is constantly being revised and modified as the legal system itself is incomplete and disjunctive, and thus dependent on market actors and their legal counsellors acting in ways that are consistent with the stated or implied intentions of the law. As will be discussed later, many parts of the legislation invite corporate activities that are not of necessity fully consistent with such legal intentions, and therefore occasionally become subject to scholarly inquiries.

Hard law, soft law, and regulatory entrepreneurship

Legal institutionalism scholars recognize that the legal system is a patchwork composed of legislation, regulatory rules, social norms, case-based court ruling, and other legal devices and tools that play a role in determining market activities and outcomes, including, e.g., innovations. Some of these legal devices are discussed as follows.[2]

2 As Deakin et al. (2017: 197) argues, "[t]he growth of a diversity of business and industrial structures makes it imperative to develop clear, distinct definitions of the different entities involved and to understand their legal structure." The introduction of a few key terms are by no means exhaustive of the legal

Abbott and Snidal (2000: 421) define *hard law* as "legally binding obligations" that are "precise" (or that "can be made precise" through adjudication or the issuance of detailed regulations) and that "delegate authority for interpreting and implementing the law." *Soft law*, in turn, denotes any kind of legal activity (e.g., contract writing) being premised on "weakened" legal arrangements that pertain to one or more of the dimensions of "obligation, precision, and delegation" (Abbott and Snidal, 2000: 422). This somewhat clunky definition, bound up with *legalese*, can be complemented by Quack's (2007: 652) description of soft law as being exemplified by "model contracts" and "other legal standards" that are developed by lawyers and other legal counsellors who are hired to assists corporations when dealing with legal affairs. In brief, soft law are activities that are conducted with the pretention of having the full legality warranted by the sovereign state, yet being activities whose legal status is either unclear or disputed. Soft law thus denotes any activity that occurs in the shadow of the legislative state and the transnational governance organizations that the state recognizes, but whose legal status is to be determined after the fact.

Based on the idea of the presence of soft law, Regan and Hall (2016) propose that there is what they refer to as *soft governance*, a "system of governance" that "differs from conventional legal regulation" insofar as "both public and private actors are involved in rule formation," and with several provisions being "voluntary," and with several cases with "no formal penalty for violations" (Regan and Hall, 2016: 2002). Furthermore, soft governance systems are premised on market participants being concerned with protecting their reputation inasmuch as they adhere to the rules to avoid being shamed, reprimanded, or otherwise suffering reputational losses that are costly in a medium to long-term perspective. It can be learned from history that policy makers may have a firm belief in such reputational losses being an effective mechanism for deterring market actors from participating in undesirable market behaviour, and that such beliefs have not been honoured by the market actors. For instance, the private ordering model that was widely considered to be robust and trustworthy prior to the 2008 finance industry crisis, based on credit rating agencies with the integrity to issue balanced and fair assessments of their clients' financial status (Besedovsky, 2018; Alp, 2013; White, 2013), proved to be inoperable and was considered one of the major causes of the largest crisis of the economic system of competitive capitalism to date (Bernanke, 2023; Fligstein, 2021). In this case, the risk of reputational loss could not mediate the financial and economic incentives that the credit rating agencies acted on the basis of, which eventually

institutionalism vocabulary, but intends to provide some operational definitions that support a more detailed understanding of the analytical framework being advocated.

resulted in over-optimistic assessments of the financial status of companies issuing stocks, bonds, securities, etc. Taken together, soft governance may be an inoperable governance model in industries prone to developing systematic risks, and being closely entangled with other industries, as in the case of the finance industry.

As soft law is by definition vague and inconclusive, legal milieus that are dominated by soft law include the possibility for regulatory entrepreneurship, the possibilities for acting *ultra vires*, outside of what is legally permitted, e.g., "outside of the firms' legitimate powers" (Hockett and Omarova, 2016: 470) in order to generate above-average rents, or, if being successful, to make these new practices legally permissible (as in the case of Silicon Valley–based companies such as Uber, actively breaching legislation and regulatory rules to promote their business concepts; Rosenblat, 2018; Thelen, 2018; Collier, Dubal, and Carter, 2018). For example, if the relevant regulatory body "credibly commits to not enforcing the law on the books," that is roughly as good, from the regulatory entrepreneur's perspective, "as formally amending the law" (Pollman and Barry, 2017: 397).

While the choice of wording, including "regulatory" and "entrepreneur," may indicate that this capacity to navigate in the grey zones of legality is an honourable thing—largely determined by the positive associations of the concept of entrepreneurship—regulatory entrepreneurship is in most cases intended to privatize returns on the basis of common goods. Regulatory entrepreneurship thus generates to a tragedy of the commons scenario, widely discussed in policy-making quarters and in economic theory (see Hardin, 1968). In the following sections, two such cases of regulatory entrepreneurship are addressed: tax avoidance and the advocacy and creation of new legal entities such as Limited Liability Companies (LCCs).

Corporate tax avoidance activities

In legal terms, it is important to discriminate between tax evasion, which is illegal, and tax avoidance, which is legally permitted but potentially associated with a violation of moral and ethical standards being widely recognized in society (Alstadsæter, Johannesen, and Zucman, 2019: 2074; Palan, Murphy, and Chavagneux, 2010: 9–10). "Legally, there is a clear difference between evasion and avoidance," Palan, Murphy, and Chavagneux (2010: 10) assert; "Tax avoidance is the gray areas between tax compliance and tax evasion." Regardless of how to draw the line between what is a case of illegal tax evasion or a legal case of tax avoidance, the magnitude of taxes being withheld from sovereign states on an annual and recurrent basis is spectacular. In the UK alone, the accountant Richard Murphy calculated that tax evasion "costs the treasury around £70 billion a year—that's seventy times more than the estimates of benefit fraud" (Jones, 2011: 165). That is, presumably low-income groups' cases of fraud committed to secure a livable income on a monthly basis is vastly overshadowed by the tax evasion that companies and high-net-worth households orchestrate on the basis of the legal engineering activities of their legal counsellors. Several scholars pay attention to how legislation, and not the least the legislation in tax havens, serves to reduce the overall welfare of citizens as in particular high-net-worth households actively plan to minimize their taxes being paid (Beckert, 2022; Tait, 2019; Harrington, 2016). The same situation is the case regarding corporate taxes, Ramanna (2020: 36) argues:

> [E]ven given the set of tax rules, corporations have created an industry of violating the spirit of those rules while complying with their letter. In fact, "tax efficiency" has become the euphemism for corporate "tax avoidance, and a whole industry, championed in sad irony by auditors, exists to enable this gamesmanship.
>
> (Ramanna, 2020: 36)

Within the European Union, otherwise being governed on the basis of the rule of law, and strict antitrust legislation to preserve market competition, a similar situation and attitude is the case, Engelen (2017) argues:

> [O]ff-shore jurisdictions like the Netherlands, Luxembourg and Ireland have been instrumental for the financialization of global capitalism by providing crucial infrastructural services to large financial agents, in the form of tax avoidance, regulatory arbitrage and the facilitation of what is called 'financial innovation,' as is indicated by the widespread use of securitization techniques to repackage mortgages, student loans, car loans and credit card debts.
>
> (Engelen, 2017: 55)

In a legal institutionalism perspective, these possibilities for tax avoidance and tax evasion are a legal matter as jurisdictions that pass legislation that provide possibilities for withholding taxable income do this on a legitimate basis, and with the intention to create new business and job growth opportunities, but when acting in this way, they create legal milieus wherein companies and capital owners can hide their wealth and avoid taxes. For instance, the state of Delaware, whose primary business is the incorporation of business ventures, passed a new law that enabled so-called Intellectual

Property Holding Companies (IPHCs) to collect income from intellectual property rights when using Delaware as its domicile, Nguyen (2021) shows:

> Delaware exists as a tax haven for intellectual property assets. Instead of creating intellectual property, Delaware *holds* intellectual property assets for corporations across the nation. As a tax haven, Delaware provides a zero tax rate on the vast income generated from the licensing, commercialization, and exploitation of intellectual property assets by intellectual property holding companies. Delaware's zero tax rate facilitates an aggressive corporate tax avoidance scheme allowing multistate corporations to avoid paying their taxes in Delaware's sister states.
>
> (Nguyen, 2021: 719)

As Nguyen (2021) remarks, a piece of legislation that may be good for Delaware incurs significant losses in tax income from any other American state whose businesses are active in the choice to domicile in Delaware. "Firms possessing intellectual property rights (IPRs) can use them to extract monopoly rents from other firms and consumers, producing interfirm inequality of profits," Schwartz (2016: 228) writes. This legal arbitrage is thus a zero-sum game wherein the one state's marginal gain comes at the price of the other state's marginal loss. Furthermore, then passing legislation of this kind, tax avoidance is gradually understood as what is a legitimate business and household practice, in turn supporting the introduction of, and wide use of euphemisms such as "tax efficiency" to justify business practices that indubitably violate the policy makers' and legislators' intentions.

To illustrate the consequences of such legal arbitrage, Schwartz (2016: 239) examines the case of Apple Sales International, a corporate entity within the Apple conglomerate. Apple Sales International had no employees until 2013, and is domiciled in Ireland, where the corporate entity collects "massive amounts of revenue from every transaction." At the same time, for legal reasons stipulated in Irish corporate tax law, Apple Sales International attracts no legal tax liability "because Apple deliberately structured it in ways that would prevent it from being legally domiciled in either the United States or Ireland for tax purposes" (Schwartz, 2016: 239). A similar case is the Coca-Cola Company, headquartered in Atlanta, Georgia, USA, but also taking advantage of Irish corporate tax legislation: "The formula for Coca-Cola is held by an Irish shell company controlled by Coca-Cola," so that the "IPR-based profit component of the value chain" is segregated legally into "a stand-alone firm"—and within that firm to a stand-alone daughter firm in a tax haven—to "maximize shareholder value and return on assets for that firm" (Schwartz, 2016: 239). Major multinational corporations such as Apple or Coca-Cola can thus take advantage of the possibilities for legal arbitrage and regulatory entrepreneurship on the basis of their capacity to hire and make use of legal advisors who are informed about the legal loopholes that are supportive of the targeted level of tax avoidance. By default, the choice to pay or to not pay taxes becomes a public relations decision of sorts, to be made by the corporate board of directors rather than some legal or moral obligation. This belief is premised on fiscal policy and tax legislation on the national level, incapable of counteracting the race-to-the-bottom corporate tax policy being enacted by sovereign states, premised on the ambition to become the state of choice to domicile in for business incorporation. Even the European Union, with its fairly strict view of corporate responsibilities, is only leniently monitoring the presence of a number of major tax havens, including The Netherlands, Ireland, Luxembourg, Malta, and Cyprus.

New legal corporate entities

Not only do corporations take advantage of legal arbitrage to minimize their corporate taxes to be paid, but they also use new legal entities such as Limited Liability Companies (LLCs) and Limited Partnerships (LPs) to circumvent or reduce the impact of the regulatory control of the sovereign state. Such new legal entities are also established on the state level (in the US) or by sovereign states to attract business ventures to domicile in the state, or to otherwise promote enterprising activities and job growth. Between 1990 and 2012, the number of LLCs and LPs increased by "more than 750 percent" in the United States—at a pace higher than any other form of economic organization, including traditional corporations, Soener and Nau (2019: 400) write. The legal reforms that permitted LLCs is an exemplary case of business lobbying to allegedly support business interests and is therefore of relevance for the legal institutionalism theory framework. The State of Panama offered "one particularly attractive model" for business incorporation in the 1960s, which combined many of the benefits of traditional incorporation with those of traditional partnerships (Soener and Nau, 2019: 402). After lobbying the legislature in the state of Wyoming, a sparsely populated state in the Rocky Mountains, and with little opposition, Wyoming adopted "the first LLC statute in the United States" in 1977 (Soener and Nau, 2019: 402). As a legal device, the LLC is a form of "hybrid business" that has neither replaced the traditional incorporated business, nor being a "simple appendage" to this corporate form. In fact, the legal-organizational structure of, e.g., LLCs combines "benefits of corporate status" like limited liability, but without the burden of "full public disclosures, rigid governance structure and double taxation" (Soener and Nau, 2019: 401). As Soener and Nau (2019: 410) notice, many legal scholars have addressed "the weak governance rules" for both LLCs and LPs "on a stand-alone basis," thus being the perfect vehicle for certain business activities intended to reward specific actors, such as the owners of the corporate stock being issued. In the State of Delaware, which followed Wyoming in legally incorporating LLCs to protect its status as being the state of choice to domicile business ventures, the paperwork needed is not burdensome, and the cost to register an LLC is most marginal, $90 for LLCs and $200 for LPs (Soener and Nau, 2019: 412).

Studies of the use of LLCs have indicated that actors in what McGoey (2021: 392) refers to as "philanthrocapitalism" have been particularly attracted by the LLC form, presumably because LLCs are subject to "far fewer disclosure stipulations" than earlier philanthropic foundations were, which in turn makes it harder to "follow the money and empirically study grant disbursements." LLCs thus bestow secrecy on philanthrocapitalist entities, which makes them less susceptible to critique regarding, e.g., their decisions and behaviours in the public sphere more generally as outsiders cannot access relevant data, mandatory to disclose by public companies. Empirical studies cast a shadow of doubt over the intended use of LLCs in, e.g., housing markets. Just like Soener and Nau (2019), Travis (2019: 146) notices that by the mid-2000s, the LLC "had become the most popular business organization in the United States," and with more new LLCs formed each year than public corporations. Studying the housing market in Milwaukee, Wisconsin, USA, Travis (2019) found that LLC ownership is "positively associated with measures of housing disrepair." An "interrupted time series analysis" shows that when "rental properties" change hands from "an unincorporated owner to an LLC owner," the rental properties "experience more rapid deterioration with no evidence to suggest these properties were on divergent trajectories prior to the change of ownership" (Travis, 2019: 143). That is, Travis (2019: 164) deduces, the legal rights associated with LLC "may undermine incentives for assiduous property maintenance among residential landlords." Furthermore, this tendency wherein new housing market entrants using the LLC legal device was "strongest in poor neighborhoods," which suggests that "the ongoing expansion of LLC ownership" may have particular consequences for housing conditions "experienced by the urban poor" (Travis, 2019: 143).

To fully understand the significance of Travis's (2019) findings, it is important to recognize that the LLC is widely understood to be an "an easy-to-use" legal device that allows owners to "circumscribe liability and protect their assets" (Travis, 2019: 147). In housing markets, especially at the low end of the market that serves families with limited and often restrained household budgets, housing assets can be acquired at a lower cost. This is the case because prior housing owners have disinvested in their property for a variety of reasons, and this results in the physical deterioration of a neighborhood's "housing stock, infrastructure, and public spaces" (Travis, 2019: 144). When housing assets are sold at a comparably low price, and especially if the location in the wider city district is attractive, there are business opportunities available: neglected housing can be renovated, and rents can be raised sharply on the basis that an investment has been done, in many cases unproportionally to the actual cost to renovate the facilities. Such business activities frequently result in what has been referred to as "renoviction" by housing studies scholars (Thörn and Thörn, 2017: 294)—renovation activities that result in *de facto* "evictions" (or "voluntary evictions") as the tenants cannot afford to pay the new higher rent.

This business model, to buy neglected housing cheaply in attractive locations, often in disadvantaged and "blighted" city districts, and to renovate to attract a new category of tenants, presumably with better possibilities for paying higher rents, is presumably more attractive if the LLC model is available. "[T]he LLC's easy-to-use liability firewall has made it easier for both professional and casual landlords to transform rental housing into an investment asset more akin to other financial products," Travis (2019: 147) writes. Although this may be regarded as an attractive business opportunity, the business practice may also run counter to affordable housing policies that the City Hall or the state has passed, and it creates additional costs for taxpayers as families being "renovicted" have the legal right to a home under all conditions. When their traditional approach to access affordable housing is being diminished by new business practices, the municipality or the state has to play an active role in supplying, e.g., public housing facilities. Therefore, Travis (2019: 164) concludes, as "LLC ownership is positively associated with indicators of property neglect," LLCs are "a source of moral hazard" (Travis, 2019: 144) inasmuch as they provide legal protection for business owners as many of their assets are protected from disclosure by, e.g., regulatory agencies. "[G]iven the anonymity and liability protections afforded by LLC ownership, cities may increasingly struggle to hold landlords accountable for substandard housing conditions or tenant abuse," Travis (2019: 165) writes. Furthermore, state governments that adopted LLC statutes "with an eye toward creating business-friendly legal environments that would spur investment," may be over-optimistic regarding the positive effects of this legal reform, as e.g., LLCs have "long been thought of as a mechanism for attracting capital to risky entrepreneurial endeavors" (Travis, 2019: 165). Seen in this view, the new corporate form is associated with legal arbitrage and regulatory entrepreneurship of the kind that, e.g., legal institutionalism scholars are interested in tracing and to fully examine in terms of their consequences for the broader economic system.

By the end of the day, regulatory entrepreneurship and tax avoidance activities are a fact of life, and only transnational governance organization and agreements passed on this international level can effectively cope with activities derived from legal ambiguities and loopholes in the legislation. What can be learnt from such cases is still that the legal institutionalism framework, which regards economic affairs as essentially being structured on the basis of legislation and the interpretation of legal statutes and rules, holds an explanatory potential regarding how economic value is generated. Economic value is determined by legal rights and legal conditions that are shared by a variety of actors, each operating in the same legal framework, and thus being exposed to the same legal and regulatory controls. Economic affairs is then not only a matter of using cognitive capacities, and the ambition to create new businesses and products and services, but also the legal conditions that are created to support such activities matter, and they matter to a great extent.

The balancing of governance on the basis of law and private ordering in advanced economies

In the legal institutionalism framework, the sovereign state holds the exclusive right to pass law and to enact international law, and consequently it is important to balance public interest and efficiency in any governance activity that pertains to market transactions and contracting. On the one side of the continuum, the sovereign state can authoritatively monitor all economic activities in detail to ensure that public interests are considered, but such a governance model would plausibly incur a considerable loss in efficiency as the whole idea of the market would cease to have an operational and practical meaning; on the other side of the continuum, a laissez-faire governance model would transfer all governance decisions to market actors to maximize so-called market efficiency on the basis of, e.g., the price system, but this type of unregulated, essentially neoliberal market system would presumably result in, e.g., public interests being neglected. In the ordinary order of economic affairs, most advanced economies are governed on the basis of a combination of market mechanisms and regulatory oversight, and the decision on how to balance these two governance mechanisms, and the devices and tools they rely on, is an ongoing concern in economic affairs. The purpose of this section is to discuss how the legal institutionalism framework does not in any way undermine or marginalize market mechanisms and devices, but rather laws, regulations, and the support for specific social norms (such as promoting an enterprising and entrepreneurial culture) act to support market devices that are already in place and in operation in the course of everyday life market transactions and contracting.

The return of private ordering: the blending of agency regulation and asset management practices

If elites are capable of influencing the legislative process through a number of mechanisms (an issue examined in more detail in Chapter 5), the question is then what the situation looks like in the executive branch, where the new legislation is implemented and intended to be followed. Political scientists, legal scholars, and other social science scholars have been concerned with what is being referred to as the "privatized welfare state" (e.g., Cordelli, 2020; Richard and Phillips-Fein, 2017; Carnes, 2013; Büthe and Mattli, 2011; Hacker, 2004; Hall and Biersteker, 2002), wherein what were once regarded as public affairs, handled by the state in the executive branch and by its agencies, are gradually becoming subject to market making and private companies actively being involved in such activities. There are also scholars who advocate such changes and who emphasize the effectiveness of private companies and the benefits of having all sorts of social activities subject to competition to optimize the use of public resources (see, e.g., Blix and Jordahl, 2020). Such activities include welfare state provision (Marwell, 2004), the financing and management of pension systems (Naczyk, 2013), or the access to and ownership over large-scale health data sets (Enriquez-Sarano, 2020).

More specifically, when law that pertains to corporate practices is implemented, the tendency has been to rely less on regulatory agencies monitoring the outcomes and consequences, and to increasingly entrust managers, such as fund managers in institutional investment firms, with such responsibilities (Lund, 2022; Lund and Pollman, 2021). Lund (2022: 80, footnote 8) defines regulation as "interventions in the private domain that are implemented in the form of rules that are intended to shape the conduct of individuals and firms." Van Loo (2020) argues that this emphasis on private ordering governance is nothing new in US policy. The Federal Trade Commission does, for instance, require that large technology companies "act in ways traditionally associated with public regulators—by policing other businesses for legal violations" (Van Loo, 2020: 469). Similarly, in the pharmaceutical industry, "policymakers can still influence private parties to regulate voluntarily" (Van Loo, 2020: 477). Say, if the law imposes "vicarious liability on the pharmaceutical company" for violations by its ingredients supplier, the pharmaceutical company may be motivated "to audit the supplier's production process even though auditing is not required" (Van Loo, 2020: 477). In the case of Pfizer, the Food and Drug Administration (FDA) acts to make this public company routinely monitor suppliers through "audits, inspections, and review of systems" (Van Loo, 2020: 493). If Pfizer detects a violation among its suppliers, it can "de-list" the supplier from the "qualified suppliers" register, or it can report violations to the FDA (Van Loo, 2020: 493). Through the use of such private ordering governance practices, there is an "increasingly narrow divide between private businesses and the administrative state," Van Loo (2020: 472) proposes. Van Loo (2020: 472) argues that this "new area of quasi-regulatory activity" is unlikely to displace the more traditional market governance activities, but he is concerned about the increased reliance on public ordering governance for two reasons. First, this "conscripted enforcement" lacks transparency and traditional measures of public involvement (Van Loo, 2020: 472), and second, there is a lack of empirical studies of how the "enforcer-firm" acts in this new role, and consequently it is difficult to formulate "strong normative conclusions" on the basis of thin or almost non-existent empirical data (Van Loo, 2020: 473).

Regarding the first issue, the corporate entity "remains exceedingly private," Van Loo (2020: 473) writes, but as corporations are directed to "write enforcement-oriented contract clauses and monitor external relationships for legal violations," the sovereign state pushes corporations to assume "a larger public role" (Van Loo, 2020: 473). If being cast in this role, it follows that policy makers, the agents representing the judiciary, and corporate directors and executives need to think hard about "what duties corporations owe to society," not the least as the predominant corporate governance mechanisms over the last four to five decades have been that the corporations should primarily create value for their shareholders (Van Loo, 2020: 473–474). Van Loo (2020) is skeptical about this scenario wherein corporations act to support social interests (no matter how precisely or vaguely that term is defined) at the same time as they act to maximize the economic wealth of their shareholders. The new private ordering governance model would have implications for the market order and market dynamics, and the quality of administrative regulation would be affected. A central preoccupation of administrative law is "the accountability of unelected bureaucrats," and the effectiveness of administrative decisions is also "crucial to administrative law" (Van Loo, 2020: 509–510), and consequently, any decisive shift in the power balance between the state and industry and corporations would presumably generate unanticipated and unintended consequences that are at risk to reduce economic and social welfare. Still, a major concern regarding regulatory affairs has traditionally been (and continues to be addressed in such terms) that bureaucrats have "insufficient skills or information," which reduce their capacity to "keep up with the private sector" (Van Loo, 2020: 511). "In theory," Van Loo (2020: 516) writes, in the absence of direct empirical study, "large firms' greater information and sophistication should make them more cost-effective than a public regulator or new class of private third-party regulators performing the same function." Unfortunately, it is plausible to assume on the basis of empirical evidence and industry-specific studies that the same predicament that befalls state administrators plausibly applies to agents employed by private corporations, Van Loo (2020) argues:

> To be clear, the firm is not necessarily an expert in all that the service provider does—indeed, a lack of expertise sometimes motivates a firm to outsource. For instance, banks have found the task of monitoring third-party vendors extremely difficult, particularly fintechs and others providing complex artificially intelligent services, such as chatbots, credit monitoring, and fraud detection.
>
> (Van Loo, 2020: 511–512)

Following from this predicament that pertains to unavoidable information costs, a key question in business regulation is what set of incentives that would optimally "deter wrongdoing," but studies of such optimal deterrence packages have to date only produced "inconclusive results" (Van Loo, 2020: 510). This means that informed agents, now being subject to both administrative rules and corporate monitoring, cannot be incentivized to act in ways that are consistent with broader economic and social interests on the basis of carefully designed deterrence packages, which leaves all participants little choice than to rely on the principle of charity and business judgment rule, which stipulates that also, e.g., supplier firms employ executives and co-workers who act reasonably and prudently even in the absence of staid and comprehensive monitoring mechanisms.

To empirically substantiate the theory of private ordering governance and its efficacy, Lund (2022) pays specific attention to the role of the so-called "Big Three" investment companies BlackRock, Vanguard, and State Street Corporation, and in terms of how new "self-regulation" activities would be able to handle long-term challenges in the economic system, including not the least the pressing environmental sustainability issue. Structural changes in the economic system of corporate capitalism have not happened overnight, but investment fund managers' entry into "the market for regulation" represents the expansion of "privatization dynamics" that have shaped policy making and legal scholarship since the 1980s (Lund, 2022: 87). These changes have broad ramifications for not just corporate America but also for "our system of democracy," Lund (2022: 87) proposes.

As investment companies are profit-maximizing, some policy makers and scholars argue that these companies act to "secure broad consensus from their clients when adopting rules" (Lund, 2022: 83). Lund (2022: 84) is skeptical regarding the efficacy of such governance practices as fund managers, who vote on corporate proposals issued by the board of directors as part of their shareholder rights (for instance, in 2020, Lund [2022: 94, footnote 93] reports, Vanguard fund managers "cast over 168,000 individual votes"), are not incentivized to "adopt socially beneficial policies" that lack broad support from their clients, and particularly not the corporate clients who supply "a large percentage of their assets under management." This means that the Big Three are likely "to mandate only tepid changes in corporate behavior," and that their rules "will not bring about the sweeping changes that may be necessary to address pressing social problems" (Lund, 2022: 84). It is thus plausible that "client tastes" will "dictate policies," rather than support "principled consideration of systematic risks or externalities," Lund (2022: 87) proposes:

> [T]he provision of regulation by a handful of for-profit asset managers, acting in response to demand from their clients, is concerning. The governance officials and executives at the Big Three who make the rules lack

> democratic accountability for their actions, and there is little oversight or transparency surrounding their policies and how they are formulated, unlike other private regulators that impact the broader market.
>
> (Lund, 2022: 88)

In addition, Lund (2022: 88) is concerned that asset manager regulation will not "further the public interest." Investors represent "the wealthier half of America," Lund (2022: 88) remarks, and corporations are likely to embrace rules regulating their conduct "for strategic reasons," including, e.g., the "desire to forestall or co-opt future government regulation." For example, over the past few decades, oil and gas companies have spent "substantial sums" to influence regulators and to undermine environmental regulation that would force these companies to "internalize externalities that harm society" (Lund, 2022: 123).

At the same time, the claim made by legal scholars such as Jeffrey Gordon, that institutional investors are incentivized to recognize social norms on the basis of the proposition that "[d]iversified institutional shareholders have an incentive to adopt social policies that will increase the value of the portfolio as a whole" (Lund, 2022: 111), have been shown to be correct in certain cases. The social norms supportive of increased gender equality in boardrooms have in fact been effectively translated into actual changes in Standard & Poor (S&P) 1500 companies in the US: from 2017 to 2020, the number of S&P 1500 firms "lacking a woman director" dropped from 179 to 30, and by 2020, "no S&P 500 company had an all-male board" (Lund, 2022: 108). Despite evidence of such landmark achievements, Lund (2022: 138) argues that institutional investors are "unlikely to adopt socially beneficial regulations that their clients oppose." Furthermore, the optimism about "this asset manager regulatory dynamic" usually stems from disillusionment with public regulation, Lund (2022: 133) proposes. Asset manager regulation does have some practical benefits vis-à-vis agency regulation, including that it is less likely to be hamstrung by "legal roadblocks" that thwart the public regulatory process (Lund, 2022: 134), but such benefits do not solve or handle the condition that institutional investors have historically failed to take a stand on a number of issues that pertain to the capacity to preserve and uphold economic and social welfare. For instance, the Big Three have failed to support new regulatory rules that would make it mandatory to disclose corporate political spending and "other deregulatory business agendas" (Lund, 2022: 138). The Big Three have also generally supported stock buybacks and merger and acquisitions activities that are associated with short-term gains for shareholders (Lund, 2022: 127, footnote 246), activities that have been argued to gradually erode the legitimacy of the economic system of competitive capitalism as such rent-seeking activities have been regarded in optimistic terms as what raise the welfare of all constituencies, while in fact they primarily benefit shareholders.

Finally, Lund (2022: 132) argues that asset manager regulation is distinctively different from "self-regulation" as the affected companies "have not agreed to be bound by their rules." This means that, e.g., Big Three governance *qua* regulation more closely resembles "other private providers of rules," such as credit rating agencies. Credit rating agencies perform a market regulatory function inadvertently inasmuch as their goal is "not to set standards for compliance," but given the consequences companies need to handle if and when their debt is downgraded by a credit rating agency, "their activity ultimately has that effect" (Lund, 2022: 132). In legal theory terms, this means that asset manager regulation is not premised on what Dworkin (1975) refers to as legal rights (being defined within a specific piece of legislation) but on policy (i.e., the objectives that are expressed by some policy). The policy goal of credit rating agencies is to establish standards for how to assess and to communicate or signal market risks regarding the issuances made by corporations on the money or credit markets, and this policy goal is premised on the belief in the value of finance market stability (and market stability in its related markets, say, the housing market or the energy market). In contrast, much market regulation is premised on rights being protected by law (as in the case of corporate legislation, which grants the authority to make business decisions to the board of directors governing an incorporated business), and the shift from agency regulation (organized and monitored by the sovereign state) to asset manager regulation is thus a hybrid regulatory form, between agency regulation and "self-regulation" that under all conditions and varying descriptions confer regulatory authority to asset managers in companies such as the Big Three. It should be remarked that this is precisely what legal scholars such as Adolf A. Berle and his collaborator Gardiner C. Means were concerned with in the New Deal era (and subject to much debate, e.g., with the Harvard law professor Merrick Dodd; see Berle, 1931, 1932; Dodd, 1932), namely the risks associated with the increased capacity of a handful of executives to wield a substantial influence on the economic system. Berle and Means and Dodd were more concerned with the decision-making authority of executives in gargantuan firms, operating in monopolist or oligopolist markets, but with the gradual and unprecedented expansion of the finance industry since the late 1990s, the focus has shifted to institutional investors and the fund managers who cast the votes and who *de jure* and *de facto* shape the economic system of competitive capitalism. The key concern here is the question of short-termism (itself an ambiguous term; Roe and Shapira, 2021) and whether such fund managers are incentivized to address the more inconvenient issues that need to be handled on short notice. In Lund's account (2022), a few modifications in the corporate system on the basis of changing social norms should not be taken as *prima facie* evidence of fund managers being concerned with handling all sorts of issues that affect economic and social welfare, simply because their job is to optimize the original investors' return at the same time as their interests and preferences are at least partially considered. By implication, it means that neither the legislature, the judiciary, or the executive branch of the sovereign state, nor the asset manager regulation model appear to have both the authority and the executive capacity to effectively address pressing issues, including not the least the environmental sustainability concern.

Political failures and governance of the corporate entity

If private ordering regulation has some limitations inasmuch as fund managers who oversee increasingly larger investment funds have some limitations regarding how to optimize the balancing of public interest and efficiency in how economic resources are generated and invested, then a return to a governance model wherein some centrally located market-monitoring agency surveils the economic system is not feasible either, the scholarly literature indicates. Fennell and McAdams (2016: 1055) say that "political failure" is no less prominent than "market failure," and that political failure "can thwart efforts at welfare maximization." Fennell and McAdams (2016: 1081) argue that economic analysts frequently incorrectly assume that what Fennell and McAdams (2016) refer to as "distributive invariance," the belief that the political decision to allocate resources differently on the basis of legal and regulatory reforms, does not reduce the overall efficiency and performance of the economic system, is the case. In contrast to this optimistic view, Fennell and McAdams (2016: 1081) argue that empirical studies demonstrate that individuals and groups "continually incur considerable political costs to win distributive fights over legal rules and non-tax policy." It is a fact of life that legislators and lobby groups fight over, e.g., free trade agreements because they intuitively understand or know on the basis of historical records that whatever the net effects would be, some individuals and localities "will lose from foreign competition," and that "the losers do not expect to be fully compensated by the winners" (Fennell and McAdams, 2016: 1081). Furthermore, the belief held and the politico-economic doctrines followed by policy makers, legislators, and the representatives of the judiciary also matter, Fennell and McAdams (2016) argue. For instance, much regulatory reforms are justified by the doctrine that "the market system reliably delivers distributionally fair outcomes to individuals," and therefore, "any shortfalls in outcomes can be readily connected to personal shortfalls of character or effort" (Fennell and McAdams, 2016: 1101). This one-sentence theory, which stipulates that "efficient markets do not let useful resources go to waste," strongly obscures the intricate and detailed legal-political and economic mechanisms that are constitutive of the advanced market economy. Therefore, to only refer to unforgiving "market devices" such as the price system to justify the loss of specific groups that do not benefit from new economic policies and legal reforms is simply to sweep the question of public interest under the carpet and to bury any criticism on current policies. On the other hand, to ignore political costs and political failures is not advisable either, as it cannot be assumed out of hand that policy makers are capable of acting in ways that would result in the optimal allocation and use of resources, Fennell and McAdams (2016: 1110) propose: "In the presence of positive political action costs, we cannot wave away the possibility that our political system will fail to achieve welfare-maximizing distributive results."

To empirically substantiate such claims, Kovvali (2023: 739) accounts for how, for instance, state-level legal reforms in the US, primarily in states dominated by Republican voters, act to undermine certain liberal values endorsed by public and private companies (see also Eichenseht, 2019). The section is cited at length:

> There has been a marked increase in the volume and intensity of state-level efforts to punish corporations acting on stakeholder interests. West Virginia has threatened to bar BlackRock, Goldman Sachs, JPMorgan, Morgan Stanley, and Wells Fargo from doing business with the state in response to the companies' reluctance to finance coal companies and projects. Texas barred financial firms from its lucrative municipal bond market if they 'discriminate' against the firearm industry or the oil industry. State lawmakers have suggested that they will use similar bans to punish banks that provide abortion-related travel benefits or cover abortion-related expenses for employees. Perhaps most strikingly, Florida sought to punish Walt Disney Co. for its opposition to the 'Parental Rights in Education' bill, also known as the 'Don't Say Gay' bill, by revoking the special district status of Disney World.
>
> (Kovvali, 2023: 739)

It would be inaccurate to describe these legal and regulatory reforms as "political failures" as they rather express a differential in what is perceived as legitimate and sound policies, as in the case of the State of Florida's ambition to kneel Disney Corporation on the basis of a minority interest expressed by the vocal Christian right that disapproves of LGBTQ rights, but Disney has steadfastly stood up for what the board of directors and executives regard as reasonable and legitimate beliefs in contemporary society. Under all conditions, such events and episodes wherein populist political campaigns act to undermine liberal freedoms, either protected by law or by social norms, it is reasonable to assume that an overoptimistic view of the political system's ability to pass laws and to implement regulatory reforms needs to be balanced against evidence that suggests otherwise. Consequently, Fennell and McAdams (2016: 1124) suggest that it is not enough for a welfarist to find "a policy vehicle for redistribution that satisfies purely welfarist criteria"; a committed welfarist must also find "a political vehicle that aligns or resonates with broadly shared forms of normative thinking to which the public subscribes." This means that in a legal institutionalist framework, it cannot be assumed *a priori* that neither private ordering governance nor political governance are of necessity the superior device for the monitoring and regulation of the advanced and highly differentiated economy. On the contrary, skilled and thoughtful policy makers need to constantly re-balance their governance tools to effectively consider both public interests and efficiency concerns, or else market failures and political failures, each located on their respective end of the continuum, are likely to result in a net loss of economic and social welfare, and presumably to a higher extent for specific groups as such a loss is rarely, if ever, equally shared across constituencies.

Summary and conclusion

In liberal society, the rule of law is the case, but as law itself is incomplete and open to interpretations and disputes, legal institutionalists argue that the rule of law needs to be understood within the institutional framework wherein the law is passed, implemented, and enforced, but also, at the same time, questioned, circumvented, and violated. As a practical matter, laws in books are one thing, and laws in a real-life economy are quite another, but to align these two modalities of law to the highest possible degree, institutional conditions do matter. From the policy makers and legislators' view, a key question is how to balance public interest, which is itself a vaguely formulated parameter as it may at the same denote a belief, a preference, or a need, not necessarily being overlapping categories, and market efficiency. In many cases, the inconsistencies and glitches that emerge or are observed as the balancing of goals are accomplished (albeit to a varying degree) are interpreted unfavourably, as what are indicative of the law or its enforcement (or both) being inaccurate or poorly formulated. In fact, such inconsistencies and glitches are suggestive, indicative of the institutional embedding of law as law seeks to optimize social and economic welfare at the same time as individual liberties and freedoms are preserved.

In the next chapter and in Chapter 4, the patent system is examined as being one domain of legislation (patent law) that reveals such inconsistencies and glitches at the same time as it acts to incentivize informed agents to uphold innovation activities on the basis of legally enforceable intellectual property rights. The point to make is then to not only engage in "fault-finding" regarding the current patent system (at the same time as flaws in the system need to be identified and eliminated to preserve its legitimacy), but to also recognize the value that such legally enforceable intellectual property rights do have for the aggregated economic and social welfare. Innovations are produced within markets and on the basis of market activities, and such markets and market activities are constituted on the basis of law. Yet, it does not then automatically follow that more precise laws that pertain to intellectual property rights would result in more innovation output as a variety of intermediary and co-produced mechanisms determine such outcomes (say, motivational factors and economic incentives), but that fact does not make the legal institutionalism view of the patent system less useful. In order to understand the mechanisms that generate innovation, the legal protection of intellectual property needs to be included in the analysis, and such an analysis demands a detailed review of the literature and an analysis of the arguments that are both supportive of the patent system as it stands and in favour of a reform of it.

3 The patent system as legal device

Introduction

The conventional view of law in legal theory, established by Pound (1910), is that laws in the books are one thing, and laws in action are quite another thing:

> [I]f we look closely, distinctions between law in the books and law in action, between the rules that purport to govern the relations of man and man and those that in fact govern them, will appear, and it will be found that today also the distinction between legal theory and judicial administration is often a very real and a very deep one.
>
> (Pound, 1910: 15)

This small shift, from what is being written, and how what is written is being interpreted and decided in the court of law, is perhaps expected to be any legal scholar's demon, a persistent source of annoyance or even embarrassment (similar to, e.g., the laboratory scientist's challenge to reproduce experimental results), but legal scholars are surprisingly unperturbed by the fact that laws are written and enforced in ways that may reveal what can be construed as inconsistencies. One plausible reason for this sanguine attitude is that laws are expected to handle a broad variety of issues and contingencies, and that this level of generality inevitably results in what non-legal audiences may perceive as noteworthy deviations between written *de jure* and enforced *de facto* law. Under all conditions, Feinman (1990: 1285) argues, legal theory "frames the way we look at problems," establishes the facts and values "we think relevant to their solution," and even specify what we "consider to be problems at all." This last observation, that the construction of problems—and non-problems, for that matter—is premised on the understanding of the object of inquiry on the basis of the theoretical descriptions that were involved when defining that very object, is important. This in turn results in a variety of analytical challenges that need to be sorted out so that all of the issues that pertain to the object of study

DOI: 10.4324/9781003460220-3

are examined. For instance, Strathern (2004: 220) notices that parts can be construed as (legal) wholes and the other way around: individuals can be examined as parts in a legal issue (e.g., as being part of a specific class of agents under specific conditions, say, as consumer, debtor, plaintiff, etc.) or as having plural roles (as having different identities at the same time, e.g., as parent and spouse, co-worker and shareholder, etc.). That is, the legality that is presumed to derive from the passing and implementation of a law accomplishes a variety of things that were not fully possible prior to the new law being introduced.

This chapter examines in more detail how the legal institutionalism framework, sketched in Chapter 2, can be applied to examine how patent law is constitutive of innovation activities, i.e., all of the activities involved to produce new innovations that serve to reduce costs, increase welfare, or fulfill any other objective that the innovator regards as his or her goal. The purpose of this chapter is thus to demonstrate how specific legislation supports activities that mainstream economic theory considers as market-based activities, and therefore to substantiate the claim that the state-controlled legislative activities are constitutive of advanced economies, not some pre-social or extra-social market that comes forth and reveals itself as soon as human actors initiate enterprising activities. In order to examine how innovations are legally coded, there still needs to be some consensus regarding what an innovation means in theoretical and practical terms, and therefore the first section draws on the influential work of Joseph Schumpeter to define an innovation within a broader institutional context, that of the economic system of competitive capitalism.

Schumpeter's theory of innovation and his innovation concept

Joseph Schumpeter's work on the role of innovations, generated by the economic figure of the entrepreneur, an indispensable component of the economic system, is elementary for the innovation management literature (albeit only to a more limited extent in the legal theory scholarship). Schumpeter (1928: 378) argues that "economic progress"—what would today be possibly addressed as "economic growth"—means essentially to put "productive resources to uses hitherto untried in practice"; "This is what we call 'innovation,'" Schumpeter (1928: 378) writes. Furthermore, Schumpeter (1928: 378) continues, an innovation "means producing at smaller cost per unit," i.e., an innovation is defined in economic terms, and more specifically in cost-reducing terms (see, e.g., Lazonick and Mazzucato, 2013: 1094).[1] Based on this idea of the innovation being the driver of economic

1 Lazonick and Mazzucato (2013: 1094) define innovation formally as "[t]he generation of higher quality products at lower unit cost at prevailing factor prices."

growth, Schumpeter addresses three theoretical implications. First, Schumpeter ([1928] 1991b: 138) proposes that the innovation process cannot be "[d]ecomposed into infinitesimal steps," i.e., the analyst must take a holistic view of the entire and, at times, seemingly boundaryless innovation process to fully understand how it unfolds and results in material consequences. Second, successful innovation is "a task *sui generis*," with its own idiosyncratic characteristics and qualities, including the capacity to combine new thinking with existing conventional wisdom, and to develop an experimental attitude that evaluates all sorts of ideas and their possible objections. The difficulties of innovating consist in "the resistances and uncertainties" that pertain to "doing what has not been done before." Third and finally, Schumpeter (1939: 100) reserves the term *entrepreneurs* for the economic agent that has the capacity to carry out successful innovation. In Schumpeter's (1928: 380) view, this "distinct type" of economic agent is "rare," and therefore entrepreneurs should be held in esteem by, e.g., policy makers and market actors.

Schumpeter's work has been highly influential, not the least because the economic system of competitive capitalism's relentless capacity to renew itself is not fully explained on the basis of the abstract category of capital (and, more specifically, finance capital), as in Karl Marx's influential analysis, but on the basis of a specific economic system actor—the entrepreneur. However, similar to Marx, Schumpeter (who otherwise defended and justified the market system) was concerned with how the economic system of competitive capitalism is inherently unstable and thus prone to generate disruptions and crises: "For Schumpeter, capitalism was protean, unpredictable, disruptive, and surprisingly fragile," Richard and Smith (2017: 98) write. Furthermore, the early Schumpeter was more concerned with how "the state should get out of the way of heroic entrepreneurs sparking a new round of growth through innovation," Schwartz (2016: 230) writes, but over time, Schumpeter became more receptive to the idea that large corporations were a source of "innovation and rising standards of living" (Lambert, 2019: 1578). In this more mature view, Schumpeter came to recognize the Keynesian idea that the state played a key role to "inject demand into the economy" and to encourage "risk averse firms to invest rather than pile up cash" (Schwartz, 2016: 230). Contemporary economic policy making is thus blending Schumpeterian ideas that pertain to the active financing and supporting of entrepreneurship and Keynesian ideas that regard the state as an important market maker on the basis of its legislative activities and the enforcement of legal rights.

Seen in this institutional context, the legal institutionalism framework presented in Chapter 2 is consistent with both economic theories: *de novo* entrepreneurship matters, but it is not the sole source of innovations as also corporations and various organizations participating in joint ventures and similar boundary-crossing activities generate new innovations. However, the recent concern in policy making and in scholarly quarters, that innovative capacities are in a state of decline (see, e.g., Decker, Haltiwanger, Jarmin, and Miranda, 2014, 2017), are largely premised in a Schumpeterian understanding of the entrepreneur, not only as an actual economic figure, but also as a kind of index of the economic system's capacity to combine new ideas so that innovations are generated. Schumpeter thus arguably remains the single most influential theorist in innovation management theory as he emphasized both the key role of entrepreneurs and the wider socio-economic, legal, and political context wherein innovations are developed. Moreover, few other major economists have been equally concerned with the fragile and protean nature of the economic system of competitive capitalism, and few others have worried more about its capacity to survive over several business cycles and the legislative and regulatory reforms that are likely to be advocated and passed over time.

Waning entrepreneurial activities: worries and concerns and long-term implications

The Schupeterian theory of the key role of innovation is consistent with overall ideas about modern society, as expressed by Rosa, Dörre, and Lessenich (2017: 54), in an ongoing state of change on the basis of three elementary mechanisms: "[a] society can be called modern when its mode of stabilization is dynamic, i.e. when it needs (material) growth, (technological) augmentation and high rates of (cultural) innovation in order to reproduce its structure and to preserve the socioeconomic and political status quo in terms of its functionality and its basic institutional and distributional order." Furthermore, Rosa, Dörre, and Lessenich (2017: 56) continue, this stability "crucially hinges on their capacity to grow, expand and innovate," a fact that the analysis of capitalist economies "often overlook and ignore." In this view, a society that ceases to innovate is not only no longer modern as stipulated by this description, but it is also at risk to derail as there is no longer any mechanism that upholds the stability of the economic system, and hence it regresses into a stationary position that undermines its legitimacy. What Pansera and Fressoli (2021: 382) refer to as the "innovation mania credo," which stipulates that "[t]he only legitimate field of action for most of the organizations that populate modern societies" is to "innovate or to die," is thus a consequence of a high-paced economic system that feeds on its own capacity to modify and renew itself. In the light of such ideologies, norms, or beliefs, it is cumbersome that the innovative capacity has been reported to be in decline. Naudé (2022: 106) speaks about a "secular decline in entrepreneurship and innovation" in advanced economies and proposes that trends are "well-documented in recent years":

> Entrepreneurial entry has declined, employment has shifted from small to larger firms, and concentration and market power have been rising. If anything, advanced economies are experiencing a very ***undynamic*** form of capitalism, amounting to a move away from the entrepreneurial toward the "ossified economy."
>
> (Naudé, 2022: 106)

Not only is there evidence of a decline in entrepreneurial and innovation management activities, addressed in the scholarly literature, but there is also evidence of declining antitrust law enforcement in the US (see, e.g., Paul, 2021; Khan, 2020; Naidu, Posner, and Weyl, 2018; Vaheesan, 2018; Wu, 2018; Masterman, 2016; Patterson, 2016) that results in smaller, more thinly capitalized, and more innovative firms being acquired by larger and cash-rich companies, which is a worrying tendency as the incentives to innovate may be in decline at the same time as the innovation rate is reduced. Cunningham Ederer and Ma (2021: 650) examine what they refer to as "killer acquisitions," which denotes the event wherein "an incumbent firm may acquire an innovative target and terminate the development of the target's innovations to preempt future competition." Rather than let incumbent companies secure future returns and economic growth on the basis of such acquisitions, Benigno and Fornaro (2017) advocate an industry policy wherein the state introduces subsidies that incentivize market-based actors to invest in R&D work. Such subsidies hold the potential to be able to "push the economy out of a stagnation trap," but the policy needs to be "sufficiently aggressive" so that agents' expectations about future growth become more positive (Benigno and Fornaro, 2017: 1428). Furthermore, policies should target "profit-maximizing agents" to avoid tax money being invested in activities with limited enterprising and innovative capacities, such as state agencies (Benigno and Fornaro, 2017: 1429). However, under all conditions, such policies supportive of innovation-led economic growth are premised on robust intellectual protection rights, primarily secured through patent law and the patent system.

An historic view of patents and the patent system

The legal institutionalism framework is broad-spanning and inclusive, and in order to fully understand how legality and legal rules come into practical use in any domain of commercial activity, it is important to study the history of legal mechanisms and devices that were gradually introduced. In a way, such a historiography is consistent with Michel Foucault's concept of genealogy, "a form of history" that can account for "the constitution of knowledges, discourses, domains of objects, etc." (Foucault, 1980: 117). As Abi-Rached and Rose (2010: 17) add, such genealogies do not provide "a continuous history, or a linear chronology, nor do they see the present as emerging from a single narrative." On the contrary, they continue, genealogies "[e]xplore the contingent interconnections between multiple surfaces of emergence of practices, techniques and knowledges that are important in their articulation and problematization" (Abi-Rached and Rose, 2010: 17). That is to say, to understand the patent system as a component of a legal institutionalism framework is to examine how it is simultaneously composed of devices and mechanisms that balance each other, and that both generate social and economic benefits and costs, albeit for different actors, at various points in time, and to varying degrees. The analysis presented in this section does not pretend to be "Foucaultian" in any specific sense, but Foucault's concept of genealogy productively apprehends the "de-centeredness" of any legal system, and it recognizes its lacunae and incompleteness, which is consistent with legal theory and legal doctrines and legal institutionalism at large.

In etymological terms, the word "patent" comes from the Latin *patere*, which means "to lay open" (Chien, 2016: 1850). The glorious city-state empire of Venice is credited for first introducing the legal protection of what today is referred to as intellectual property, more precisely in 1474. By 1500, "legal fictions" were already being devised to "accommodate the patenting of inventions" and "assignment of literary properties," Eisenstein (1983: 83) writes. These legal reforms were, if nothing else, supportive of individualism and the autonomy of the actor as "individual initiative was released from reliance on guild protection" (Eisenstein, 1983: 83). On the other hand, with the passing of intellectual property rights, "new powers were lodged in the hands of a bureaucratic officialdom" (Eisenstein, 1983: 83). MacLeod (2002) examines the patent legislation in England and its role in the industrial revolution, and suggests that legal intellectual property right reforms moved in lockstep with economic growth and the establishment of an industrial economy. In contrast, Sullivan (1990) argues that there is only limited evidence of any causal relation between legal reforms and innovative activities; in Sullivan's account, the English industrial revolution was caused by a variety of changing economic, social, and political conditions, which make it difficult to grant, e.g., patent law any foundational role in the economic development that occurred in the 1600–1800 period.

In the US, the first modern patent act was passed in 1793, conveniently named "the 1793 Patent Act" (Demaine and Fellmeth, 2002: 372). In the Patent Act of 1836, passed by US Congress, there was a "greater emphasis on novelty" (Demaine and Fellmeth, 2002: 372). Thomas Jefferson intended that patents should be issued "only for new and useful products of invention and creativity," as opposed to "mere mechanical skill or exercise of the imitative faculty" (Demaine and Fellmeth, 2002: 372). That is, Jefferson's conception of patent law emphasized "ingenuity" as a precondition for patentability. Despite Jefferson's admiration of the work of John Locke (discussed in more detail in Chapter 5), the Lockean notion of labor as "conferring a *right* in the resulting work" did not guide the American formation of intellectual property laws, Demaine and Fellmeth (2002: 377) clarify.

In Europe, post-revolutionary France had enacted a new patent law in 1791, and patent laws were enacted in Austria in 1810, in Russia in 1812, in Prussia in 1815, in Belgium and the Netherlands in 1817, in Spain in 1820, in Bavaria in 1825, in Sardinia in 1826, in the Vatican State in 1833, in Sweden in 1834, in Württemberg in 1836, in Portugal in 1837, and in Saxonia in 1843 (Machlup and Penrose, 1950: 3; see also Barnett, 2021, for an historical overview of patent system disputes and legal reforms). Despite such legal reforms being passed, there was no consensus among economists regarding the value and justification of the patent system. In countries such as England, France, Germany, Holland, and Switzerland, the controversy was at "its height" between *circa* 1850 and 1875 (Machlup and Penrose, 1950: 1). In Germany, the critique of the patent system centered on the idea that patent law serves as a protectionism device, and free-trade arguments were used by economists who were "almost unanimous in the condemnation of the [patent] system" (Machlup and Penrose, 1950: 3). Furthermore, trade associations and chambers of commerce submitted reports "recommending reform or abolition of the patent laws" (Machlup and Penrose, 1950: 3). Similarly, in the Netherlands, having a long and successful tradition of free trade and commercial and intellectual liberties (see, e.g., Burke, 1994; Dutch banks were even lending money to countries that waged war against the Dutch state, and without any major political repercussions), the "antipatent movement" was even more than elsewhere linked with the free-trade movement, and in July 1869, "the patent law was repealed" (Machlup and Penrose, 1950: 5). These controversies indicate how the economic and moral soundness of the patent system was questioned when its broader institutional conditions were examined in detail. However, Machlup and Penrose (1950: 5–6) write that the success of the antipatent movement in Europe was not lasting as the advocates of the patent system "organized a mighty counteroffensive":

> The techniques of propaganda employed in the years between 1867 and 1877 were quite remarkable for the time. New societies for patent protection were formed, resolutions were drafted and distributed to the daily press, speakers were delegated to professional and trade association meetings, floods of pamphlets and leaflets were released, articles were planted

> in trade journals and reproduced in daily papers, public competitions were announced with prizes for the best papers in defense of the patent system, petitions were submitted to governments and legislatures, international meetings were held and compromises were made with groups inclined to endorse liberal patent reforms.
>
> (Machlup and Penrose, 1950: 5–6)

As a consequence of these activities, the tide changed and, in 1877, a uniform patent law for the entire German Reich was adopted. Several other countries reformed their patent legislation to promote risk-taking, venturing, and economic welfare.

The advocacy of the patent system drew on basically four different ideas, having their own intellectual roots and political and moral philosophies. First, it was claimed that an innovator has "a natural property right in his own ideas" (Machlup and Penrose, 1950: 10). This was basically a so-called *droit morale* argument, grounded in the legal doctrine of natural rights. The second idea was that legal rules or social norms that pertain to justice "require that a man receive, and therefore that society secure to him, reward for his services in proportion as these services are useful to society" (Machlup and Penrose, 1950: 10). In this view, the innovator who makes the world a better place on the basis of his and eventually her (the innovator was largely assumed to be a male, as indicated by the quote) intellectual and practical ingenuity, then society has a *moral responsibility* to compensate this innovator in equal terms. Both the first and the second idea were thus expressed in a deontic vocabulary that pertains to morality and ethics. The third idea expressed was that industrial progress is "desirable to society," and therefore society needs to establish legal incentives for innovators and capital owners (whom innovators often rely on to finance their development work) to engage in risky and time-consuming innovation and business activities (Machlup and Penrose, 1950: 10). This argument was premised on the assumption that only limited economic progress would be generated unless a patent system (or similar) would be introduced, which critics of the patent system portrayed as an empirical question to be examined, and not as some stipulated principle that would *per se* justify the patent system. The fourth idea was that if industrial progress is desirable, as it is conducive to economic and social welfare (as stipulated by the third idea), and if there will be individuals with extraordinary capacities to innovate and to enroll finance capital owners in their business ventures under all conditions, then the value of the patent system derives from the fact that it makes innovation ideas that were originally held in secrecy publicly available, yet being associated with an exclusivity of use clause that benefits the patent owners. This disclosure of intellectual ideas would then presumably further propel innovation work activities in both the original field of expertise but also, when being combined with other types of expertise or skills, in adjacent or emerging fields (Machlup and Penrose, 1950: 10). This fourth idea is arguably closest to the contemporary legal theory view of the patent system, which recognizes the incompleteness of the patent system in both its written and practical forms, but still stipulates that a patent system provides several benefits vis-à-vis the situation wherein no patent system would be in place. Such benefits include not the least the establishment of a market for innovation ideas, wherein specific innovation ideas can be used by non-originators, who thus contribute with new or better materializations of the underlying innovation idea.

It is noteworthy that the patent system has been justified on the basis of both moral and substantial (i.e., economic) arguments and that "moral rights" have consistently been rejected as an authoritative justification of the patent system, primarily because innovations are social in nature (discussed in Chapter 4), whereas natural rights pertain to elementary negative freedoms, such as the right to one's own body and similar human rights. At the same time, as soon as the patent system is justified through either policy or principle goals (Dworkin, 1975)—both being dependent on institutional conditions that pertain to the innovation, or the innovation idea being examined, say, in litigation cases—this advocacy paves the way for empirical studies of whether the patent system fulfills the role its advocates presume is the case. As Hara (2003) says, speaking about new drug development in the pharmaceutical industry as a specific form of patent-protected innovation work activity, the innovator is always embedded within an institutional structure that is both supportive of and hindering innovations to materialize:

> [A]ctors are not isolated from wider and quite stable social relationships. Institutions and structures such as organizational structures, organizational capabilities, corporate strategies, regulatory systems, clinical trails, patent systems, production economies and market structures affect the process of shaping drugs.
>
> (Hara, 2003: 182)

Furthermore, much analyses of innovation work activities, and not the least successful innovation work activities, succumb to the *post hoc ergo propter hoc* fallacy, the claim that just because something happened at some point in time wherein another condition was observed (say, an innovation was produced at the same time as a patent system was in operation), then it does not logically follow that the condition being accounted for caused the thing observed to happen. That is, based on a temporal ordering of events being observed, co-occurrence is confused with causality. As we learn from history, innovations that are widely embraced today were not necessarily widely acclaimed and embraced at the time when they were first introduced, as documented by Nye (2006):

> At first, Samuel Morse had trouble convincing anyone to invest in his telegraph. He spent five years "lecturing, lobbying, and negotiating" before he convinced the US Congress to pay for the construction of the first substantial telegraph line, which ran from Washington to Baltimore. Even after it was operating, he had difficulty findings customers interested in using it. Likewise, Alexander Graham Bell could not find an investor to buy his patents on the telephone, and so he reluctantly decided to market it himself. Thomas Alva Edison found few commercial applications for his phonograph, despite the sensational publicity surrounding his discovery. . . . In the mid 1970s, a prototype of the personal computer, when first shown to a group of MIT professors, seemed rather uninteresting to them. They could think of a few uses for it, and they suggest perhaps it would be most useful to shut-ins. In short, the telegraph, the telephone, and phonograph and the personal computer, surely four of the most important inventions in the history of communications, were initially understood as curiosities.
>
> (Nye, 2006: 41)

Such historical cases or anecdotes are indicative of how, e.g., the patent system is not only dependent on the legal texts written and printed in books, and the law enforcement activities justified on the basis of such laws and actual cases under consideration, but also fundamentally determined by social and historical conditions that shape a society's capacity to innovate.

Legal patent theories and the role of patents in the economy

Kitch (1977: 265), a Chicago law and economics scholar, writes that "the patent system" performs a function not previously handled, i.e., "to increase the output from resources used for technological innovation." In order to generate technological innovations that are protected by patents, the developer needs to develop what Kitch (1977: 266) refers to as a "prospect," the expression of a "particular opportunity to develop a known technological possibility." If a prospect that expresses a specific idea is available to several actors with the skills and competencies needed to materialize what is described in the prospect, then the chances of the new knowledge materializing into innovations increase. Furthermore, Kitch (1977: 266) argues, these individuals, presumably participating in company-based activities, do not need to be revealed to one another, but the activities can continue without being disclosed. This idea that one single prospect that contains some specific patented or "patentable" innovation idea would be able to generate innovation activities in several locations, after being disclosed, is what justifies patent law in Kitch's (1977) account. Kitch (1977: 266) refers to this view of the patent system as the *prospect theory*, as new patents do not necessarily need to be associated with an idea being proved to work in practice at the stage when the patent application is submitted, but primarily being assertorial inasmuch as it holds the promise that the innovation idea expressed in the patent application has the potential to materialize at some future point.

Fromer (2016: 1715) emphasizes that prospect theory, regardless of its empirical substantiation (which is weak, as discussed later), is consistent with Supreme Court decisions. In, e.g., the court case *Kewanee Oil Co. v. Bicron Corp.* (1974), the Supreme Court emphasized that the information disclosed in patents "add to the general store of knowledge [and is] of such importance to the public weal that the Federal Government is willing to pay the high price of . . . exclusive use for its disclosure" (US Supreme Court, *Kewanee Oil Co. v. Bicron Corp.*, 416 U.S. 470, 481 (1974). cited in Fromer, 2016: 1715). Furthermore, the Supreme Court statement added, the exclusive use of the patent granted by the court "[w]ill stimulate ideas and the eventual development of further significant advances in the art" (US Supreme Court, cited in Fromer, 2016: 1715). In other Supreme Court cases, such as *Universal Oil Prods. Co. v. Globe Oil & Refining Co.* (1944), the exclusive right to use a patent is explicitly portrayed as a *quid pro quo* for disclosing ideas that could support "further significant advances in the art":

> [T]he *quid pro quo* [for the patent grant] is disclosure of a process or device in sufficient detail to enable one skilled in the art to practice the invention once the period of the monopoly has expired; and the same precision of disclosure is likewise essential to warn the industry concerned of the precise scope of the monopoly asserted.
>
> (US Supreme Court, *Universal Oil Prods. Co. v. Globe Oil & Refining Co.*, 322 U.S. 471, 484 (1944), cited in Fromer, 2016: 1715. Emphasis added by Fromer.)

In these cases, the Supreme Court established the doctrine wherein "patent protection is viewed as providing *ex post* incentives to prompt efficient maturity of the patented invention," Cotropia (2012: 1900) writes.

In contrast to the prospect theory of patent, the *reward theory* is premised on the more intuitively acceptable idea that the patent system should act as a legal device that "enables an inventor to capture the returns from his investment in the invention" (Kitch, 1977: 266):

> We tend to think of an invention as the thing an inventor has made or accomplished, and the rule seems to imply the inventor is confined to

> that. But the rule is misleading, because the invention as claimed in the patent claims and the physical embodiment of the invention are two quite different things.
>
> (Kitch, 1977: 268)

In fact, the patent system does not require "a finished, commercially relevant invention," but merely requires "something that works," Kitch (1977: 270–271) writes. This means that the reward theory offers "an incomplete view of the functions of the patent system" (Kitch, 1977: 266) inasmuch as the commonsense view that a patent granted would correspond to some demonstration of how the patent would work in practice is not consistent with how the patent system is both legally designed and operating. Of course, the question of what "something that works" would mean in legal and practical terms has been a source of long-term legal disputes, i.e., a patent cannot be granted on the basis of pure fiction or speculation, but some kind of plausible argument, supportive of the content of the patent application, needs to be presented. However, such statutes and rules do not *per se* change the fact that the patent officer who handles the patent application needs to be in the position to understand and to determine when "something works" and when it does not. The quality of the patent assessment procedure is therefore at the very heart of the patent system, and the prospect theory or the reward theory models (or alternative theories) that justify it.

More recently, Lemley (2016a) has examined the role of the patent system in innovation activities. In the US Patent Act of 1952, it is stated that the definition of an invention "incorporates both conception and reduction to practice," and thus defines the inventor sometimes as "the person who conceived of an idea," while on other occasions as "the one who reduced the idea to practice" (Lemley, 2016a: 1172). This ambiguity has been widely addressed in the patent law studies literature. A key concern is that there is a deviation between *the conception of the idea* and *its materialization*, which creates possibilities for, e.g., so-called patent trolls to intervene in the process and to unduly (some commentators say) benefit from work conducted by others (Lemley, 2016a: 1173). As Lemley (2016a: 1172) remarks, "precisely because those inventors haven't yet figured out what works," their patent claims "tend to be more general," which gives them broader rights than those who "take the time to build and patent a working invention." Intuitively, it appears as if patent law is rewarding individuals who do not care to do the hard work, whereas those who "take the time" to materialize the innovation idea are subject to penalties. Seen in this view, the patent system needs to be justified on the basis of policy ideas, legal theory propositions, or empirical evidence that demonstrates its efficacy. Lemley (2016) chooses the legal theory and court case ruling path, and points at Supreme

Court decisions that have established the current legal practice and the patent system it supports.

In the nineteenth century, the Supreme Court held that an invention was "not complete" until it had been "reduced to practice" (Lemley, 2016a: 1174). On this view, to qualify something as an invention requires reducing an idea to "a tangible thing" that actually works for its "intended purpose," i.e., that it "achieves something useful in the world" (Lemley, 2016a: 1175). To be an inventor then, it is not enough to have ideas and to advance knowledge on the basis of such thinking, but to make the world a better place also demands that such ideas can materialize to prove their worth. This attitude and legal doctrine would be revised during the twentieth century. Lemley (2016: 1176) cites the Supreme Court's 1998 decision in *Pfaff v. Wells Electronics, Inc.*, wherein the court concluded that "[t]he primary meaning of the word 'invention' in the Patent Act unquestionably refers to the inventor's conception rather than to a physical embodiment of that idea." Lemley (2016) summarizes the change in legal doctrine:

> For courts and scholars that take this view, the primary contribution of an invention is the idea itself. Various people can implement the idea once it is disclosed, but no one could do so without the initial mental act—the conception of the idea itself. . . . Indeed, one purpose of the patent system might be to permit people with ideas to sell those ideas to others who will test or implement them.
>
> (Lemley, 2016a: 1176)

In the new legal doctrine, ***practical utility***—a key term in the engineering science ideology that generated the patent system in the first place—is downplayed and is displaced by the economic theory concept of a market for innovation ideas, wherein new ideas and the complex reasoning they express would *per se* have a market value regardless of their documented practical value. In fact, the presence of such a market for innovation ideas is what justifies the new patent law enforcement, and while several legal scholars recognize this doctrine as being potentially useful and conducive to net economic and social welfare, it also generates a series of legal and practical concerns, discussed in more detail later.

One of the most debated components of patent legislation is what is referred to as "prophetic examples." When a patent applicant has an idea but "no way of knowing whether that idea works," courts have permitted the applicant to refer to an *Gedankenexperiment* (with German Physicist Ernst Mach's term), a "thought experiment" that is practically speaking "essentially guesses as to what would happen if [the innovator] were to build and test his invention" (Lemley, 2016a: 1179). This is a notably generous legal device in the patent system, granting comprehensive legal rights on the basis of informed guesses that do not need to be accompanied by any robust empirical evidence, but that confers a legal protection on the basis of the patent application assessor's decision as to whether the prophetic example is plausible or a case of mere fiction.

The patent system and the role of social norms

Although the patent system is rarely, if ever, justified on the basis of moral rights and an accompanying deontic vocabulary, it does not mean that social norms and beliefs that pertain to what is legitimate to patent are irrelevant in the legal institutionalism perspective. For instance, in the field of life science research work, scholars and researchers regarded their work as being a "public good" resource for a long period of time, which in turn made patenting, *de jure* and *de facto*, a form of privatization of scientific know-how morally questionable. Such beliefs and preferences were also reflected in official statement and in regulatory rules. In the 1879–1911 period, the American Medical Association (AMA) regarded patented medicines, by definition, as "unethical." A "monopolization of medical preparations" through the use of patents was "to grow fat on human misery," AMA stated (cited in Cramer, 2015: 71). When Herbert W. Boyer, at the University of California at Berkeley and at San Francisco, and Stanley N. Cohen, at Stanford University, developed the recombinant DNA technology in the early 1970s, a major step forward for genetics research, Herbert W. Boyer claimed that Cohen would never have "dreamed of the notion of patenting" their research findings (cited in Hughes, 2001: 548). When Stanford eventually decided to patent the research finding, Boyer was also met with a certain degree of hostility at his universities, Smith Hughes (2001) proposes:

> The personal hostility directed at Boyer left enduring scars and suggested the novelty and precarious state of corporate relationships in academic biology at the time. He was an early target of the tensions that were to erupt throughout academia in coming years as universities and scientists at the forefront of molecular biology sought to capitalize on commercial opportunities.
>
> (Hughes, 2001: 558)

Anyway, regardless of the reputational loss incurred on Boyer and Cohen, the patenting of the recombinant DNA technology was nothing short of a "legal revolution," Demaine and Fellmeth (2002: 306) argue: "This invention spawned further advancements in genetic research, including the discovery in 1983 of a generally applicable method for cloning genes for polypeptides where the amino acid, DNA, and mRNA sequences were not completely known." In hindsight, even the most skeptical scientists would admit that the patenting of the new technology productively contributed to the establishment of the genomics research field, which in turn increased the medical know-how and expertise in quantum leaps. At the same time, the patenting of the recombinant DNA technology was still a significant moment wherein the "value systems in the sciences" changed, away from what sociologist Robert Merton had referred to as the ideal of "disinterestedness" or (non-pejorative) "communism" (Sunder Rajan, 2012: 6).

Fueled by both the commercial interests shown in the new biosciences and the endogenous growth of life science research in the university system, the patent system has been pragmatically modified to enable new possibilities for patenting new biological species, previously being widely understood to be "non-patentable." The landmark decision made by the Supreme Court in the *Diamond v. Chakrabarty* case in 1980, "[w]hich allowed patent rights on a genetically engineered microorganism that could break down crude-oil spills" (Sunder Rajan, 2012: 2–3), paved the way for a whole new class of patent, perhaps best described as "sequences of biological life." Prior to the *Diamond v. Chakrabarty* Supreme Court ruling, the so-called "product of nature doctrine" (Carolan, 2010: 115), which prescribed that naturally occurring species could not be patented, dominated patent law. In 1988, Harvard University acquired a patent for the so-called onco-mouse (also being protected by trademark rights), a transgenetic mouse developed on the basis of gene knock-out bioengineering technology to provide a laboratory animal that develops certain forms of cancer "within weeks," thus assisting the clinical in vivo research-based work to develop cancer therapies. In Europe, patent offices and courts refused to grant Harvard a patent for the onco-mouse on the basis of a European patent law rule that prohibited the patenting of "plant and animal varieties or the essentially biological processes for the production of plants and animals" (Bud, 1983: 216).

Although biologically engineered species are today widely patented and seen as patentable, there are some concerns regarding the consequences of this legal reform. Carolan (2010: 111) argues that patent law creates the "illusion of an immutable, ontologically independent object" on the basis that a certain description of a biological entity or process is consistent with patent law and patent office assessment practices. Such a "socio-legal maneuver" is necessary if such objects "are to be distinguished from the unwieldy (and thus unpatentable) realm of the natural world" (Carolan, 2010: 111). Biagioli (1999: 13) expresses the idea accordingly:

> It is becoming increasingly common for scientists (mostly geneticists) to patent natural objects, but they do so by making them potentially useful by carving them out of their state of nature. Nature becomes patentable by being turned into something that is less natural and more useful.
>
> (Biagioli, 1999: 13)

By implication, following these liberal legal reforms, the boundaries of what is patentable and what isn't become blurred. "Patents are increasingly stretched out to cover 'ideas' that twenty years ago all scholars would have agreed were unpatentable," Boyle (2003: 39) proposes. The "most troubling of all," Boyle (2003: 39) adds, are the attempts to introduce intellectual property rights "over mere compilations of facts." These types of reservations are commonplace when the patent system is being examined, either by legal scholars (as in the next chapter) or by science and technology scholars (as in this section). Under all conditions, the patent system needs to be understood within the institutional context wherein it was first formulated, implemented, and enforced when necessary.

Long-term implications of the patent system and its moral rights vestiges

Following the legal reforms of the patent system, including the Bayh-Dole Act in the US, the university became a major market force in terms of its patenting activity. The number of patents issued to universities "roughly tripled" between the mid-1960s and the mid-1970s (Berman, 2012: 95), and in the period 1976–1998, there was an "eightfold increase" in university patents (Powell and Snellman, 2004: 204). "Universities increased their share of patenting from less than 0.3% in 1963 to nearly 4% by 1999," Mowery (2009: 37) reports. Still, regardless of this upsurge in patenting activities, many academic researchers were only modestly concerned with patenting their research findings, Vallas and Kleinman (2008) show:

> [M]any of our respondents could not be bothered to patent their research findings, and only a minority was personally involved in direct commercial ventures of any sort. Rather, the major constraints on the sharing of information and materials that we observed stem from more subtle, indirect changes in the normative context in which academic science is conceived and conducted.
>
> (Vallas and Kleinman, 2008: 296)

As Kleinman and Vallas (2001: 467) have reported previously, apart from "the handful of commercializable projects" that generate "the bulk of the royalties," the great majority of academic researchers invest time in the patent application process that "might more profitably be spent undertaking new investigations." "[O]nly a small minority of these academic scientists was actively engaged in start-ups, the pursuit of patents, consultant arrangements or other commercial endeavours" (Vallas and Kleinman, 2008: 292). Vallas and Kleinman (2008) and Kleinman and Vallas (2001) are agnostic regarding the reasons for this lukewarm interest in patenting research findings, but a rational apathy in combination with vestiges of the public's moral right to access research findings funded by tax money or tuition fees, and a skepticism towards what has been called "academic capitalism" (e.g., Slaughter and Leslie, 1997) more widely, may be plausible explanatory factors for this condition. One scientist cited by Colyvas and Powell (2007) claimed that research work cannot be reduced to be a matter of univocal "ownership rights" without something essential being lost in the process:

> "I don't want to sign a letter saying that I was just another laboratory worker," commented a university of Michigan professor to Nature in 1980 when the now famous recombinant DNA patents were under scrutiny. . . . The patenting process, which required disclaimers on the patenting application from co-authors and other scientists that they were not investors, contravened scientific conventions of dissemination and credit.
>
> (Colyvas and Powell, 2007: 222)

Academic scholars may be less interested in patenting their research activities (despite overall patenting activities soaring over the last five decades), but the venture capital industry and the field of business enterprising have good reasons for being pleased with the patent law reforms being introduced over the last half century. Pagano and Rossi (2009: 670, Fig. 2.) show that the share of intangible assets held by S&P 500 corporations has grown over time, from 16.8% in 1975 to 32.4% in 1985. By the mid-1990s, 68.4% of S&P 500 firms' assets were intangible, and by 2005, the measure stood at 79.7%, thus raising sharply to account for close to four-fifths of all assets, i.e., composed of patents, intellectual property rights, the skills of the employees, etc. Research on the venture capital industry, such as Kertum and Lerner's (2000: 674) study, shows that "venture capital is associated with a substantial increase in patenting." More recently, this association has been proved to be causally related to initial venture capital investments in, e.g., start-ups: "[w]e can conclude that the causality runs mainly from VC investment to a firm's patenting, not vice versa" (Safari, 2017: 510). That is, venture capital investors demand that the companies they commit their funds to should patent their intellectual assets. "[T]he effect of VC investment on firms' patenting is about five times higher in the weakest IPR than the strongest IPR in our data," Safari (2017: 511) found in his study, and Bernstein (2015: 1369) reports that the number of patent citations captures "the economic importance of the innovation," as it presumably correlates with a firm's "market value." Such data and studies of venture capital investment provide strong evidence that the patent system does play a role in protecting intellectual property and innovation ideas in start-ups and other thinly capitalized firms that produce new innovations. At the same time, there are empirical studies that point at the discontinuity in corporations between the number of patents and innovative output on the one hand, and scientific research activities, on the other hand:

> [I]nnovation clusters around highly cited scientific discoveries do not result in highly cited patents, indeed, patent clusters around important science produce less cited patents. This provides support for . . . [the] finding of conflicting logics between the selection of valuable scientific ideas and valuable technologies.
>
> (Gittelman and Kogut, 2003: 378)

Gittelman and Kogut (2003) show that a venture capital firm's alleged procedure to select companies to invest in on the basis of the number of citations of the scientific publications related to the innovation under development is unreliable, and that the number of scientific citations is a poor proxy for innovative capacities; in fact, there is a negative relationship between "scientific capabilities" and "the innovation effort." Expressed differently, "scientific ideas are not simple inputs into invention," as "important scientific ideas" and "influential patents" follow different and "apparently conflicting evolutionary logics," Gittelman and Kogut (2003: 380) summarize. Venture capital firms select companies to invest in on the basis of the imputed quality of the scientific publication (assessed in terms of documented citations), but this proxy for innovative capacities is misconstrued. One consequence would be that highly valuable so-called "smart money" (Sørensen, 2007) would be misallocated in ways that potentially reduce economic and social welfare in comparison to the case where a more accurate assessment of entrepreneurial capacities and a more efficient allocation would be accomplished.

Secondary effects of the patent system: registered patents as assets and collateral

Corporations do not only use the patent system to protect their investments in intellectual property, but also actively use the patent system to capitalize on their intellectual property rights, as assets are possible to trade or use as collateral when, e.g., raising funds to finance innovation work. In the legal institutionalism perspective, patents are legally coded claims that pertain to innovation ideas that are associated with legal protection, and therefore a registered patent is considered a firm-specific asset that is associated with, under certain conditions, a calculable economic value. Somaya (2012) addresses the patent system in such terms:

> Governments confer patent rights to protect the creative efforts of inventors and thereby preserve incentives to make and commercialize

> inventions. . . . Patent rights are primarily protected by national laws and institutions, and in many Western democracies these property rights have had a long history and are deeply embedded within the legal system.
>
> (Somaya, 2012: 1085)

As several commentators remark, many, if not most, patents are associated with only limited economic value or prospects of generating revenues on the basis of a patent on file if the innovation idea would materialize (Moore, 2005):[2] "It is well known that most patents generate little *ex post* value to the firm," Kline, Petkova, Williams, and Zidar (2019: 1345) write. At the same time, it is important to notice that in addition to the legal protection granted to patent owners, and the creation of a market for innovation ideas on the basis of licensing contracts, the patent system also acts to establish a secondary market wherein registered patents serve as an asset and, by implication, as a collateral in the finance market, e.g., when start-up firms raise new funds to finance their development work. This means that it is important to consider corporate strategies as being at least partially determined by the patent system and its rules.

Somaya (2012: 1086) remarks that in this perspective, the "appropriability from patents" is not "automatic or exogenous"; rather, it is "endogenously determined by firm strategies and actions." The "strategic management of patents" includes a variety of activities, such as the "signaling and information disclosure strategies" and the managing of patents as "real options" (Somaya, 2012: 1086). Somaya (2012: 1086) identifies three patent strategy domains: (1) acquiring and maintaining patent rights, (2) licensing (or sharing) patents, and (3) enforcing and litigating patents. That is, via the patent system, companies hold assets that are protected by property rights, and such assets can be licensed, but they may also need to be protected against infringements. Mann (2018) adds a fourth activity, and that is how such assets are part of "patent portfolios" that act as collateral for secured debt. Mann (2018: 25) found that 16% of patents registered by US corporations "have been pledged as collateral" at some point, and that

2 Moore (2005: 1523–1524) uses a study design to assess the perceived value of a patent on the basis of the patent holder's willingness to pay the fees needed to keep the patent on file. "Whether a patent is likely to be maintained by its owner is indicative of the long term value of the patent," Moore (2005: 1550) stipulates. Moore (2005: 1526) found that "53.71% of all patentees do allow their patents to expire for failure to pay one of their maintenance fees," which would then mean, under the current description, that slightly above half of all patents on file are regarded as having limited value by the patentee. This proxy for economic value (expressed as the cost of paying the fees in comparison to the value of preserving the legal protection of the innovation idea) can of course be disputed in terms of its accuracy and validity, as in the case wherein a certain patent would have a considerably higher value for more informed or resourceful market actors than for the patentee short of such skills and capacities. Nevertheless, Moore's (2005) proxy indicates how patentees assess the economic value of their assets and the value of having them legally protected.

the frequency of patents being pledged as collateral has "increased rapidly in recent years" (Mann, 2018: 28). For a patent to have a collateral value in the eyes of the lender, the patent must demonstrate what Mann (2018) calls a certain level of "generality," which means that the patent must be cited in either other patent texts or in scholarly publications within a specific technological field so that it signals that the patent is of relevance and value for the industry. Furthermore, when a lender accepts a patent as collateral, the lender can file a record with the USPTO that provides public notice so that "a third party cannot purchase the patent and subsequently claim ignorance of the security interest" (Mann, 2018: 27). Mann (2018: 28) found that one standard deviation in generality (i.e., an increased citation rate above the statistical mean) is associated with a 1.2% greater probability that the patent is "pledged as collateral." Furthermore, Mann (2018: 27) says that small-sized innovative firms tend to be thinly capitalized, i.e., are "credit constrained," and with the lack of access to collateral being one primary reason for this predicament. The patent system thus provides the auxiliary benefit to increase the collateral value of patents, which in turn—if the patent can display an adequate level of generality—can enable debt financing and investment in the development work conducted in innovative firms.

Ma, Tong, and Wang (2022) argue in a similar manner that "accumulated innovation assets," such as patents, include a "large amount of knowledge," and at the firm level, patents are thus treated as assets that can, e.g., be sold off during a so-called Chapter 11 bankruptcy. In their study design, Ma, Tong, and Wang (2022: 6673) retrieved data from all Chapter 11 bankruptcies filed by U.S. public firms from 1981 to 2012 to examine how patents are used by firms to re-finance the development activities. Similar to Mann's (2018) findings, Ma, Tong, and Wang (2022: 6672) found that firms undergoing a Chapter 11 bankruptcy were seven times more likely to sell their "core patents" than "nondistressed firms" were. Furthermore, this use of "collateralized patents" is more pronounced after the year 2000 (Ma, Tong, and Wang, 2022: 6672), which is possibly indicative of how the finance industry has differentiated at this point in time so that it could calculate the collateral value of core patents. Under all conditions, strong legal creditor protection, which is the legal basis for Chapter 11 bankruptcies (for an overview of the Chapter 11 bankruptcy device and its use, see, e.g., Simon, 2022), creates and assists functional markets for patents, Ma, Tong, and Wang (2022: 6671) argue: "creditor-driven sales" have important implications for the "market for technology and technology diffusion." For instance, as will be discussed in the next chapter, so-called Patent Assertion Entities (PAEs)—which some commentators refer to as "patent trolls"—can acquire patents at a specific market rate, which serve, in the ideal case, to transfer know-how and rights to new corporate entities that may have better possibilities for developing and materializing an innovation idea. Alternatively, critics say, PAEs on the contrary impose costs on the market system as patent infringement litigations and court cases demand significant resources.

The studies that Mann (2018) and Ma, Tong, and Wang (2022) report indicate that the patent system not only generates legal rights that are supportive of innovation activities and a secondary market for innovation ideas, but that it also has implications for finance markets and the work to raise funds to finance innovation work. The empirical question is then whether the stock of patents on file with, e.g., the USPTO contains information that is valuable for market actors such as innovators, so that the desirable level of generality that makes the specific patent qualify as collateral can be achieved and documented. Furthermore, such generality would also matter for the price to be paid for registered patents that firms undergoing Chapter 11 bankruptcy restructurings wish to sell. These issues will be discussed in the next chapter, but at this point it may be remarked that the patent system as a legal and institutional creation generates several possibilities and has consequences for not only how specific innovation ideas are protected, but also for how the firms that are granted such legal rights can use patents as assets to finance their innovation work. The patent system thus has both manifest and latent functions, in Merton's (1957) parlance: some of its consequences are immediately accessible and intuitively understandable, whereas some are secondary and reveal themselves only after other legal and institutional changes may have taken place or if, e.g., financial markets differentiate, say, as in the case of patents being sold at a higher frequency after year 2000, as documented by Ma, Tong, and Wang (2022).

Summary and conclusions

Organizations and markets are populated by actors who use all their know-how, skills, and ingenuity to compete over limited resources and to generate a profit on the basis of revenues earned. Elementary economic theory easily confuses the presence of such actors with the more abstract mechanisms and devices that are constitutive of economic affairs and the regularities observed, including that of legislation and regulatory rules, and the various private ordering devices such as contracts and related "soft law" rules that structure economic transactions as they are repeated over time. Based on the legal institutionalism analytical framework, the purpose of the third chapter of this volume is to review the literature on patent law to better understand how this specific legislation, intended to both provide intellectual property protection to inventors and to create a secondary market for innovation ideas, is being written, interpreted, and enforced in the domain of the market. One of the intended theoretical benefits of this analytical procedure is to demonstrate that market making and market regulation is partially accomplished on the basis of legal devices such as patent law, and that despite being incomplete and subject to systematic criticism from legal scholars and other relevant market actors, the market is a legal-institutional creation that must not be confused with either an idealized image of the market as an information-processing device (and that itself needs to be explained in terms of its genesis) or, on the basis of sheer mythology, as in the case of the claim that markets are pre-social or even "naturally occurring" phenomena. As will be discussed in the final chapter of this volume, this legal institutionalism view paves the way for a political view of how new legislation is passed. Advanced and highly differentiated economies, such as the contemporary economic system, are premised on a variety of conditions and resources, whereof laws and regulations, which express political beliefs and ambitions, remain a centrepiece. As this institutional order generates considerable economic and social welfare (if resources generated are distributed reasonably fair), these issues are not only of some peripheral and academic interest, but are at the center of public interests.

4 Patents as the legal coding of innovation ideas

Introduction

In the previous chapter, patent law and the patent system were introduced as legal devices that intend to support innovation activities on the basis of both providing a legal protection of the intellectual work invested in developing, expressing, and formalizing an innovation idea and to make such innovation ideas publicly available via the patent system and the administrative agencies involved, e.g., patent offices. This chapter presents a review of the patent law literature (in the widest sense) to demonstrate both the strengths and the weaknesses of the patent system as it is currently backed by patent law and its enforcement given the broader institutional conditions that pertain to this piece of legislation. It is argued that the patent system may be far from optimally designed, which indicates that certain legal reform may be justified, but also that, on balance, it is more helpful to have an incomplete or non-optimal patent system than to have no such patent system and legislation in place at all. A key concern for legal scholars is opportunistic behaviour that is premised on the trade of patents wherein so-called patent trolls (unsurprisingly being a pejorative term) can take economic and financial advantage of the work conducted by innovators but without productively contributing to the innovation activities. However, such legal arbitrage may be tolerated as it is part of the design of a market for innovation ideas that policy makers and legislators at the point where the legislation was passed believed would support higher innovative output, and hence net economic and social welfare. Whether these misgivings regarding the current use or misuse of the patent system can be substantiated or not is subject to intense scholarly debate in legal scholarship quarters. This chapter and the next, Chapter 5, address these concerns primarily on the basis of the legal literature (in this chapter) and political philosophy and political science writings (in Chapter 5) to make some tentative conclusions regarding the role and value of patent law and the patent system.

DOI: 10.4324/9781003460220-4

Legal theory debates regarding the patent system

A patent is the legal protection of any agent that issues a patent application that would leave the explanation of the underlying innovation idea "in the open," i.e., to be publicly available for any person who wishes to develop and materialize the innovation idea. The concern is that not all patents granted provide this capacity to leave potentially useful information in the open. From a legal point of view, the question is then when a patent expresses a genuine innovation idea and when it does not: "Given the invention's central role, determining what exactly is the invention being considered becomes crucial to any patent inquiry," Cotropia (2012: 1860) writes. This issue results in disagreement regarding what principles and theories of innovation the patent system should be structured around:

> Although disagreements exist in many areas of patent law, two of the most pronounced disagreements in recent years involve evaluating the patent document itself. The first disagreement is the process of interpreting patent claims—single sentences found at the end of the patent. Patent claims define the area of exclusivity granted by the patent. . . . The second disagreement is the viability and independence of the written description requirement for patentability.
>
> (Cotropia, 2012: 1864)

Cotropia (2012: 1861) here distinguishes between two types of definitions of innovation: the "external invention" and the "claim-centered invention." Under the external invention description, the technical information and discussion "contained in the patent's specification define the invention." The specification is therefore considered to be the "more robust part of the patent" inasmuch as it includes "descriptions and drawings of the state of the relevant technology," references to what "has been done before," any specific implementations of the invention known to the inventor, and "a general description of the purpose or goal of the invention" (Cotropia, 2012: 1861). The claim-centered invention, in contrast, is defined by "the patent's claims," wherein a claim is "a single sentence at the end of a patent that describes what the inventor wishes to have exclusivity over" (Cotropia, 2012: 1861). Although these two definitions of an innovation are based on different legal principles, both theories suppose that patent protection is "[a]t least centered on the inventor's actual inventive activities and understandings, not on a legal fiction such as the patent claim" (Cotropia, 2012: 1862). Nevertheless, regardless of all the legal theory implications in all their intricate details, both theories justify the patent system on the basis of an analytical model that discriminates between the *conception* and the *materialization* of the innovation idea. Conception is legally defined by the

Supreme Court as the "formation in the mind of the inventor, of a definite and permanent idea of the complete and operative invention, as it is hereafter to be applied in practice" (*Hybritech Inc. v. Monoclonal Antibodies, Inc.*, 802 F.2d 1367, 1376 (Fed. Cir. 1986), cited in Cotropia, 2012: 1876), but what the materialization of the innovation idea would mean remains obscure in patent law and in available court cases. It is clear, though, that the patent system does not rely on any factual evidence of the innovation idea being patented as capable of materializing "in the arts." That is, the patent system is premised on legal fiction wherein an image of the materialized innovation idea serves as a placeholder, an entity to be developed at some point in the future. This legal doctrine in turn generates considerable debate and research in legal scholarship quarters, actively seeking to amend or reform patent law, so that it is more consistent with legal principles and becomes supportive of economic and social welfare.

Lemley (2015) argues that the difficulties involved in making the patent system theoretically and legally consistent, despite including elements of legal fiction, have resulted in legal scholars and other proponents of the current patent system introducing natural and moral right theories to once and for all bury the debate about the moral authority of the patent system itself. That is, Lemley (2015) insists, for these scholars, it would be better to have a patent system that is based on the wrong premises but widely accepted than to have a patent system that is partially based on empirical evidence and good legal theory conscience but under continuous debate. To Lemley, this appears to be a misplaced genre of scholarship that he dismisses as "faith-based" intellectual property rights. Lemley (2015) is skeptical of faith-based legal theories that stipulate that intellectual property (IP) is "an end in itself"—that IP is some kind of pre-political right "to which inventors and creators are entitled" (Lemley, 2015: 1338); "even many economists have begun to talk not in terms of evidence and cost-benefit analysis, but of property in ideas as an end in and of itself," Lemley (2015: 1337) writes.

One of the features of faith-based intellectual property rights is that several legal scholars and other commentators argue that "[t]he optimal rules of IP can be derived from the theory of real property rather than from evidence" (Lemley, 2015: 1345). As evidence is complicated to obtain, it is more convenient to simply stipulate that intellectual property can be asserted on the basis of the claim that it is a form of real property, a proposition that Lemley rejects out of hand: "IP is not like real property or chattels in any meaningful sense" (Lemley, 2015: 1339). The convergence of intellectual property rights and property rights more generally is problematic from a legal theory point of view as intellectual property rights "impose significant costs on freedoms we value," from "free speech" to the ability to make and sell products in a market economy, and on the freedom to make "the very kinds of inventions that give rise to the right in the first place"

(Lemley, 2015: 1343). Unfortunately, in the faith-based intellectual property rights doctrine, all of these objections become unnecessary and time-consuming digressions from the greater question—to what extent and how legal rights and legislation add to social and economic welfare—but Lemley (2015: 1346) warns that a too early closure of this debate is at risk to create considerable harm to the economic system. Lemley's (2015) defense of an ongoing scholarly debate regarding the role of any legal system, and patent law and the patent system more specifically, is commendable, and as will be demonstrated in the remainder of this chapter, there is in fact a lively and animated debate in legal scholarship quarters regarding how to both justify the patent system and how to amend it to better meet its stipulated policy goals.

Ex ante and *ex post* justifications for patent legislation

Lemley (2004) makes an important distinction between *ex ante justifications* and *ex post justifications* of the patent system. The former term denotes how the patent system is justified on the basis of its capacity to bestow property rights on the patent applicant before the innovation idea has materialized, i.e., it is ideas and conjectures regarding the practical value of the innovation idea being examined that are being legally protected. In contrast, *ex post justifications* are extended legal rights granted to an agent that already holds one or more patents and that has developed products and services that are now being considered for additional legal protection. Lemley (2004: 130) explicates the term:

> [C]ommentators and courts have invoked new justifications for intellectual property protection. These arguments focus not on the incentive to create new ideas, but on what happens to those ideas after they have been developed . . . refer to both of these new arguments as *ex post* justifications for intellectual property because they defend intellectual property rights, not on the basis of the incentives they give to create new works, but on the basis of the incentives the right gives its owner to manage works that have already been created.
>
> (Lemley, 2004: 130)

The *ex ante* justification of the patent system is based on what is commonly referred to as *disclosure theory* in patent law and in its enforcement in litigations and in courts: "the value of disclosure is largely axiomatic," Devlin (2010: 407) writes. By and large, disclosure theory identifies two benefits associated with the disclosure of innovation ideas. The first benefit derives from the capacity to facilitate "cumulative invention": "follow-on innovation" accounts for "the vast majority of technological breakthroughs,"

Devlin (2010: 407) argues, which underlines the importance of making inventors "compelled to explain their discoveries." By disclosing their innovation ideas and providing explanations for why the innovation idea would presumably work in practice, the disclosure theory stipulates that the free circulation of innovation ideas supports increased innovative activity and thus, in the next instant, of net economic and social welfare. The second benefit is that the patent application clarifies "the boundaries of an invention" (Devlin, 2010: 407), i.e., the information "conveyed by patents also serves an important role in demarcating the contours of a patentee's property interests," Devlin (2010: 407) writes. This second benefit is a more disputed claim (and will be discussed in more detail later) as the boundaries of the innovation are difficult to predict and anticipate, not the least on the basis of the so-called prophetic examples that patent applications can include under US patent law. Regardless of these objections and empirical evidence that cast a shadow of doubt over this alleged benefit, patent law's disclosure function stipulates that "an inventor must provide not only a sufficiently concise explanation of his invention as to enable others to recreate it (the 'enablement' requirement) but also the optimal method known to him of practicing it (the 'best mode' requirement)" (Devlin, 2010: 409). Taken together, the disclosure theory argument is premised on the idea that the patent system "allows information to percolate through society and makes it available for a range of valuable uses" (Devlin, 2010: 409); "this is the conventional and commonly understood function of disclosure," Devlin (2010: 409) concludes.

All of the theoretical and practical concerns taken aside, this *ex ante* justification of the patent system's disclosure function is widely recognized among legal scholars and policy makers. Regarding *ex post* justifications, there is less consensus. The question is whether patent system regulations should also consider—in addition to incentivizing the disclosure of innovation ideas in the first place—to what extent the patent system's role is to provide "incentives the right gives its owner to manage works that have already been created" (Lemley, 2004: 130). In the case of *ex ante* justification, supported by disclosure theory, intellectual property rights such as patents are widely understood as a "necessary evil" if a free circulation of innovation ideas is to be enabled (as opposed to all such ideas being carefully guarded trade secrets; Morten, 2023), and consequently, what Lemley (2004: 131) refers to as "the incentive theory of intellectual property" dictates that intellectual property rights "should be granted only where necessary." In contrast, Lemley (2004: 131) argues, recent advocacy of *ex post* justification of extended patent rights is more tuned to the idea of letting "greater" and perhaps "unlimited duration and scope" of intellectual property rights become a standard. This argument is essentially premised on the idea that anything that has some economic value should be subject to legal protection so that the originator of the idea that generates economic value would be able to prolong the period where he or she has exclusive rights to use the innovation idea and its materialization. "The *ex post* justifications seem to provide economic support for the legions of new intellectual property owners who claim a moral entitlement to capture all possible value from 'their' information—a view that scholars have derided as 'if value, then right,'" Lemley (2004: 131) writes. Lemley is skeptical about such *ex post* justification because it rests on a misunderstanding of the value of private ordering, and therefore represents an "anti-market" position inasmuch as the argument is primarily supportive of incumbent actor interests (Lemley, 2004: 132). Rather than being theoretically consistent and supported by empirical evidence, *ex post* justifications are grounded in the proposition that incumbent firms serve, e.g., public interest on the basis of extended property rights protection, which is a claim that Lemley (2004) rejects:

> Even if we thought creators would be good managers, there is no reason to believe that the grandchildren of creators will be. If we are to grant perpetual rights to a curator of a work to get efficient management, and not because of any sense that we must further encourage creativity, it seems far more logical to give such control to a professional versed in such management.
>
> (Lemley, 2004: 137–138)

In the end, "empirical evidence strongly supports the intuition of the market, not the arguments of the lobbyists and *ex post* theorists," Lemley (2004: 136) summarizes.

To better explain this position, Lemley (2004: 140) argues that the claim that the original inventor would be better equipped to supply new innovations than the market would be, i.e., to hold the belief "that merely because a company made an initial invention, it would be better informed than the host of companies who might otherwise compete to improve the invention" (Lemley, 2004: 140), remains an empirical question (which Lemley argues has been proved to be an incorrect assumption or proposition), and that it is better to substantiate *ex post* justification claims on the basis of a coherent theoretical model. Lemley thus refers to economic theory (see, e.g., Romer, 1990) that distinguishes between excludable and rivalrous resources, and non-excludable and non-rivalrous resources. Romer (1990), who is concerned with the question of how economic growth is generated on the basis of a combination of technological change, incentives, and legal conditions, explains the difference between two terms:

> Economists studying public finance have identified two fundamental attributes of any economic good: the degree to which it is rivalrous and

> the degree to which it is excludable. . . . A purely rival good has the property that its use by one firm or person precludes its use by another; a purely nonrival good has the property that its use by one firm or person in no way limits its use by another.
>
> (Romer, 1990: S73–S74)

Resources that are excludable can only be accessed by individual market actors owning the resource, or holding contractual rights that specify such exclusivity: a good is excludable "if the owner can prevent others from using it" (Romer, 1990: S74). Furthermore, "excludability is a function of both the technology and the legal system," Romer (1990: S74) says. A classic example is the right to extract valuable minerals from a mine, a right that excludes other market actors from extracting from the same source. Rivalrous resources are in turn competing with each another, as in the case of cotton textiles versus synthetic textiles that can be used to produce similar garments, but at costs that vary over time and with different quality. The idea of the "tragedy of the commons" (Hardin, 1968), widely used to justify that non-excludable resources need to be protected by ownership rights to be used in a reasonable manner, has been invoked to justify *ex post* patent rights, but for critics of extended rights, such arguments are misplaced as innovation ideas are primarily informational assets, and information is a typical case of a non-excludable and non-rivalrous resource:

> Information goods . . . are neither excludable nor rivalrous. They are nonrivalrous because the supply of an information good is limitless. Once revealed, a method for solving a renowned problem, a formula for a new drug, the source code underlying valuable software, and an infinite variety of other examples are available for all to utilize. Such information goods are also nonexcludable, which means that preventing third parties from learning of one's discovery and employing it for their own gain is inordinately difficult.
>
> (Devlin, 2010: 413)

As information "cannot be depleted," the tragedy of the commons argument falls, Lemley (2004: 143) says. As opposed to limited natural resources (such as ore or silver extracted from a mine, of limited supply), the consumption of information is non-rivalrous inasmuch as it "simply cannot be 'used up'" (Lemley, 2004: 143). Given this condition, grounded in economic theory, proponents of extended anti-market ex post justification of more strict property rights need to explain need on what basis it is advisable to give the favour of "strong, perpetual exclusive rights" (Lemley, 2004: 142) to incumbent market actors. Devlin (2010) also considers the value of such legal protection of innovation ideas and/or innovations, but regards them as justifiable only insofar as they provide exclusive rights for a limited period of time, so that the patent holder can acquire compensation that is reasonable, given the resources and efforts committed to develop the innovation idea in the first place:

> We normally trust free market forces to ensure allocative efficiency, as competitive conditions force companies to drop prices toward marginal cost. While marginal cost pricing creates socially desirable static efficiency, it creates insolvency in the presence of fixed costs. Given information goods' nonexcludable nature, many innovators will have difficulty maintaining a monopoly over their commercialized inventions.
>
> (Devlin, 2010: 414)

In the end, Lemley (2004) argues in favour of abandoning *ex post* justification claims as they are neither empirically substantiated nor supported by elementary mainstream economic theory propositions, but primarily reflect the interest of incumbent companies that for the most part already hold a significant number of patents. Lemley (2004: 148) notices that *ex post* justification claims are premised on two views of the market that are inconsistent and incommensurable: "On the one hand, supporters of *ex post* justifications for intellectual property are very quick to conclude that the market will not produce efficient outcomes," Lemley (2004: 148) writes: proponents of *ex post* justification claims "[e]mbrace the public goods or tragedy of the commons theories of market failure without detailed inquiry into whether or not such market failures actually exist." On the other hand, Lemley continues, proponents of *ex post* justification claims

> have an abiding faith in the knowledge, rationality, and good faith of the individual companies in whom they would vest control over the distribution of information, and appear completely unconcerned that transaction costs might prevent them from making efficient use of the power we would vest in them.
>
> (Lemley 2004: 148)

These two claims combined generate a confusing view of the market, wherein *ex post* justification claims are in the first place determined by a preference for "private ordering," while in the second place they reject "market ordering" (Lemley, 2004: 148): companies acting in the market are assumed to act with prudence on the basis of the legal right they are granted and act to maximize economic and social wealth, and yet the market system they are part of cannot be trusted to handle innovative activities in an effective manner.

In summary, the disclosure theory that justifies *ex ante* legal protection plausibly contributes to increased economic welfare, as policy makers predict. In contrast, proponents of *ex post* justification do not substantiate the claims made, which means that "strong support exists for the basic idea underlying the current patent regime," Devlin (2010: 416) proposes: "This system operates to ensure that innovators escape the public goods dilemma by maintaining exclusivity over their inventions and thus reap a sufficient *ex post* return to have induced their research efforts *ex ante*." The patent system and the legal protection of intellectual property right thus needs to be justified in ways that consider all of the possibilities for externalities and legal arbitrage so that it can optimize its ability to fulfil the policy goals it allegedly serves.

New legal doctrines and their consequences: the Leahy-Smith America Invents Act reform

Abrams and Wagner (2013) argue that the heroic figure of "the garage inventor" is an American icon and part of the American business folklore. The image of "the solitary genius tinkering away in order to perfect her idea captures our imagination," Abrams and Wagner (2013: 518) write, and they refer to "a long line of world-changing inventors," including Thomas Edison (operating in Menlo Park and West Orange, New Jersey), Bill Hewlett and David Packard (in Palo Alto in the Bay Area, California), and Steve Wozniak and Steve Jobs (in Los Altos, also in the Bay Area, California). In Abrams and Wagner's (2013: 518) account, this glorious American tradition of independent innovators is now under pressure as new patent legislation has been implemented. Until March 16, 2013, when the so-called Leahy-Smith America Invents Act (AIA) was passed in US Congress, the United States used a "*first-to-invent* (FTI)" priority rule, which indicated that "when there was a dispute as to patent priority, the party that had the inventive idea first was entitled to the patent" (Abrams and Wagner, 2013: 519). With the new legislation, the FTI rule is being displaced by "a *first-to-file* (FTF) rule," which on the contrary "relies on the date (and possibly time) when a patent application was filed with the U.S. Patent Office for the priority determination" (Abrams and Wagner, 2013: 519–520). This means in practice that the patent office and the courts that handle legal dispute consider it irrelevant whether an idea under patent application assessment has been developed at some earlier point, or by some other innovator, as the new legislation grants patent rights strictly on the basis of the documented date of the patent application on file. Lemley (2016: 1180) describes the AIA as the "most substantial overhaul of the patent system in the past sixty years," and as being a legal reform that "incentivizes inventors to promptly disclose their ideas to the public" (Lemley, 2016a: 1181). It is noteworthy that the United States was "the last country" to make this change in its patent system (Abrams and Wagner, 2013: 520). Under all conditions, AIA further underlines the centrality of the market for innovation ideas as a source of economic and social welfare, but the legislation also reduces the demands for evidence regarding the practical applicability of novel innovation ideas, Lemley (2016: 1182) proposes: "[w]hile the 1952 Act didn't give enough encouragement to build and test, the AIA gives none at all."

Abrams and Wagner (2013: 520) are concerned with the consequences of this legislative reform and argue that under the FTF rule, "a successful patentee must not only invent," but also "win the race to draft and submit a patent application that satisfies the requirements of the patent law." This in turn demands investment, which means that in the day-to-day course of business life, smaller or more thinly capitalized firms such as start-ups are likely to be disadvantaged in the new FTF regime: "Companies with significant research and development (R&D) operations are more likely to have patent attorneys on staff with experience working with the company's inventors," Abrams and Wagner (2013: 520) suggest. To provide empirical evidence supportive of such concerns, Abrams and Wagner (2013: 531) collect and examine patenting data from Canada, the second-to-last country to implement a patent law that includes an FTF rule. The benefit with this comparative study design is that the American and Canadian societies are fairly similar on several measures, i.e., the enterprising activities and "entrepreneurial spirit" in the two jurisdictions can be assumed to be comparable. Furthermore, the Canadian and American "transitions from first-to-invent to first-to-file" patent systems are, Abrams and Wagner (2013: 527) propose, in a broad sense, "identical." In the study, data from the Canadian Intellectual Property Office (CIPO) and the United States Patent and Trademark Office (USPTO) was collected (Abrams and Wagner, 2013: 536), with the US serving as the "control group" (Abrams and Wagner, 2013: 531). The U.S. and Canadian data sets are similar, and both include "information on application date, patent grant date, inventor, assignee, patent number, number and word count of claims, and technology classification" (Abrams and Wagner, 2013: 538).

The descriptive statistics reveals that "[t]here were 6.32 patents granted per 1000 Canadians and 3.59 patents per 1000 Americans" (Abrams and Wagner, 2013: 538). When examined within a cost-benefit framework, "[t]here were 294 patents granted in Canada per billion dollars (1989 U.S. dollars) of annual GDP compared with 162 patent grants in the United States per billion dollars of annual GDP" (Abrams and Wagner, 2013: 538). Such descriptive statistics do not reveal very much about the efficacy of the legal reform, but Abrams and Wagner (2013: 536) cite a previous study that showed that "the changes in the law seemed to channel patenting behavior towards larger businesses." Such results are also provided in Abrams and

Wagner's (2013) sample. The first significant result is that "the Canadian change to FTF generally harmed individual inventors." Abrams and Wagner (2013: 521) argue that it is difficult to rule out that these changes are not due to "general long-term trends," such as "an increase in R&D funding among larger entities," rather than being caused by the priority rule change itself. To examine the impact of the legal reform, Abrams and Wagner (2013: 521) use an econometric difference-in-difference methodology to compare "the difference between the differences in individual grant rate in the United States and Canada" and to isolate the net effect of the Canadian law change. Based on this analysis, Abrams and Wagner (2013: 521–522; emphasis in the original) find that there is "a substantial decline in patents granted to individuals due to the change in priority rule: *about a fourteen-percent drop*." This means that the change to the FTF rule, as mandated by AIA, is plausibly harmful for smaller and thinly capitalized firms that would have benefitted from more robust legal protection of intellectual property.

The second significant finding is based on a "linguistic analysis" of patents submitted for review, before and after the change of the law. To operationalize this analysis and to determine whether the patents have changed after the legal reform (and to rule out that patent application quality has deteriorated, or alternatively, increased), Abrams and Wagner (2013: 522) use "word count, sophistication of words, and similar measures as proxies for how much information a patent conveys." Based on this analysis, Abrams and Wagner (2013: 522) report that they find no evidence of "a substantial impact of the law change on patent quality." On balance, the empirical results being reported indicate a "[s]tatistically significant and substantial reduction in patents granted to individual inventors subsequent to the Canadian law change" (Abrams and Wagner, 2013: 550).

The AIA and the FTF rule is premised on a prospect theory, the policy idea that solid property right rules and patents support economic venturing more widely, also operating on the basis of a market for innovation ideas that enables individuals, smaller firms, or thinly capitalized firms to develop ideas that they can sell to companies with deeper pockets and that access the competencies needed to make such ideas materialize. Consequently, it is important to recognize all implications from the results. Abrams and Wagner (2013: 525) agree that there were flaws in the old system, e.g., the FTI priority rules established in §102(g) of the 1952 Patent Law were "highly complex" and involved several careful definitions of what terms such as "reduce to practice," "conception," and "reasonable diligence" would mean in practical terms. In contrast to the FTI rule, the FTF rule is "(relatively) simple and straightforward" (Abrams and Wagner, 2013: 526). However, this simplicity, *per se* potentially supportive of increased patenting activity, comes at the expense of some classes of innovators, including that of "individual innovators" presumably being disadvantaged. "There are good reasons to believe that organizations with more resources will be, on balance, more able to file patent applications quickly," Abrams and Wagner (2013: 528) propose:

> [I]t is clear that the rate of individual patenting has been decreasing in the United States over time, it is widely believed that individuals and small entities have an important impact on the innovation ecosystem—perhaps an outsized impact. This is for several reasons. First, there is some evidence that the inventions from smaller entities are more likely to be disruptive in nature, moving the pace of technological change forward. Second, in some industries, such as high technology and pharmaceuticals, small companies and individuals serve as important innovation inputs into larger, established companies. Finally, even if small entities are no more effective than their larger counterparts at innovation, the distribution of patent rights—and thus marketplace power—has important consequences.
>
> (Abrams and Wagner, 2013: 530)

Based on their comparative study of the consequences of the Canadian legal reform in 1989, Abrams and Wagner (2013: 530) thus call for more research regarding the medium- to long-term consequences of the changes in the patenting system:

> As a statute, the AIA remains unclear. Numerous commentaries speak to the potential complexities and statutory ambiguities. Only as courts work through the AIA's challenges and contours will we definitively know its scope and content. However, these details and intricacies pale in comparison to the broad-based structural change inherent in the AIA.
>
> (Abrams and Wagner, 2013: 528)

One complementary empirical approach is to examine how AIA is actually being implemented and enforced, an issue that more recent legal scholarship research projects have been able to examine. One such issue is to what extent patents that are granted include useful information so that such patents can, in fact, as stipulated by the underlying legal doctrines that justify AIA, be traded in the market for innovation ideas. Several studies address this central feature of the patent law, discussed in the following sections.

Do patents disclose useful knowledge or information?: examining the use of prophetic examples

Lemley (2016: 1187) remarks that both the 1952 Patent Law and the 2011 AIA Patent Law are premised on the idea that "the patent document teaches the world how to make and use the invention." Unfortunately,

Lemley (2016a: 1187) adds, "patents rarely provide much in the way of useful scientific knowledge in most industries." For instance, scientists working in private companies tend to "look elsewhere than patents " for such insights, i.e., the public disclosure mechanism that is the very basis for the legal protection of the idea being submitted for patent protection review is questionable on empirical grounds. Lemley (2016a: 1187, footnote 88) provides anecdotal evidence regarding the limited perceived value of patent documents from his own research work in the field: "I often ask the former scientists and engineers in my patent class whether they ever read patents as a way of doing scientific background reading. The question provokes a chorus of denials and giggles at the very idea" (Lemley, 2016a: 1187, footnote 88).

Several other legal scholars have commented on the alleged limited practical utility of the prophetic examples included in patent applications. "Counterintuitively, the information-revealing function of the patent system is largely illusory," Devlin (2010: 410) writes: "Numerous studies and anecdotal reports reveal that the patent system's performance in disseminating information is disappointing at best" (Devlin, 2010: 410). This means that proponents of disclosure theory may have the wrong idea about the role of prophetic examples: "As a primary function of that system, disclosure is both ineffective and potentially poisonous to larger social goals," Devlin (2010: 403) argues. "To a surprising degree, inventors simply ignore patents," Devlin (2010: 403–404) adds. This is the case as the sheer volume of outstanding patents, coupled with "the lack of specificity in many claims," makes an "exhaustive search of the prior art expensive" (Devlin, 2010: 403–404). Furthermore, of all the patents being granted, only a small majority has been proved to have any commercial value, which is, at the end of the day, what most industry-based researchers are concerned with. Not even in the pharmaceutical industry, where patents are unusually valuable because of the mind-boggling development costs of a new therapy, "only a minority of patents prove to be profitable" (Devlin, 2010: 416). Regardless of these concerns, Devlin (2010: 416) argues that the patent system has a value, not as a storage of valuable knowledge, but as the legal device that incentivizes market actors to innovate: "[I]t remains clear that eliminating the patent system would stymie dynamic efficiency and choke innovation" (Devlin, 2010: 416). Furthermore, "the patent regime" should primarily be construed as "a tool for incentivizing the invention and commercialization of easily appropriated technology," Devlin (2010: 404) clarifies.

The ability to balance disclosure theory claims (which Devlin, 2010: 406, regards as "secondary" to the incentive theory) and incentive theory claims is thus a complicated legal affair, as an oversupply of information that is only marginally useful in innovative activities may misallocate resources to lengthy information searches that result in limited value added. Under these conditions, to examine the current patent system's capacity to minimize information that is distracting and misleading remains a legal theory question of certain prominence, and therefore the following sections will review the legal theory literature that addresses this concern.

Case Study One: patent applications and their use among nanotechnology researchers

Ouellette (2012: 546) refers to disclosure theory as the basis for the current patent system and says that under this theoretical description, "patents are awarded as a quid pro quo for disclosing the invention (rather than keeping the information secret, such as with trade secrets)." This theory is widely endorsed by the courts, and the Supreme Court has often cited disclosure as "one of the main purposes of the patent system" (Ouellette, 2012: 554–555). In contrast, some scholars have been more skeptical regarding the substance of this proposition and have consequently "criticized its prominence as a justification for the patent system" (Ouellette, 2012: 546). This critique is centered on three basic observations and arguments: (1) actual patents contain "little valuable technical information"; (2) "willful infringement rules" cause innovators to "avoid reading patents"; and (3) only inventions that "would be disclosed anyway are patented" (Ouellette, 2012: 555). Ouellette (2012) is concerned with the first argument in particular, and she starts with citing US patent law to demonstrate that the patent application being examined "shall include" some written information about how the innovation idea can be of practical use and value:

> The specification shall contain a *written description* of the invention, and of the manner and process of making and using it, in such full, clear, concise, and exact terms as to *enable* any person skilled in the art to which it pertains, or with which it is most nearly connected, to make and use the same, and shall set forth the *best mode* contemplated by the inventor or joint inventor of carrying out the invention.
>
> (35 U.S.C. § 112, cited in Ouellette, 2012: 550; emphasis added by Ouellette)

When being submitted to the patent office, which grants the right to intellectual property protection to innovation ideas, the application is assessed, §112 prescribes, by "a skilled person" addressed as a "person having ordinary skill in the art" (referred to the acronym "PHOSITA" (Ouellette, 2012: 551). A major concern is then to what extent the PHOSITA does in fact have the state-of-the-art expertise in, e.g., advanced scientific disciplines, and how well the PHOSITA can determine whether the empirical application of the innovation idea is plausible or pure fiction. As this condition constitutes a systemic uncertainty that cannot be handled easily at only a limited cost, this issue is often widely accepted as a fact of life. As a practical matter, Ouellette (2012: 563) refers to one empirical study that shows that "patents were the third most important information source" for scientists, ahead of "public meetings or conferences, competitors' products (via reverse engineering), joint ventures, trade associations, recent hires, licenses, and contracts with other firms" (Ouellette, 2012: 563).

To further substantiate the claim that patents do in fact include information that is useful, and thus sought after by scientists, Ouellette (2012: 568) submitted a survey to more than 1,000 nanotechnology researchers working in the industry, and received responses from 214 researchers, at a response rate of *circa* 20%. In this sample, the respondents had, on average, published 14 papers and had submitted two US patents in the past two years (Ouellette, 2012: 569). In addition, the respondents listed six reasons for not using patents as a source of information or reliable knowledge, with respondents arguing that patents are "(1) confusingly written; (2) unreliable; (3) duplicative of journal articles; (4) out of date; (5) difficult to find; and (6) in conflict with the open culture of science" (Ouellette, 2012: 571). Regarding argument two, some respondents viewed patents as unreliable on the basis of the "lack of peer review" (Ouellette, 2012: 571), a quality control mechanism at the very core of the scientific ideology that nanotechnology researchers endorsed and actively promoted. Regardless of these concerns, the empirical material indicates that 64% of respondents have read patents, and of these respondents, 70% looked at patents for "technical information." Of the respondents that had read patents, 62% of these respondents did so to determine "whether their research was patentable" (Ouellette, 2012: 574). That is, a majority of those who paid attention to patents at all did so to be able to navigate in the patent system, not to find any significant research findings or useful information. In addition, 40% of the respondents in the sample who looked at patents wanted to see how other researchers solved a particular technical problem, and 44% wanted to research a general scientific topic.

These results show that nanotechnology researchers are primarily using patents to learn how to use the patent system, or to learn how to solve specific technical problems, and these findings may be construed as evidence supportive of the disclosure theory under certain conditions. For instance, only 38% of the patent-reading researchers (i.e., 1 in 4 of the responding researchers) said yes to a question about whether patents are "reproducible" (Ouellette, 2012: 576). This in turn indicates that most nanotechnology patent application examples are more of conjectures, thought experiments, or loose reasoning than based on solid scientific evidence. Despite this assessment by the patent-reading researchers, Ouellette (2012: 548) still emphasizes that nanotechnology researchers do in fact actively look for patents for information that can guide their research work:

> Given that we have a patent system . . . the relevant question is whether the benefits of strong disclosure outweigh its costs . . . and this article demonstrates that disclosure has stronger benefits than previously appreciated. These benefits probably outweigh any incremental loss in innovation incentives caused by further strengthening disclosure.
>
> (Ouellette, 2012: 548)

In the end, Ouellette (2012) concludes, the AIA and its emphasis on a disclosure-and-reward model assist the development of a market for innovation ideas, which in turn supports a better allocation of economic resources as people with innovation ideas can be connected with people with the money and the skills needed to transform ideas into materialized innovations.

Case Study Two: the use of prophetic examples to substantiate innovation ideas

Gugliuzza (2016) and Freilich (2019) examine the use of what is referred to as prophetic examples within AIA and what unintended consequences the introduction of this legal device have for the innovation policy that AIA expresses. Gugliuzza (2016: 1226) proposes that the Federal Circuit (US federal courts with specific legal responsibilities, including the handling of patent rights) has ruled that "a patent can be enabled by mere 'prophetic examples,'" i.e., on the basis of basically "educated speculations about how one might make the invention," as well as in cases that "allow an inventor to establish priority even if the inventor was unsure whether the invention would work." In Gugliuzza's (2016) account, these are fairly vague terms given the weight of the legality of a patent right, granted after a successful examination and acceptance. As Gugliuzza (2016: 1227) remarks, "the core purpose" of patent law is "utilitarian" insofar as it "enhances social welfare by incentivizing the development of new and useful technology." The empirical question is then to what extent the use of prophetic examples in fact support an increased innovative output, or, in case of a lack thereof (caused by, e.g., a limited supply of venture capital and other exogeneous conditions), do prophetic examples at least provide more pronounced incentives to innovate?

Freilich (2019) delves into this issue, and to better position her study, she cites an actual case that stirred some emotions when being revealed:

> In May of 2005, a team of scientists made headlines after the prestigious journal *Science* published a report that they had cloned human embryos.

> Only a few months later, the team was making headlines for a different reason: the data in the paper had been faked; *Science* retracted the paper and the team's leader, Dr. Hwang Woo-Suk, was fired and spent two years in prison for violating bioethics rules. Almost ten years after the retraction, Dr. Hwang received a U.S. patent on his discredited technique. Other scientists were 'shocked' by the news that Dr. Hwang obtained a patent for falsified data.
>
> (Freilich, 2019: 665–666)

The response from the fellow geneticists is intuitively understandable: if being caught fabricating data, which is a violation of good scientific practice rules and scholarly norms at the highest degree, then it is expected that patents based on such fake data should be withdrawn. Perhaps surprisingly, as Freilich (2019) writes, the USPTO and other patent offices do not regard such data as of necessity being fraudulent in the legal sense of the term: on the contrary, fictional data are instead treated as "equivalent to factual data" (Freilich, 2019: 666). This kind of counterintuitive legal practice needs to be explained in more detail to be fully understood and to be regarded as justifiable. The first point to make is that "fictional experiments" are commonly called "prophetic examples" in patent law, and they are a legal device that supports the goals of utilitarian patent legislation (Freilich, 2019: 666). As a matter of fact, Freilich (2019: 667) writes, "it is possible that the [US] PTO has granted hundreds of thousands of patents based on hypothetical experiments and we know nothing about it."

In order to understand how the legal device of the prophetic example was first introduced and thereafter tolerated as a necessary evil (or worse) in the patent system, the history of the patent system should be accounted for. At the earliest period of time when the patent system was in operation, most US patents were "mechanical or electrical" in substance (Freilich, 2019: 675). As mechanical and electrical inventions are "relatively predictable," which suggests that a skilled engineer, reading a patent disclosing one model of an apparatus, "could predict how variations of the disclosed apparatus would perform" (Freilich, 2019: 675). In the early twentieth century, the field of organic chemistry burgeoned, and the number of chemistry patents skyrocketed, which put more pressure on the patent system to revise the doctrine that patents could be communicated via drawings or illustrated by drawings. For instance, although a drawing of, say, a molecule shows its structure and can convey other information, it is not always clear from that structure "how to synthesize the molecule or what the molecule's uses might be" (Freilich, 2019: 676). To better assist the patenting of chemistry-based innovations, the patent office increasingly recognized the use of "examples," including "experimental protocols" that support organic chemistry claims "in the same way that drawings traditionally had for mechanical patents" (Freilich, 2019: 676). This new use of examples was only gradually established, and as Freilich (2019: 677) remarks, "for the first 50 years in which prophetic examples were used, the USPTO had no official rules concerning the practice." While the patent law has become more formalized over several legislative reform cycles, there is still to this date fairly limited court case ruling information available to learn from: "Overall, case law on prophetic examples remains sparse," Freilich (2019: 681) writes. This means that the central legal device, the prophetic example, upon which the decision to grant significant legal rights to the patent applicant rests, remains legally ambiguous in terms of how both participants in markets for innovation ideas regard this information and how the courts rule on the basis of this information in the case of, e.g., disputes over alleged patent infringements. For the layperson and other outsiders in the patent law field, this is a noteworthy condition.

Based on these observations, Freilich (2019: 667) seeks to substantiate the claim that prophetic examples do in fact serve a productive role as intended, i.e., to assist the sharing of innovation ideas so that ideas can either materialize on the basis of self-interested research activities or otherwise generate new ideas or knowledge that contribute to innovative output, and/or to generate net economic or social welfare. Freilich's (2019: 667) study design includes chemistry and biology patents as such patents are often on file with industries that commonly generate experimental data. Experimental data are regarded to be closer to the conventional scientific knowledge production procedures that are used in the sciences and that are accounted for in the journal articles being submitted for peer review in scientific journals. In total, Freilich (2019: 668) examined 2,214,558 patents and applications, a sample that contains no less than 12,300,156 such entities in total. The results of the study indicate that in the case of chemistry and biology patents, "at least 17% of examples are prophetic" and, of patents with examples, "at least 24% contain some prophetic experiments" (Freilich, 2019: 668). This means that prophetic examples are widespread enough to "seriously impact patent law," Freilich (2019: 668) proposes. Furthermore, Freilich (2019: 669) reports that she finds that "there is little evidence that prophetic examples benefit patentees on a population level":

> Patents with more prophetic examples are narrower than patents with fewer prophetic examples. Similarly, patents with more prophetic examples are less valuable than patents with fewer prophetic examples. Finally, although small companies should benefit disproportionately from the ability to use prophetic examples, they do not. I found that small companies are significantly less likely to use prophetic examples as compared to their larger counterparts.
>
> (Freilich, 2019: 669)

Therefore, on balance, the results provide weak evidence of the benefits of prophetic examples, whereas the evidence "for their *harms* is much stronger," Freilich (2019: 669) writes.

In addition to these results that indicate that prophetic examples have limited value in the patent system, Freilich (2019: 669) examines another downside risk, that scientists, if they look at patents for valuable information, would be misled by low-quality prophetic examples. Also on this parameter, the results are daunting: Freilich (2019: 698) randomly selected 100 of the studied patents and found that no less than 99 "were not cited in a manner that made it clear that the cited information was prophetic." Of specific concern is the fact that in dynamic scientific fields such as nanotechnology (Ouellette, 2012), or in chemistry and biology research, wherein new ideas and knowledge are being generated on a day-to-day basis, information that may be inaccurate is easily being reproduced via cross-referencing, which makes it vital that the input information is correct and verified on the basis of experiments and/or peer-review procedures:

> Since the citing document gets cited in turn by others, prophetic examples create a chain where few readers would be aware that the underlying data are fictional. Additionally, patents are now frequently mined by databases that automatically extract information from patents.
>
> (Freilich, 2019: 699)

Freilich (2019: 669) does not mince her words regarding how prophetic examples are read and cited in research work: "False information is infiltrating the scientific community by way of prophetic examples"; prophetic examples are "[m]isleading, inaccurate, and present in low-value patents that may hinder downstream research," Freilich (2019: 710) adds. Apparently, such findings calls for reform, but banning prophetic examples would presumably be a too drastic legal change, Freilich (2019: 670) proposes. A less pervasive reform would be to rename prophetic examples so that the name used to a lesser extent "carries a ring of accuracy and infallibility" (Freilich, 2019: 670), e.g., the scientific term *hypothesis* would for instance be more accurate to use:

> Instead of banning prophetic examples entirely, it is better to require patent applicants to provide an explanation for why their hypothesis is likely to be correct and allow examiners to weigh that explanation in assessing whether the enablement and written description requirements are met. This effectively renders wild guesses valueless but still gives credit to predictions based on sound underlying principles.
>
> (Freilich, 2019: 725)

In summary, Freilich's (2019) research results do not indicate that patents serve the role predicted by disclosure theory, i.e., that the information being part of new innovation ideas can be revealed to other actors so that it supports a market for innovation ideas. The use of prophetic examples is only vaguely related to state-of-the-art practice, and it is difficult for scientists who look at patents to obtain useful information. To figure out whether the information provided is solid and trustworthy, or merely expresses a conjecture or some piece of fiction, is associated with informational costs and the work demands skills and experience. These research results call for important questions to be asked and answered regarding the design of the patent system, arguably first being developed to handle mechanical and other engineering-based innovations, but not necessarily being in line with the demands for legal rights in an advanced knowledge-based economy.

Case Study Three: the "replication crisis" and the patent system

As patents are of specific importance for, e.g., chemistry and life science disciplines, and for the pharmaceutical industry in particular, wherein the development of a new drug costs billions of dollars and demands ten years of development work, patents that are based on experimental research are of specific interests. Freilich (2020) examines to what extent patents permitted by the USPTO include methodological descriptions that can be of practical value for any scientist who wishes to use patent information as part of the development work. This assessment of patent data methodology descriptions is complicated by the fact that many, if not most, experimental activities has been shown to be difficult to replicate: "Studies attempting to replicate preclinical experiments have found that almost 90% of experiments from well-respected, peer-reviewed journals are not replicable," Freilich (2020: 433) writes. Unfazed by these facts, Freilich (2020: 434) "hand-coded" a random sample of 500 preclinical experiments from patents and patent applications, and "scored their methodological quality." Freilich (2020: 435) focused on life sciences patents specifically because "these patents are the most likely to contain experiments" and because "the replicability crisis" addressed in the scientific literature is "most often discussed in the context of life sciences research" (Freilich, 2020: 435). The results indicate that the descriptions "have very poor methodological quality": "Only 62% of experiments in patents in my sample disclosed sample size, 12% were randomized, 4% were blinded, 2% conducted replicate studies, and 63% had statistical analysis of any kind," Freilich (2020: 434) summarizes. Freilich's (2020) study thus contributes to a scholarly literature that indicates that the patent system does not include rules or demands that incentivize patent applicants to include information that would make it more likely to reproduce the data that is claimed to support the innovation idea. If the patent is understood to be a quid pro quo to compensate for the disclosure of the innovation idea, then the information accompanying the patent application should preferably have some practical value to support a functional market for innovation ideas, as the policy makers and legislators intended.

Based on her results, Freilich (2020) discusses some legal implications. As Freilich (2020: 435) argues, "[a] foundational assumption of patent law is that inventions work," but if most inventions in patents "do not work and are not replicable," then there is arguably little value in disclosing innovation ideas in the first place. Furthermore, such a patent system would be burdened by "patents on technologies that do not work," which would generate costs in excess of the social value generated. In this scenario, Freilich (2020: 436) writes, patent assessors would be overwhelmed by patent applications, and their work would result in "patent thickets"[1] that would provide further incentives for patent trolls to engage in litigation activities. Regarding non-monetary effects, including the lack of trust in the patent system that in the eyes of informed market actors (e.g., company-based researchers) operates on the basis of mere fictional descriptions of experiments, Freilich (2020: 442) argues that "irreplicable studies" are demoralizing to scientists, but they also affect the public as "the public's trust in scientific research diminishes." In the end, therefore, some legal reform is needed that reduces these risk and the costs they generate.

The unintended consequences of the patent system: the role of Patent Assertion Entities (PAEs), "patent trolls," and others

Under all conditions, in the "cognitive capitalism" (see, e.g., Haskel and Westlake, 2017; Akerlof and Shiller, 2009; Thrift, 2005; Giere and Moffatt, 2003) economic system that has been developed over the last decades, the patent system is a centerpiece of the legal system that supports enterprising and economic venturing, regardless of its theoretical inconsistencies and practical glitches. "We issued six times as many patents in 2014 as we did three decades before," Lemley (2015: 1343) reports. Based on such empirical data and observations, the concept of "overpatenting" (Asay, 2017: 5) has been introduced. Although patenting activity may be understood as an index of enterprising, and thus signals a viable economic system, several commentators have been concerned that many of these patents filed do in fact counteract the legislator's intentions (see e.g., Parikh, 2023).[2]

1 The term *patent thickets* denotes "dense, overlapping webs of patents" owned by some legal person, and that make it difficult to commercialize an innovation idea because products "may overlap with large numbers of patented technologies" (Cohen, Gurun, and Kominers, 2019: 5473). The concept of patent thickets is thus used as an essentially pejorative term as it is associated with opportunistic behaviour on the basis of legal rights associated with intellectual property. Patent thickets are particularly prevalent in the software, semiconductors, and electronics industries, which Cohen, Gurun, and Kominers (2019: 5483, footnote 48) consequently refer to as the "thicket industries."

2 When examining legal arbitrage in the field of patent law and within the patent system, it is important to recognize that any specific legal framework provides such possibilities. For instance, in bankruptcy law, a number of recent scholarly publications have called attention to how market actors actively use the

Cotropia, Kesan, and Schwartz (2014) examine what they refer to as Patent Assertion Entities (PAEs), their role in the economic system, and how they affect how patent law is interpreted and enforced. The concern is that during the last two decades, "the landscape of patent litigation" has "radically shifted," Cotropia, Kesan, and Schwartz (2014: 649) argue: entities that do not manufacture products have become "important players in the patent litigation system." Such PAEs are in many cases suspect of being either so-called "Non-Practicing Entities" (NPEs), or "Patent Monetization

---

bankruptcy legislation to achieve benefits in ways that presumably violate the legislators' intentions (Skeel, 2023; Ellias, 2023; Seymour, 2022; Skeel, 2020; Casey and Macey, 2020; Macey and Salovaara, 2019). Simon (2022: 1157) examines a number of legal cases wherein so-called Chapter 11 bankruptcies are used to avoid liabilities that become overwhelming for the corporate entity or majority owners. Simon (2022) refers to market actors who rely on the Chapter 11 bankruptcy device as an exit option as "bankruptcy grifters," which indicates that the bankruptcy law and system are used in an inadequate manner. The ability to use Chapter 11 bankruptcies in this way is "not created by the Bankruptcy Code," but specific judges grant them access to the bankruptcy system on the basis of legal decisions that are questionable (Simon, 2022: 1157). Simon examines a number of cases, including Purdue Pharma's much-debated bankruptcy case, wherein liabilities associated with the opioid epidemic in the US that was formally declared by regulatory agencies in 2017 were avoided by leaving $4.5 billion "on the table" when Purdue Pharma received protection within a Chapter 11 bankruptcy procedure. A similar case of legal arbitrage is the Catholic Church Dioceses in Portland, Saint Paul, Minneapolis, Tucson, San Diego, Wilmington, Davenport, and New Orleans that have all "turned to federal bankruptcy to deal with pending liability related to sexual abuse" (Simon, 2022: 1200). In all, Simon (2022: 1200) continues, "more than twenty parishes have sought relief in bankruptcy—in some cases, hours before trial was set to start." LoPucki (2022: 248) reports that Belk, a Charlotte, North Carolina–based department-store chain with $3.7 billion in annual revenues, filed a Chapter 11 petition in the Houston division of the United States Bankruptcy Court for the Southern District of Texas in February 23, 2021. The court, which actively sought cases of this kind—"Houston was the hot new destination for big bankruptcy forum shopping with just under a 50 percent market share" (LoPucki, 2022: 248)—received the petition in the evening and began restructuring Belk's debt the following morning, ultimately reducing it by $582.2 million (LoPucki, 2022: 264), but without giving the creditors any chance to be informed, to ask questions, or to protect their contractual rights. The Purdue Pharma, Catholic Church dioceses, and Belk cases were unified in the use of the Chapter 11 bankruptcy device to escape overwhelming debt, but in a manner that clearly violated "the spirit" (Pistor, 2022: 345) of the legislation. In Simon's account, bankruptcy grifters act like "a Trojan horse in the bankruptcy system, undermining the integrity of the bankruptcy process at the expense of claimants who will lose procedural protections and rights." LoPucki (2022) is equally skeptical about the bankruptcy system's regress "into lawlessness": "[T]he bankruptcy courts have no authority to ignore the law. Routine disregard for the law creates a gangster-like atmosphere in which the case placers not only appear to be, but actually are, above the law," LoPucki (2022: 252) writes.

In addition to the more lax use of the bankruptcy system, Dick (2021: 1336) examines what she refers to as "hostile out-of-court private loan restructuring." Dick (2021: 1338) proposes that "recent Chapter 11 cases" suggest that it is becoming "more difficult to reach consensus among ever more fractured lender groups," with minority lenders in some cases forming "ad hoc groups to oppose the restructuring and advance alternative transactions." Under such conditions, "hostile restructurings" have been used as an alternative to the court-based bankruptcy system, but Dick (2021: 1338–1339) is concerned that such market practices have the potential to "destroy value, impair the smooth functioning of the capital markets, and introduce and amplify the distributional concerns that have traditionally plagued bankruptcy restructurings." By and large, the incompleteness of bankruptcy law and market-based regulatory rules create new possibilities for corporate entities and other economic entities to escape liabilities. Such practices may justify legal reforms or more strict regulatory oversight if legal arbitrage impose externalities and costs in the economic system.

Entities" (PMEs), or, more simply put, "patent trolls"—market actors that seek to extract rents through the patents they hold, but otherwise not being involved in any productive activities intended to result in innovation output. Cotropia, Kesan, and Schwartz (2014: 650) say that this category of market actors includes a large variety of organizations, ranging from universities, individual inventors, and failed start-ups to "companies formed by venture capitalists seeking to exploit the inventions of others" (Cotropia, Kesan, and Schwartz, 2014: 650).

If legal scholars and other proponents of the patent system are concerned with the efficiency of the market for innovation ideas, there are worrying market data being reported by Cotropia, Kesan, and Schwartz (2014): studies show that PAEs cost the economy "tens of billions of dollars," a figure calculated on the basis of a "confidential survey" of defendants (Cotropia, Kesan, and Schwartz, 2014: 651). Furthermore, another study found that patent trolls filed "62% of patent lawsuits in 2012," which represents a significant increase from the 29% filed in 2010 (Cotropia, Kesan, and Schwartz, 2014: 652). Although such figures may appear to be alarming for proponents of the current patent system, a key issue here is how to access and how to construe reliable data that demonstrate that PAEs wield a negative influence on the patent system and the economic system at large. "To us, the fundamental barrier to thoroughly understanding these competing narratives is the lack of granular and transparent data that attempts to properly account for the various types of PAEs," Cotropia, Kesan, and Schwartz (2014: 654) say.

As was discussed earlier, one group of scholars argues that one of the explicit policy goals with the creation of a patent system is to generate a market for innovation ideas (the patent as a *quid pro quo* for disclosing innovation ideas so that they become public), and the presence of market actors who use their legal rights being enshrined by patent law cannot be taken as a prima facie evidence of this patent system revealing dysfunctions. Another group of scholars disputes such claims. Lemley and Melamed (2013) are widely concerned with what they refer to as "patent trolls," picking up the Scandinavian and Nordic folklore figure of the "almost human" but deceitful, dumb, and at times dangerous creature of the troll, lurking in the woods but occasionally interfering with human communities, to describe these market actors—a not entirely flattering choice of metaphor. Lemley and Melamed (2013: 2119) point at costs and efficiency issues when framing the problem to regulate the market for innovation ideas: "A recent academic study calculates that trolls cost society approximately $30 billion per year and have cost a total of $500 billion over the past twenty years" (Lemley and Melamed, 2013: 2119). Another study published in 2009 estimated that 19% of patent lawsuits "were filed by patent trolls" (Lemley and Melamed, 2013: 2122), which accounts for a considerable aggregated legal cost as litigation processes are both costly and time consuming. Furthermore, patent trolls are active to a varying degree in different industries; for instance, "patent trolls are particularly common in the software industry," Lemley and Melamed (2013: 2123) say. When looking at the cost side of the equation, it appears as if patent trolls are a primary driver of innovation costs, as there is little evidence that trolls "[s]ignificantly increase rewards to inventors" (Lemley and Melamed, 2013: 2125).

Lemley and Melamed (2013) suggest that the presence of patent trolls and the costs they generate for innovators and the legal system is not some exogeneous condition, but is to be understood as a symptom of a below-optimal design of the patent system, and that provides possibilities for free-riding on the basis of legal arbitrage: "The growth of patent trolls, coupled with the costs of practicing entity licensing and litigation, suggests systemic problems that are not limited to trolls" (Lemley and Melamed, 2013: 2170):

> In a world in which everyone can patent every little thing, royalty stacking[3] is a fact of life. Troll suits bring into sharp focus the fact that much patent litigation does not represent a working market for ideas as much as a market for government-granted permissions to control or tax independently developed technologies. And the endless parade of trolls reflects the endless parade of patents granted on every new idea (and many not-so-new ideas) and the profit opportunities they provide.
>
> (Lemley and Melamed, 2013: 2149)

In practical terms, patent trolls are often companies that acquire patents from original patent owners at low cost, because these patent owners are "unwilling or unable to assert them," or because they "lacked the resources or sophistication to do so," Lemley and Melamed (2013: 2149) say. In this account, patent trolls and PAEs appear to be an entirely undesirable and unattractive consequence of a patent system that was originally designed to support a market for innovation ideas.

Although the costs for litigation may be measured and assessed as being significant, such metrics need to be assessed against the (fictive) costs of not having any market for innovation ideas in place at all, proponents of the current patent system are less concerned with the erosion of the system on the basis of active PAEs and any other actors who wish to have their legal rights enforced. As Lemley and Melamed (2013: 2120) also admit, patent

3 "Royalty stacking" denotes the "[t]he phenomenon in which disparate owners of complementary technologies license their patents at their profit-maximizing monopoly price and cause a cumulative reduction in welfare" (Shrestha, 2010: 124). Companies that own patents can make a return on these legal assets by licensing a variety of companies the right to use the patent, thus creating a business model based on the creation of a portfolio of patents.

trolls are not "a unitary phenomenon": "We see at least three different troll business models developing, and those models have different effects on the patent system" (Lemley and Melamed, 2013: 2120). In fact, companies that act to aggregate a stock of patents and that use these legal rights to extract rents may play a market-marker role inasmuch as they provide incentives for would-be innovators to patent their innovation ideas, even if they know *ex ante* that they do not access the resources or the expertise needed to protect their patents against infringement:

> [M]any of the problems associated with trolls are in fact problems that stem from the disaggregation of complementary patents (patents that cover technologies used together in the same products) into too many different hands. That in turn suggests that aggregators might be reducing, not worsening, these problems.
>
> (Lemley and Melamed, 2013: 2121)

Shrestha (2010: 115–116) takes a more sanguine view of PAEs and NPEs than Cotropia, Kesan, and Schwartz (2014) and Lemley and Melamed (2013) do, and argues that a substantial scholarly literature shows that "NPEs enhance innovation and competition by providing capital to independent inventors and creating an efficient market for trade in technological information." Shrestha (2010: 117) examines patent data from the USPTO and "infringement litigation information" from Stanford Law School's Intellectual Property Litigation Clearinghouse (IPLC) database to examine whether there has been sharp growth in patent troll litigations, as e.g., Lemley and Melamed (2013) claim is the case. The study included "patent infringement" suits between January 1, 2000 and March 21, 2008 (Shrestha, 2010: 121), and the analysis of the "NPE patents and their litigation behavior" provides "a generally favorable picture of NPEs" (Shrestha, 2010: 118):

> These firms own patents that are of significantly higher value or importance than other litigated patents. NPE patents also rank higher than the litigated patents that share the same technological class in every value measure employed in the analysis. Finally, the study of NPE litigation behavior shows that the success rate of NPEs in patent infringement litigation is quite similar to that of other litigants.
>
> (Shrestha, 2010: 118)

In Shrestha's (2010: 118) assessment, the results suggest that policy makers should "exercise caution" before creating laws that "hinder the ability of NPEs to effectively perform their role in fostering innovation." In fact, NPEs do play an active and productive role in acting as a marketmaker inasmuch as they ensure that innovators who do not hold the resources needed to protect patents from infringements are given a chance to have their rights legally determined, which is one of the several benefits that patent law was intended to provide, according to its proponents. As empirical research has demonstrated that the value of patents owned by "independent inventors" is "highly variable"—some patents are very valuable, whereas others are less so—NPEs can perform an "important function" by "sifting through the patents owned by independent inventors" and by identifying "the most valuable ones" (Shrestha, 2010: 128). Over time, by repeatedly analyzing and buying patents, NPEs become "experts at differentiating between valuable and trivial patents," which is an expertise that independent inventors could not accomplish on their own on the basis of social dilemmas and free-riding concerns (see, e.g., Olson, 1965). Based on this market-making activity, NPEs act to reward the inventors as stipulated by patent law and intended by the legislation (Shrestha, 2010: 128): "By making patents liquid and reducing information asymmetries between buyers and sellers of patents, NPEs help create an efficient market for patents" (Shrestha, 2010: 130). Based on these results, and inferences made from available legal doctrines, policy goals, and conventional wisdom, Shrestha (2010: 149) argues that "[l]egislators should not be swayed by those who use NPEs as scapegoats for the problems of the current patent system and as a justification for reforms that could have drastic consequences for the broader inventive community." The patent system may be far from perfect, but the actors (e.g., NPEs and PAEs, and the independent innovators with whom they collaborate) should not be held culpable for the difficulties involved in constructing a robust patent system that relies on descriptions and speculations regarding the value of the innovation idea being protected by intellectual property rights.

Equally concerned with providing empirical evidence regarding the role of NPEs and PAEs in the patent system, Cotropia, Kesan, and Schwartz (2014) present a study that includes all patent infringement lawsuits filed in "two complete calendar years," 2010 and 2012. The "raw data" from these years included 3,553 and 5,600 lawsuits, respectively (Cotropia, Kesan, and Schwartz, 2014: 662). In the end, after some infringement cases were eliminated from the sample, the final data set contained 2,520 patent infringement lawsuits in 2010 and 5,185 patent infringement lawsuits in 2012 (Cotropia, Kesan, and Schwartz, 2014: 666). Based on the analysis of the material, Cotropia, Kesan, and Schwartz (2014: 655) found, contrary to previous reports, that "there has not been any explosion of PAE litigation between 2010 and 2012." In fact, Cotropia, Kesan, and Schwartz (2014: 655) continue, "[o]verall, the often-repeated 'explosion' of PAE litigation from 2010 to 2012 is almost completely a myth." Similar to Shrestha's (2010) argument that PAEs and NPEs do play an important market-making role, and that these market actors should not be blamed for the legal difficulties involved in establishing a watertight patent system as that would be to shift blame from legislators or regulators to market actors, Cotropia, Kesan, and Schwartz (2014: 653) take a more positive view of PAEs role in the patent system and the market for innovation ideas that they are allegedly supportive of:

> Defenders of PAEs have offered several purported benefits. They claim that PAEs provide liquidity in the marketplace for patents. They permit inventors who are otherwise excluded from the marketplace—because, for instance, they are individuals who cannot manufacture products, or they are companies that tried yet failed to manufacture—to obtain some return on their investment.
>
> (Cotropia, Kesan, and Schwartz, 2014: 653)

In the end, a fairly complex image of the patent system emerges, including the market for innovation ideas being sketched on the basis of legal theories, legal doctrines, and empirical data. NPEs and PAEs are often portrayed as being culpable for patent system deficiencies, but this critique is presumably based on what is referred to as the "Nirvana Fallacy" (Eisenberg, 1989: 1525), wherein an ideal, fictive state devoid of any friction, inertia, transaction costs, and tensions is compared to an actual real-world economy situation, which of necessity makes the ideal case appear to be more attractive, simply because it has been described exclusively on the basis of its attractive and desirable features. In order to avoid this fallacy in policy making and in legislative affairs, it is important that the patent system is constructed on the basis of realistic assumptions regarding how the patent system works and what kind of loopholes and possibilities for legal arbitrage that can possibly be the case, despite the best intentions to handle such legal glitches. As Haber and Lamoreaux (2021: 23) write, "[i]t is naive to believe that any system devised by human beings to apportion economic surplus is going to be frictionless." For all their imperfections, US-style patent systems spread "because they had multiple advantages" (Haber and Lamoreaux, 2021: 23).

More recent studies following the upsurge in NPE litigations after 2015

Cohen, Gurun, and Kominers (2019) argue that after 2015, intellectual property right infringement litigation activities have increased considerably, and that it is essentially NPEs that propel these changes. According to a report issued by the US Government Accountability Office in 2013, three factors contributed to the rise in IP litigation: (1) the number of patents (especially software-related patents) "with unclear scope" has increased; (2) courts have "granted large monetary awards in infringement lawsuits," even for ideas that make only "small contributions to a product"; (3) markets place a "larger valuation on patents" than they did previously (Cohen, Gurun, and Kominers, 2019: 5462). Based on a data set that includes NPE litigation cases, Cohen, Gurun, and Kominers (2019: 5461) demonstrate that NPEs "appear to behave opportunistically" inasmuch as they "target firms that are flush with cash" and firms that have recently reported "positive cash shocks." Furthermore, NPE-initiated litigations target firms that earn their profits from business segments "having nothing to do with the allegedly infringing segments" (Cohen, Gurun, and Kominers, 2019: 5461). These legal activities observed are mostly what Cohen, Gurun, and Kominers (2019: 5461) refer to as "the behavior of large 'patent aggregator' firms." These activities contrast against small inventors' lawsuits, wherein defendants' cash holdings "are not a significant factor" (Cohen, Gurun, and Kominers, 2019: 5461). Besides being a significantly expanding legal activity, NPE litigations do not have the favourable outcomes for the market for innovation ideas that their proponents claim is the case. Cohen, Gurun, and Kominers (2019: 5461) report that they find evidence that firms losing to NPEs (either in court cases or through settlement) reduce their research and development investments "by roughly 20% going forward relative to *ex ante* identical firms." That is, the legal activities of NPEs do not provide any allocative benefits as court cases or settlements are premised on a zero-sum game market model wherein the NPEs' extraction of financial capital from companies legally violating the patent rights held by the NPE comes at these companies' expense, but also result in a reduction of future investments in R&D activities that follows. In the medium- to long-term view, predatory NPEs thus accomplish a downward shift in R&D investment appetite, which is at risk to harm long-term growth and economic and social welfare as new innovations are more costly and more legally demanding to produce. "The best available estimates suggest," Cohen, Gurun, and Kominers (2019: 5462) summarize, that "only a small fraction of the damages won by NPEs are actually paid back to innovators."

Kiebzak, Rafert, and Tucker (2016) report that between 2004 and 2012, the number of patent lawsuits in the US "more than doubled," from circa 2,500 to over 5,000 annually. In nominal terms, in 2012, more than 12,600 defendants were involved in such lawsuits. Based on a database material, wherein PAEs that are so-called frequent litigators are identified, defined as "an entity that has filed twenty or more patent lawsuits" (Kiebzak, Rafert, and Tucker, 2016: 222), the legal action of such PAEs and their consequences are examined. An analysis of the sample reveals that no less than 61% of all defendants that were sued by a PAE "had sued eight or more times," compared to 16% that were sued by a PAE "had sued less than eight times" (Kiebzak, Rafert, and Tucker, 2016: 222). Furthermore, the legal corporate structure of PAEs is complex as such firms "often hide under multiple shell companies and names" (Kiebzak, Rafert, and Tucker, 2016: 222), which makes it complicated to identify them precisely by name. Under all conditions, it is plausible that the class of frequent litigators are "large-scale patent aggregators" that operationally and strategically use the legal system as a device to extract economic value from innovating firms.

Kiebzak, Rafert, and Tucker (2016: 218) report that there is a robust statistical relationship between venture capital investment and patent litigation activity that is non-linear: "our parameter estimates suggest that there is an inverted-U-shaped relation between the extent of patent litigation and entrepreneurial activity." At a low level of patent litigation, an increase in patent litigation is associated with increased venture capital investment, while at high levels of patent litigation, an increase in patent litigation is associated with decreased venture capital investment (Kiebzak, Rafert, and Tucker, 2016: 218). Expressed in other terms, as venture capital investment is the life blood of entrepreneurial activities, more active PAEs are associated with "lower levels of entrepreneurial activity," presumably on the basis of a more limited appetite for investing finance capital in industries where PAEs are active (Kiebzak, Rafert, and Tucker, 2016: 219). Furthermore, the data indicates that litigation activities differ between industry sectors, and with the "'Bio and Pharma' space" being comparably well protected, and with venture capitalists funding companies in the sector receiving far fewer "PAE demand letters" than in, e.g., the computer and software industries (Kiebzak, Rafert, and Tucker, 2016: 226). In the computer and software industries, wherein patents "may have fuzzier boundaries," inadvertent patent infringement is more likely to occur, and as a consequence, defendants are more exposed to the risk of receiving PAE demand letters (Kiebzak, Rafert, and Tucker, 2016: 227).

The implication is that the economic loss following lower entrepreneurial activity (e.g., lower investment in R&D results in fewer new innovations being produced) needs to be weighed against the value of having a market for innovation ideas, populated by PAEs and similar market actors that hold legal rights that they enforce via primarily the litigation mechanism. Kiebzak, Rafert, and Tucker (2016: 229) calculate that the "average total cost" of a patent lawsuit involving PAEs, including settlements and legal fees, ranges from $1.75 million per lawsuit for firms with revenues "less than $1 billion" to $8.79 million per lawsuit for firms with revenues "greater than $1 billion." Given the nominal increase in patent litigation cases between 2004 and 2012, the aggregated direct and indirect costs are considerable, especially if venture capitalists refrain from investing in, e.g., the computer and software industries as they assess the risks of losing money in—from their point of view—unproductive litigation cases, initiated by frequent litigators that regard this legal practice as a key component of their business model. Kiebzak, Rafert, and Tucker (2016) thus provide first-hand evidence that patent litigation cases do play a role in a variety of industries, and in the computer and software industries in particular.

Based on their empirical data examined, Cohen, Gurun, and Kominers (2019) and Kiebzak, Rafert, and Tucker (2016) provide a more negative view of NPEs and PAEs than, e.g., Shrestha (2010) does. In their assessment, the evidence reported appears to be most consistent with the view that NPEs, on average, behave as "patent trolls": "NPEs chase cash and have a real negative impact on targeted firms' innovative activity" (Cohen, Gurun, and Kominers, 2019: 5462). Under all conditions, one of the elementary purposes of the patent system, as declared on numerous occasions by the Supreme Court, is to create incentives to disclose innovation ideas, which in turn should be part of the field of expertise that the patent purports to contribute to. If market actors such as NPEs and PAEs act consistently with this policy goal, they cannot at the same time be lambasted for acting in ways that reveal inconsistencies in the patent system, which they have not been able to design or influence in detail, scholars who reported the earlier studies suggest. In contrast, more recent studies, such as that reported by Cohen, Gurun, and Kominers (2019), present a more skeptical view of the legal activities conducted by NPEs. The overarching conclusion may therefore be that it is more reasonable to modify and reform the patent system (e.g., by introducing more strict demands regarding the content and scope of the patent as such to reduce the impact of patent thickets), rather than to impose additional and more complex regulatory rules that may have the unintended consequence of lowering the incentives to innovate or to apply for patents to protect intellectual property, which would presumably reduce innovative activities at large. Unsurprisingly, the patent law studies literature contains a variety of such research projects and reported results.

Proposals regarding how to improve the patent system

Given the observations reported in the literature reviewed in the previous sections, several scholars have argued that legal and regulatory reforms are called for. Price and Rai (2016) advocate legal reforms in the field of biopharmaceutical research and patenting on the basis of this argument, and in the next section, such arguments in favour of legal reforms will be examined in more detail.

Case One: biologics research, antibody therapies, and the patent system

Lemley (2004) is skeptical regarding what he refers to as *ex post* justification of extended legal protection as such "anti-market" campaigns risk to reduce economic and social welfare as incumbent market actors are over-protected in ways that hinder an efficient and fair use of available resources, and not the least public informational goods. Price and Rai (2016) argue that in the field of biopharmaceutical research, such claims are legitimate and plausible regarding their anticipated outcomes, but that concerns for the welfare of the population may justify such legal reforms anyway. Price and Rai (2016: 1026) speak of the shift in the industry from small-molecule drugs to the larger and more complex class of biologics therapies as being a challenge as the patenting system is out of step with how this new class of therapies are developed, and not the least how they are manufactured. "[D]rug companies are increasingly turning to very large drugs: biologics produced by living cells," Price and Rai (2016: 1026) write. The class of biologics therapies include "therapeutic proteins, toxins and antitoxins, viruses, blood and blood products, gene therapy products, and whole cells, among others," Price and Rai (2016: 1033) explain. Biologics are complex macromolecular therapeutics, "produced by living sources" rather than through chemical synthesis (Price and Rai, 2016: 1033), which means that this class of therapies is also manufactured in ways that differ substantially from small-molecule drug production: "[c]ells are grown in large-scale vessels, making the biologics in a complex and variable production environment" (Price and Rai, 2016: 1043). Furthermore, once the production is completed, the protein must be isolated and purified "in several steps" (Price and Rai, 2016: 1043).

The concern is that the development costs are considerable (despite being, as several authors have remarked, either inflated vis-à-vis, e.g., regulatory agencies [Light and Warburton, 2011] or otherwise compensated for as pharmaceutical companies have persistently proved to have considerably higher bottom-line results than comparable industries [Lexchin, 2006]), and in combination with the scientific and technical difficulties involved when producing biologics therapies, the patent system is considered as a barrier to the full-scale exploitation of this class of therapies. Price and Rai (2016: 1027) write that biologics have an "average daily cost in the United States that is 22 times higher than small-molecule drug therapies," which presumably mirror higher development and manufacturing costs. Furthermore, unlike small molecules, many complex biologics products "cannot be fully characterized by current techniques for analyzing the end product" (Price and Rai, 2016: 1028). Therefore, Price and Rai (2016: 1028) continue, "slight variations in the manufacturing process can change the quality, safety, or efficacy of the final product." The concern is that the proactive approach that several countries make mandatory, to impose "price regulation of originator products," serves to protect end-users from paying a price premium on therapies that are protected by patents, but this governance model does not solve the underlying issue: how to develop new biologics therapies and how to make the manufacturing process more predictable and cost-efficient so that market prices can be pushed down.

Price and Rai (2016: 1029–1030) argue that the price regulation device "mistakenly views the problem as one of natural monopoly," while the problem is instead related to "information sharing"—an issue that the price regulation device does not consider. One key issue is then how to enable and assist better information sharing at the same time as the incentives to patent biologics ideas and results are preserved, Price and Rai (2016: 1030) argue: "[P]olicy interventions encouraging greater information disclosure and generation, both by individual originator firms and through public-private consortia, would yield both cost efficiencies and innovation gains." But, again, to simply require "more disclosure" would likely lead the originator firm to abandon "the patent path" altogether (Price and Rai, 2016: 1031), e.g., by resorting to the trade secret device to protect intellectual assets (Morten, 2023).

To navigate between these two challenges, Price and Rai (2016: 1052) advocate a patenting system wherein information sharing regarding biologic manufacturing practices can be channeled in a meaningful way, as such a patent system would have the potential to "accelerate biosimilar development." Such a reform would not only put higher demands on patent offices such as the USPTO in terms of acquiring expertise on biologics manufacturing methods, but it should also more actively involve the US Food and Drug Administration (FDA), which already has the competence to assist biologics-producing companies (see, e.g., Eisenberg, 2007). "Because the FDA already serves as the gatekeeper for regulatory approval, and already has the necessary expertise to evaluate disclosure of biologic characteristics and manufacturing methods, it could ensure that manufacturers actually disclose the relevant information," Price and Rai (2016: 1053) argue. Such a system would balance the need for the legal protection of ideas being generated and developed, and the wider social demand for new and cheaper biologics therapies in an era wherein it is increasingly costly to identify new small molecules that reveal the therapeutic efficacy and safety demanded by the FDA and other regulatory agencies. Still, such a legal reform needs to effectively balance *ex ante* and *ex post* justifications, as Lemley (2004) has called for.

Price and Rai's (2016) argument can be regarded as a statement in favour of an industry that already reports significant above-average profits and is routinely being governed under the common "public good" or "public interest" banner. Both the public and policy makers that the voters (ideally) elect and assign the role to pass new legislation have an interest in new therapies being available at a reasonable market price, so such arguments presumably do not fall on deaf ears. On the other hand, Price and Rai's (2016) text can be read as a genuine attempt to grapple with the information-sharing issue that, e.g., Ouellette (2012) and Freilich (2019) have proved to be an actual concern for scientists—how to acquire meaningful information and knowledge from the patent system that grant substantial legal rights to applicants, in many cases on the basis of ideas that are difficult to substantiate in some practical and material manner. Under all conditions, Price and Rai (2016) argue that the patent system cannot be assumed to be once and for all fixed on the basis of certain statutes, rules, and standards, but that legal reforms may be called for so that the patent system plays the role its proponents say it would: to balance incentives to invest time, money, and effort in developing new innovation ideas, to make innovations materialize, and to maximize the possibilities for these ideas ending up in the right hands, i.e., among highly skilled and resourceful organizations, and professional communities that can explore the full potential of the innovation idea. Under these conditions, the patent system should support innovation not only in principle but also in practice, and preferably handle issues such as property rights and information costs so that the outcome from the activities involved in such innovation work are optimized.

Lemley and Sherkow (2023) call for similar legal reforms regarding patents that protect antibody drugs. The market for antibody drugs is currently valued at US$145 billion, a figure more than triple "the entire global music and movie markets combined" (Lemley and Sherkow, 2023: 1002). Consequently, how patents that protect antibody drugs are designed, among the most valuable intellectual property rights ever granted to any company or organization, matters greatly. A biochemical entity, an antibody or a so-called T-cell receptor, are not monolithic proteins but are "incredibly diverse," and each human being is likely to have "tens of billions of different variations of immune receptors circulating in their blood at any given time" (Lemley and Sherkow, 2023: 1002). As antibodies are composed of "*billions* of different proteins, more than the number of genes in the genome—*ten million times over*" (Lemley and Sherkow, 2023: 1045), it is complicated to patent an antibody on the basis of its formal structure, which has been the dominant doctrine in patent law on the basis of conventional chemistry expertise regarding, e.g., molecular structures. However, unlike in the case of "typical 'small-molecule' drugs," scientists have long identified antibodies "not by their precise molecular structure but by what they *did*" (Lemley and Sherkow, 2023: 998). In the early days of the industry, when scientists often "knew little about the precise molecular and genetic structures of antibodies" and lacked the tools to identify such structures, "the law permitted broad patents covering any antibody that bound to a particular target with a certain specificity" (Lemley and Sherkow, 2023: 998). The only practical way to describe newly discovered antibodies was thus to identify such characteristics. Indeed, to characterize antibodies "atom by atom" is both impractical and essentially pointless, akin to "describing a fighter jet by listing every nut and bolt" (Lemley and Sherkow, 2023: 998).

Today, the situation has changed as it is now easier to identify the "physical sequence" of a newly discovered antibody in the laboratory (Lemley and Sherkow, 2023: 998). Following such scientific advancements, American courts, which traditionally allowed a patentee to describe and claim a new antibody "by reference to its functional characteristics" (Lemley and Sherkow, 2023: 1016), have gradually abandoned this legal doctrine. Beginning in 2004 with the two cases *Amgen Inc. v. Sanofi* and *Juno Therapeutics, Inc. v. Kite Pharma, Inc.*, the courts "renounced antibody exceptionalism" (Lemley and Sherkow, 2023: 1020), i.e., antibodies could no longer be patented exclusively for their function. In the former case, *Amgen*, the court held that the disputed claims "were invalid under the enablement requirement," because Amgen's claims were "broad functional claims that provided little guidance on how to recreate the full scope of the invention, anti-PCSK9 antibodies, without undue experimentation" (Lemley and Sherkow, 2023: 1029). In the second case, *Juno*, the court concluded that Juno's claims "lacked sufficient written description," because—even though the patent included "working examples of Juno's engineered immune receptor"—the fact that "other functional receptors" existed and were not disclosed in the patent made "the disclosure not 'representative' of the scope of the claims" (Lemley and Sherkow, 2023: 1029). Lemley and Sherkow (2023: 1033) argue that the Amgen and Juno cases "cements the court's structural turn," its return to structural descriptions of antibodies to be included in patent applications. In the previous legal doctrine, antibody claims "were consistent with other cases in which a patentee invented something new but didn't know exactly what it was made of or precisely how it worked" (Lemley and Sherkow, 2023: 1016), but with the advancement of new and more precise scientific methods, such a vagueness in the patent description was no longer tolerable. Lemley and Sherkow (2023: 1045) thus speak of an *antibody paradox* under the new court ruling doctrine, which denotes the situation wherein the more researchers learn about antibodies and their structure and their functional role in the human immune system, the less can be claimed in a patent application as the court regards such an improved scientific understanding of antibodies as what justifies stricter patent rules. The concern is that even if antibodies are technically speaking chemistry, and "chemistry is all about molecular structure" (Lemley and Sherkow, 2023: 1038), it does not follow that this legal principle can be meaningfully applied to antibodies: antibodies are molecules, and so they are chemistry, albeit chemistry on a scale "large enough that atomic identity is impractical" (Lemley and Sherkow, 2023: 1038):

> Pathbreaking biologics innovation today concerns sequencing and optimizing a single antibody. And there is no clear relationship between the structure of any of those billions of proteins and the binding function they perform. There simply cannot be a valid claim to a structural genus under this theory.
>
> (Lemley and Sherkow, 2023: 1046)

That is, even if the courts have promised that claims directed to antibody genera are not dead "if the patentee just discloses enough structural similarity," that promise has so far "proven illusory" (Lemley and Sherkow, 2023: 1046). As a matter of advancing science, Lemley and Sherkow (2023: 1046) continue, "there is good reason to think that it will always be illusory." Given the importance of this type of therapies and their market value, it is of utmost importance that the courts established patent law rules that do not undermine the further development of this class of drugs, Lemley and Sherkow (2023) emphasize:

> Because antibody patents are so valuable, invalidating even one can cost a company billions of dollars and changing the law of antibody patents can send shock waves through the industry. Patents are widely viewed as a necessary incentive lever to bring forms of the technology from bench to market.
>
> (Lemley and Sherkow, 2023: 1011)

Just because life sciences companies know more about the antibodies they produce, it does not follow that this production has become a routine activity. On the contrary, to scale up the production of antibodies therapies to be able to push down the per treatment or per annum treatment costs (which can be astronomical for the time being) is a key scientific and hence legal challenge for the coming period of time (Lemley and Sherkow, 2023: 1051).

Case Two: the value of dynamic patent disclosure reforms

Fromer (2016) argues that the disclosure theory, which, to repeat, considers the patent as a *quid pro quo* for the disclosure of innovation ideas, does not explain the desirable secondary market for innovation ideas. In Fromer's (2016: 1715) account, several scholars argue that the patent system's disclosure function is "poor and does not achieve its objective of stimulating innovation," and therefore legal reforms are called for. Fromer (2016: 1717) is concerned that the work to fully develop the innovation idea into an actual innovation is accounted for and being disclosed at a too early stage, in many cases "at the time a patent is filed." This procedure is counterintuitive because most complex ideas demand additional work to prove their value and economic and social worth:

> So much of the innovation process, from refinement to prototyping to market research to mass production, has yet to occur at the moment of patent filing. Yet the law does not require disclosure of so much of this valuable information related to a patented invention. That is, patent disclosure is early and static.
>
> (Fromer, 2016: 1715–1716)

The underlying legal principle of the patent system is that *ideas* are provided with legal protection, not the intended or anticipated innovation to be developed on the basis of that idea. This legal principle is referred to as the *constructive reduction to practice*: "Constructive reduction to practice means that patent filing can occur well before an actual prototype—let alone a commercialized product—has been made" (Fromer, 2016: 1720). The constructive reduction to practice principle implies that much of the work to be conducted is in fact to be done when the patent application is already submitted and on file with the patent office, but this elementary condition is unfortunately not being reflected in the demands regarding the prophetic examples that are included in the patent applications. "Given that patenting tends to happen very early on, it is often only much later that a patented invention makes its way to the marketplace," Fromer (2016: 1720) argues:

> Even when the innovation timeline is more compressed, so much happens between invention and commercialization: refinement of and changes to an invention, prototype development, integration with industrial design, development for cost constraints, market testing, marketing, distribution, and further refinements over time in response to customer feedback.
>
> (Fromer, 2016: 1721)

In this manner, patent law reforms share the same structural features as policy making do more widely: policies express intentions and desirable outcomes in a world characterized by uncertainty, and that includes relevant social actors with cognitive limitation and changing preferences that depend on context and situation. Therefore, both laws and policies are of necessity incomplete and leave much to be determined to the judiciary, regulatory agencies, and the officials that are held accountable for the implementation of the law. In the case of the patent system, the disclosure theory prescribes that it is better to have innovators to disclose their ideas than to not disclose them, and in order to incentivize such disclosure, legal rights are conferred to the patent applicant, but in what way this patent system should realize the purportedly beneficial goals being stipulated in the theory is far from evident. In hindsight, when the patent system is examined in terms of the value of the prophetic examples it provides, the informational value of such descriptions seems to be marginal, presumably resulting in much work being conducted on the basis of inaccurate or even false premises (Freilich, 2019; Allison and Ouellette, 2016). In many cases, issues that pertain to the practical implementation become a mere afterthought in the policy-making process or, in this case, the legislative process (see, e.g., Riles, 2011).

To amend the patent system, Fromer (2016: 1722) proposes a reform that includes a "dynamic patent disclosure," i.e., that patentees are "required to divulge all inventions commercialized by the patentee or a licensee of the patentee." This means that it is mandatory that the patentee discloses how the innovation idea was commercialized at the point where such accomplishments are made, so that other actors can access that information and develop innovations on the basis of such new information. Such a "dynamic disclosure" would "help improve the disclosure function of the patent system, all in the name of stimulating further innovation," Fromer (2016: 1723) argues. Fromer (2016), similar to Price and Rai (2016), optimistically portrays the patent system as being capable of not only granting legal rights to the patent applicant at one discrete point in time, but also to more dynamically monitor how already patented ideas are developed over time as more money and efforts are invested in translating innovation ideas into actual innovations.

Summary and conclusion

In the third chapter, the legal institutionalism framework was introduced to underline how market making and market regulation are legally coded practices, organized by the sovereign state's legislature, judiciary, and executive agencies (such as regulatory agencies overseeing specific markets, say, the finance market). Within this framework of analysis, a great number of specific legal and regulatory practices are located and continuously modified and changed, and in this chapter, one specific legal framework, that of patent law (and, by implication, intellectual property rights more widely) is examined. The review of the literature indicates that patent law is implemented with a variety of policy goals being considered, including the ambition to provide enforceable legal rights that incentivize inventors to disclose their innovation ideas, and the goal to create a market for innovation ideas. As the literature review demonstrates, at times such policy goals are either by their very nature difficult to reconcile, as in the case of so-called patent trolls being able to enforce their legal rights, derived from the first patent law objective expressed previously, but without making any substantial economic or intellectual contributions to the innovation work being conducted, or having unintended consequences that were difficult to fully anticipate from the vantage point where the new legislation was first passed.

The legal institutionalism framework does recognize that laws and regulatory rules are of necessity incomplete, and therefore need to be interpreted by informed actors to be implemented and enforced in ways that are consistent with the legislators' intentions and to be aligned with law enforcement practices in litigations and court cases, handled by the judiciary. This small but noticeable deviation between "laws in book" and "laws in real-world economies" prompt animated discussions regarding the need for orchestrating legal reforms to amend the situation. As was noted in the case of patent trolls and the allegedly too-generous intellectual patents protection of would-be but essentially passive patent owners, any call for legal reforms on such grounds are not necessarily recognized as there is a shortage of accurate empirical data, which precludes a conclusive assessment of the situation, and because different groups of legal or innovation management scholars make different inferences from the data that is publicly available or constructed from such public data. This in turn results in ongoing discussions regarding the efficacy and moral legitimacy of current legislation, e.g., patent law. It would be over-optimistic to assume that such scholarly debates would finally be muted by legal reforms, as such legal reforms inevitably create new possibilities for both legal arbitrage and opportunistic behaviour, which plausibly result in another cycle of second-order scholarly analyses and commentaries.

Under all conditions, the legal institutional framework provides the analytical benefit that it articulates an explanation for *how* and *why* markets are constructed, at the same time as it recognizes that any legislation is incomplete, and preferably embedded in social norms that are both supportive of the legislation but also further justified as they are now supported by the authority of a formal law (as in the case of the "no littering in the park" norm, that may be further strengthened if a litterer can be subject to penalties such as fines on the basis of a law being introduced, i.e., to litter is not only an act that breaches a norm, but is also a legal offence as littering is to act against the law as it is written and enforced). Such analytical benefits are complemented by actual legal studies activities that show on the basis of formal analyses of legal texts and paragraphs, or on the basis of empirical studies (of either actual market practices, or court cases being published) that the law needs to be interpreted and acted upon to matter in a practical and economic sense of the term.

At the end of the day, the legal institutionalism framework rests on the policy makers' political agendas and stipulated programs, which locates the question of law in a political context wherein the power and the access to economic resources become of key importance for the understanding of why certain laws are passed and enforced, whereas other legal proposals are simply dropped in the legislative process. The fifth and the final chapters of this volume thus shift the focus from economic (in Chapter 1) and legislative affairs (in Chapters 2 and 3) to examine the politics of legislative activities from a more political science–oriented perspective. As will be demonstrated, policy makers who pass laws on the basis of policy ideas are not insulated from the interests of actors having a stake in the market activities that are being subjected to, e.g., legal or regulatory reforms. Whether this condition is actually conducive to increased economic and social welfare is a question that has been addressed on the basis of a variety of theoretical frameworks and study designs, but without reaching any consensus. The conventional wisdom is, at this point, that the democratic deficit in legislative affairs correlates with increased economic inequality. The question is then whether increased economic inequality is the price to be paid for upward shifts in economic and social welfare (as conservative commentators are prone to believe and to claim), or if increased economic inequality is *per se* a condition that may generate social unrest and the radicalization of certain social groups on the basis of the (not entirely unfounded) belief that they are excluded from sharing the economic wealth that is generated through joint efforts and specific team production activities organized inside, e.g., a corporation. The fifth chapter does not provide any definite answers to such pressing political questions, but merely calls for an analysis of how specific legislation such as the patent legislation examined in this volume may be of relevance for how such questions are answered, and not the least for how such questions are formulated in the first place.

5 The ethics and political economy of intellectual property rights

Introduction

Much of the critique of the patent system and the calls for its reform (discussed in Chapter 4) is premised on the idea of justice, and more specifically the idea of justice as fairness, as developed in detail by, e.g., John Rawls in his influential *A Theory of Justice* (1971). In Rawls's (1958: 166) conception, justice denotes "a complex of three ideas," namely "liberty, equality, and reward for services contributing to the common good." Furthermore, justice is premised on social institutions and what Rawls refers to as "practices" (Rawls, 1958: 164). That is, justice as fairness is what can be achieved or accomplished if this concept is considered in practical terms, Rawls (1985) proposes:

> [T]he aim of justice as fairness as a political conception is practical, and not metaphysical or epistemological. That is, it presents itself not as a conception of justice that is true, but one that can serve as a basis of informed and willing political agreement between citizens viewed as free and equal persons.
>
> (Rawls, 1985: 230)

While Rawls's theory of justice as fairness has been influential in political philosophy and political science, it has also been subject to extensive criticism. Judge (2021: 197) argues that Rawls's liberalism is premised on a paradox: it essentially relies on a market distribution at the same time as Rawls cannot justify "these arrangements within the confines of the theory," i.e., Rawls wishes to introduce the concept of fairness that counteracts the effects of market distribution *ex post* that violates his own concept of justice. Consistent with Rawls's liberal credo, such a concept of fairness requires a theory that validates "a pure procedural approach to distribution that all reasonable citizens would accept" (Judge, 2021: 204). Unfortunately, Judge (2021: 204) says, "no such theory is available." Consequently, Rawlsian liberalism

DOI: 10.4324/9781003460220-5

is "incommensurable with actual political and economic life, regardless of how elegant, economical, efficient or well-arranged it might be as a theory" (Judge, 2021: 204). As Feinberg (1973) remarks, in the practical terms that Rawls otherwise recognizes and includes in his theory under the label "practices," "every reform of an imperfect practice or institution is likely to be unfair to someone or other." That is, to change the rules "in the middle of the game," even when those original rules are not altogether fair or universally endorsed, "will disappoint the honest expectations of those whose prior commitments and life plans were made in genuine reliance on the continuance of the old rules" (Feinberg, 1973: 268). Therefore, the "practices" that Rawls appears to regard as merely being a matter of the implementation of a theory of justice as fairness appear to create important hurdles for his "ideal theory."

John Mackie, who advocates a moral relativism position inasmuch as he states that "there are no objective values" (Mackie, 2013: 22), argues that morality is necessary to be able to regulate "interpersonal relations" and to "control some of the ways in which people behave towards one another." To make a governance activity operable, humans want their moral judgements "to be authoritative" for other agents as well as for themselves: such an "objective validity" of such morals "would give them the authority required" (Mackie, 2013: 30). However, this preference for morals to be universally accepted (or acceptable) as they would support specific policy goals and governance activities, being a desideratum, should not be confused with this preference being grounded in some objective value, or the concept of objectivity more largely (Mackie, 2013: 30): "It is fairly easy to confuse the way in which a thing's desirability is indeed objective with its having in our sense objective value," Mackie (2013: 30) says. Consequently, it is advisable to think of what Mackie (1978: 351) refers to as "moral entities"—values or standards, or "whatever they may be"—as what "belong within human thinking and practice." This means that the positing of rights or norms is no more obscure or questionable than the positing of goals or obligations (Mackie, 1978: 351). Under this description, the analyst should not look for "objective truth" in a "moral system," and Rawls's liberal theory of justice as fairness thus becomes inoperable as there are no objectively true rights or universally accepted rules that such a theory of justice can be founded on. In practical terms, Mackie (1978: 354–355) writes, the diversity of preferences, lifestyle choices, and ideas and beliefs in human societies makes any universalist claims to justice a piece of fiction or some unattainable ideal. People do not, in the course of everyday life, base their decisions or actions on some universally valid theory of justice from which they can deduce what decisions to make or what actions to take, but they rather pragmatically seek to navigate in social milieus that are overdetermined by social norms, morals, rules, "dos-and-don'ts", "no-no's," etc., that all influence how people behave and relate to each other:

> People differ radically about the kinds of life that they choose to pursue. Even this way of putting it is misleading: in general people do not and cannot make an overall choice of a total plan of life. They choose successively to pursue various activities from time to time, not once and for all.
>
> (Mackie, 1978: 354–355)

In this view, Rawls's liberalism is either vacuous or illusive as it ignores the true essence of a liberal society, that of the ability of its members to *individually* make decisions within the realm of the law and the rich variety of norms and rules that regulate their day-to-day decisions and actions.

At the same time, that Rawls's theory of justice is presumably an inoperable ideal theory does not mean that the concepts of justice and fairness would not matter in everyday life in a specific society. As Dworkin (1980: 202) remarks, as a practical matter, individuals do choose "a mix of justice and efficiency with an eye to maximizing their individual utility under conditions of dramatic uncertainty," i.e., they are trading off gains in their prospects, so conceived, against losses "in the just character of the society." More recently, Schaefer (2023) has agreed on this point, proposing that "values and policies are chosen simultaneously" in the course of everyday life activities:

> A citizen's view of public morality will affect her support or rejection of constitutional and institutional rules. Similarly, these constitutional and institutional rules will affect the material conditions of a citizen's life, including her social and political experiences, thus affecting her evaluation of public-moral rules.
>
> (Schaefer, 2023: 287)

This means that it makes sense to speak of a trade-off between "justice and culture," or to speak of a trade-off between "justice and social wealth" (Dworkin, 1980: 203). People do want to honour justice as a valuable concept and as an ideal, but absolute justice may be an unattainable goal inasmuch as it would presumably reduce social welfare if it is instrumentally and unrelentingly pursued. In pragmatic terms, people recognize justice, but at a level of justice that is meaningful and tolerable. From this proposition, it follows that concepts such as justice and fairness need to be defined independently of concepts such as wealth maximization and economic welfare: it is not enough to say that, e.g., distributive justice is whatever state of affairs obtained by wealth maximization as such a claim that wealth maximization leads to distributive justice is a tautology (Dworkin, 1980: 212).

In everyday life, people are preoccupied with their day-to-day activities, which means that there is limited interest in theorizing what justice as fairness would mean in propositional terms: what matters is that justice as fairness can contribute to the overall sense of things being just *and* the aggregated social and economic welfare. What scholars such as Judge (2021), Feinberg (1973), Mackie (1978), and Dworkin (1980) wish to accomplish is to provide the basis for a *dynamic* theory of justice as fairness that fully recognizes the variety of beliefs, preferences, etc., that characterizes a liberal society premised by the freedom to act under the rule of law and social norms, rather than to endorse an *ideal* theory of justice as fairness that cannot fully accommodate a stipulated freedom as it is premised on some agreement regarding what norms or rules to follow and to be considered as being universally valid or significant. That is, justice is not a matter of achieving some steady-state position wherein all members of society act on the basis of shared beliefs, but to develop a legal system that apprehends and accommodates the diversity of views so that the idea of justice as fairness can be preserved at the same time as social and economic welfare are maximized. Based on these propositions, this chapter addresses the moral, ethical, and political views of patent law and the patent system, and in order to reach some point where the legitimacy of the patent system can be asserted, a variety of arguments and perspectives need to be recognized. "If justice has any meaning at all, it refers at least to the allocation of various rights to control physical resources," Palmer (1990: 856) proposes, and this is arguably what the patent system is designed and managed to accomplish, to allocate the rights to control physical resources that are involved in materializing an innovation idea.

Beyond the practical usefulness of the patent system: the broader role of intellectual property rights in a liberal society

The prior sections indicate that the legal studies literature shows that the patent system does in fact play a central role in generating a market for innovation ideas, but it also proposes that there are many possibilities for improving, reforming, and modifying the patent system as it reveals many inconsistencies and loopholes that generate unintended consequences for various market actors. In Chapter 2, the legal institutionalism perspective, wherein patent legislation is part of the legal environment of the corporate entity, was introduced. The corporate entity often (albeit not necessarily) participates in innovation activities—and acts as a "practicing entity," in Lemley and Melamed's (2013) parlance—and consequently it is important to intellectually justify why the state imposes such a legal framework on market actors, especially as elementary neoclassical economic theory stipulates that paternalist legal rules should be seen as an infringement on the economic liberties of market actors, an issue and position discussed in the first chapter. This section reviews the legal literature that addresses how political philosophy has been introduced as the basis for legal rights and new legislation, and how such legal doctrines may in fact be inconsistent with political philosophy dictums. If that is the case, better and more logically consistent arguments need to be brought forward, as legal rights cannot only be justified on the basis of social beliefs in the conventional sense of the term, but also need to be consistent with more comprehensive political theories that pertain to the elementary rights of humans and how legal rules are justified, despite being paternalist and an infringement on liberal rights, otherwise being held in esteem.

The moral authority of intellectual property right legislation

Palmer (1990: 817) argues that most of the arguments for and against intellectual property rights emanate from the belief in the benevolence of the "free-market system" and the private property legislation that such a free-market system demands, at least in principle. In this doctrine, "liberty" and "property" may be irreconcilable inasmuch as "copyrights" and "patents" are property, but they also "seem to restrict liberty," Palmer (1990: 818) writes. Palmer (1990: 818) defines *intellectual property rights*, following the regular legislation, as "rights in ideal objects, which are distinguished from the material substrata in which they are instantiated" (Palmer, 1990: 818). Palmer (1990: 820) is concerned that the mainstream advocacy of the free-market system considers intellectual property rights only as being secondary to the vindication of the market system *per se*, which Palmer refers to as "the 'piggy-back' theory" of intellectual rights, wherein "intellectual property right obtains its moral force from its dependence on a more conventional right of property." Based on this proposition, Palmer (1990) addresses two legal theory principles. First, any claim that considers intellectual property rights as derived from a general right of property implies that such intellectual property rights would be based on what Palmer refers to as "Moral Desert Theories" (i.e., *droit moral* theories), a legal theory class that assumes that rights are either derived from "natural rights" or "moral rights" (Palmer, 1990: 827). Such theories propose, based on the seminal work of John Locke (to be examined in more detail shortly), that every person has the right to his or her work on the basis of natural and thus moral rights. Palmer (1990) denies that intellectual property rights can be justified on such grounds (for reasons to be explained), but he also adds that there is a difference between "property rights in tangible objects" and intellectual property rights (that pertains to intangible resources). The former class of rights "do not restrict liberty at all"—they simply *restrain action*, which is their very *raison d'être* in classic legal theory—whereas intellectual property rights, in contrast, "do restrict liberty" (Palmer, 1990: 831).

Following a similar thread of argument, Waldron (1992: 881) argues that the idea that, say, some author's work "should be completely original" rather than being "derivative," either on the basis of a moral or a legal requirement, "would strike most sensible observers as supererogatory." Referring to the court case where George Harrison, the former guitarist of The Beatles, was ruled in a court case to have "infringed the plaintiff's rights" (Waldron, 1992: 882) when using a certain chord progression structure in his song *My Sweet Lord*, similar to that of the song *He's So Fine*, recorded by the American "girl group" the Chiffons, Waldron (1992: 882) argues that it is unreasonable to stipulate that creative works of art should be considered in such strict legal terms:

> One who fails to trace the particular provenance of a combination of notes that happens to "work" for him can hardly be regarded as thief. He is more like someone who has stumbled onto another's property where there is no clear boundary fence.
>
> (Waldron, 1992: 882)

Under the current intellectual property right legislation being recognized in the Harrison court case, a certain chord progression structure that is part of the communal resource of the (Western) tonality musical system would be considered as subject to intellectual property right. This in turn expresses a legal principle or doctrine that undermines the idea of music being a social and communal resource to freely draw on as part of liberal freedoms and as a member of a society, otherwise being recognized and protected. That is, under such a legal doctrine, Waldron (1992: 883) writes, "[t]hose who own and propagate stories, songs, images and ideas lay a sort of trap for the people whose lives are touched by their productions." By implication, a systematic overprotection of certain individual accomplishments on the basis of shared cultural resources is at risk to undermine all sorts of human ingenuity and creativity, Waldron (1992) proposes:

> It is not ideas that circulate in the maelstrom of modem culture—at least, not ideas considered as pristine propositional entities untainted by the form in which they were expressed. On the contrary, forms and expressions circulate—just listen, for instance, to the similarities in the speech of any two teenagers chosen at random—and they pervade each person's sense of what it is that he in particular wants to say or produce.
>
> (Waldron, 1992: 882)

In the end, when such conditions are considered, free-market theory arguments that construe intellectual property rights as a sub-species of traditional property rights appear to be logically and normatively inconsistent, and they overlook the legislators' intention when protecting intellectual property.

This line of argument takes us back to the work of John Locke, whom free-market theorists are fond of citing but unfortunately do not care to read in detail and in its wider historical and political context, several legal scholars argue. For Locke, the principle of "self-ownership" serves "several important functions," Palmer (1990: 832) argues, including being "the foundation of liberty"—"indeed, it is synonymous with liberty," Palmer (1990: 832) says. As *liberty* is a grand term in the political philosophy and political science vocabulary, and consequently also included in elementary economic theory, this term is widely understood to be unified and indubitably part of the elementary legal principles that regulate a liberal society and the market economy that such a society supports. However, on closer inspection, Locke's theories introduced a number of philosophical complications that need be addressed. Craig (2002: 3) argues that a single-minded reliance on John Locke's work results in an understanding of intellectual property rights that undermines Locke's own liberal beliefs and ambitions. For instance, John Locke's "labour acquisition approach" results in a "notion of entitlement" regarding intellectual property rights such as copyrights, which expresses a natural rights claim and the introduction of a deontic vocabulary that describes moral rights that are inconsistent with a liberal society. That is, after her proper analysis of the Lockean natural right argument, Craig (2002) advocates the introduction of other political philosophy principles and propositions being more consistent with how contemporary civil society is organized and operates (a question also addressed by, e.g., Barron, 2012, discussed later).

Craig (2002: 48–49) starts by claiming that it is important to read Locke's work in its historical and political contexts, and that such an analysis shows that "it is not entirely clear that Locke drew the libertarian conclusion attributed to him." In fact, Locke developed his property theory—now widely portrayed as a cornerstone of the liberal society and its market-based economy—to refute Sir Robert Filmer's argument that "God gave the world to Adam." Filmer's conjecture ultimately served to support "the unlimited authority of monarchs," a conclusion that Locke did not regard as being consistent with good philosophical conscience (Craig, 2002: 48–49). In fact, Craig (2002: 49) argues that the interpretation of Locke outside of this historical debate results in a logically inconsistent theory, which also legally undermines the vision of a liberal society and its market system: "[a]bsolute property rights acquired through labour do not survive the transition to civil society," Craig (2002: 49) proposes. The key target of Craig's critique is the natural rights vocabulary and discourse, and the deontological private property theory that Locke's work purportedly represents. When society departs "from the state of nature," other legal principles are of more relevance than deontic discourses, Craig (2002) proposes:

> What is not clear is exactly why we should force ourselves to stumble through the assumptions and unnecessary restrictions imposed by the invocation of natural law reasoning, rather than avoiding them and being honest about the end-point that is sought. . . . [I]t makes little sense to tie up an instrumentalist agenda with deontological reasoning, particularly where the deontological approach advanced is far from self-evident and riddled with ambiguities.
>
> (Craig, 2002: 55)

In our everyday life in liberal societies and market-based economies, intellectual properties cannot be considered to be protected by neither natural nor moral rights, as intellectual work and the ideas they include and express do not emerge from outside of social life and human culture. On the contrary, intellectual work is inherently and indubitably based on and derived from shared social and cultural resources, and such resources cannot be protected by exclusivity rights as, e.g., private property can. For example, a musician may hold the property right to exclusively play the guitar she once bought, but the songs composed when playing the guitar cannot be treated as an entity being equally protected from the use of others, as several persons may sing a particular song at the same time, whereas only one person (for practical reasons) can play a specific guitar at the same time. As Palmer (1990) and Craig (2002) argue, it is philosophically and legally inconsistent to derive intellectual property rights from general property rights as they pertain to different types of rights. More specifically, to consider intellectual property rights as a subclass of general property rights would undermine the very basis for the liberal society that, e.g., John Locke wanted to defend and to preserve over time. "The Lockean justification for copyright rests upon the assertion that the original author is entitled to the exclusive rights in her work, having exerted mental labour in its creation" (Craig, 2002: 9). Yet, Craig (2002: 9) continues to say that "[i]t seems obvious that labour is not, simply as a matter of fact, constitutive of property"; "In a great society, not all labor is rewarded; and not all of the rewards to labor are in the form of property rights" (Palmer, 1990: 834). Therefore, the derived Lockean theory rests on "the false sense of bifurcation between public and private, and between the individual and the community" (Craig, 2002: 4), and when such inaccurate assumptions are accepted as being elementary principles, the legislation that follows from the adherence to such political or legal principles generates externalities and dysfunctions.

Craig (2002: 13) argues that "a utilitarian conception of copyright," in turn grounded in what she refers to as a "rights-fetishism," wherein "rights to the products of intellectual labour come to be regarded as independent absolutes, as an end in themselves" (Craig, 2002: 43), results in a legal system wherein "presumptions of moral entitlement" inevitably distort rather than facilitate "a nuanced understanding of the copyright system" (Craig, 2002: 3). For instance, when examining case law, wherein copyright interests are addressed, it is not uncommon for a court "[t]o preface its argument with a sentimental passage depicting the author's position in terms of entitlement, effort, and labour, and to juxtapose this depiction against a portrayal of the defendant as lazy, opportunistic, parasitic, or merely inconsequential" (Craig, 2002: 44–45; see also Conley, 1990). In such cases, intellectual property rights such as copyrights are understood in *moral terms*, rather than being a legal device that should not restrain the liberty of the secondary user of, e.g., a literary work (say, a biographer or a literature theory scholar). In contrast, a more modern conception of copyrights would ensure that the liberty to use such cultural (and thus communal) resources are supported by the law, both as it is written and enforced. This alternative view of intellectual property rights not only needs to be explained and justified on the basis of empirical cases, but should preferably also be aligned with political philosophy propositions that justify such legislation.

All intellectual work is based on communal resources that are nonexclusive: a Kantian view of intellectual property rights

To move beyond theories derived from Locke's philosophy, and to theoretically assert that intellectual property rights differ from general property rights, some new analytical model needs to be introduced and advocated. Craig (2002: 34) says that the work process that generates outcomes that are associated with intellectual property rights is more "collective rather than individual," and that this fact makes it theoretically difficult to explain how "a property right can be accorded to an individual on the basis of individual labour." As the "fruit of intellectual labour" has "no definable boundary" (Craig, 2002: 34), i.e., human culture is an "interdependent" and a communal resource, intellectual works are "necessarily the products of collective labour and so ought to be owned collectively," Craig (2002: 35) proposes. Craig (2002: 58) argues that it is important to overturn a utilitarian theory of intellectual property rights and to, *volte-face*, start with collective liberties rather than with imputed individual natural and moral rights to justify intellectual property rights:

> If, in contrast, analysis began with the public interest in the production and exchange of knowledge, ideas, and intellectual works (the public-work link), and reasoned backward to defend the author's right of control

> in terms of encouragement (the author-work link), then the presumptive force would lie with the freedom to use and not the right to exclude.
>
> (Craig, 2002: 58)

Craig continues:

> [T]he notion is rooted in the idea that the subject matter of copyright—literary, artistic, dramatic, and musical works—is fundamental to what it means to be human, and what it means to belong to society. Tied up in this process of intellectual creation, exchange, and response are various human ideals ranging from personal development and self-fulfillment to constitutional rights and the democratic ideal.
>
> (Craig, 2002: 6)

Barron (2012: 2) picks up the challenge to address intellectual property rights in such terms, and she shares the belief in the need to theoretically justify an intellectual property rights system: "In common law jurisdictions, the copyright system has on the whole tended to be justified in liberal-utilitarian terms, more particularly in terms of its contribution to achieving an efficient allocation of society's scarce resources," Barron (2012: 2) writes. If collective liberties are granted a privileged position in the liberal and democratic society, simply because such qualities provide every individual with their greatest possibilities for contributing to optimal collective welfare, then intellectual property rights need to be considered in new terms: "Given the oligopolistic structure of markets for cultural commodities, bloated copyrights produce a 'permission culture' that chills expression. . . . The negative liberty of individuals is thereby endangered" (Barron, 2012: 4). Barron (2012) argues that the conventional view of individual freedom is rooted in British liberalism doctrines, such as the work of John Locke and, thereafter, John Stuart Mill:

> When contemporary liberals refer to autonomy, they generally have in mind the vision of positive freedom set out by John Stuart Mill in his classic essay *On Liberty:* personal autonomy as the free development of 'individuality' through the self-cultivation of one's natural potentialities.
>
> (Barron, 2012: 11)

Similar to Palmer (1990) and Craig (2002), both being critical of the natural and moral rights vocabulary derived from Locke's (and Mill's, in Barron's, 2012, account) political philosophy writings, Barron (2012) attempts to formulate a new political theory of intellectual property rights, and she refers to the work of Immanuel Kant to better anchor intellectual property rights legislation in a political philosophy framework. Barron argues that

Mill's conception of autonomy is "very different from" and in many ways "at odds with" Kant's account of moral autonomy, described as "the *submission* of subjectively experienced wants, and inclinations to the jurisdiction of an objectively valid moral law" (Barron, 2012: 11–12). Mills' concept of freedom presupposes "a process of 'intelligent self-mastery,'" through which we decide between "our wants" with a view to satisfying those "that will realize our potentialities most completely." For Kant, action is conditioned by wants or inclinations not being entirely autonomous, but being "heteronomous," i.e., defined and experienced within a specific social field, including its practices and beliefs (Barron, 2012: 12). More specifically, as Brandom (2007: 652) writes, Kant treats *judgment* as "the smallest unit of awareness," and as judgment is inherently social in nature, determined by collectively agreed-upon social norms, expressed as rules at a varying degree of formalization that regulate everyday social life, judgment is expressive of a normative "discursive intentionality" (Brandom, 2019: 9). The capacity to pass judgment is thus elementary in social life, and this capacity is in turn related to, e.g., the legal system in intricate ways, Barron (2012) proposes.

Barron (2012: 22) cites Kant's works such as the essays "An Answer to the Question: 'What is Enlightenment?'" (published in 1784) and "What is Orientation in Thinking?" (published in 1786), to address how Kant expresses what might be called the "supreme principle of rational thinking" (Barron, 2012: 22). In "What is Orientation in Thinking?," Kant proposes that "to think for oneself means to look within oneself (i.e. in one's own reason) for the supreme touchstone of truth" (Kant, cited in Barron, 2012: 23), an elementary proposition in his political philosophy:

> To employ one's own reason means simply to ask oneself, whenever one is urged to accept something, whether one finds it possible to transform the reason for accepting it, or the rule which follows from what is accepted, into a universal principle governing the use of one's reason.
>
> (Kant, 1786, What is Orientation in Thinking?, cited in Barron, 2012: 23)

Similar to the English liberal thinkers, Kant too recognizes individual freedom as a key moral and legal principle, but for Kant (and also, one generation later, for Hegel), such an individual freedom is only the starting point for a more advanced and differentiated society to emerge on the basis of the collective sharing of ideas, beliefs, etc. "[E]ach person should reason in a way that recognizes—in oneself and in everyone else—the freedom to think for oneself, while at the same time acknowledging the necessity to think in community with others," Barron (2012: 25) explains. For Kant, in contrast to proponents of English liberalism, intellectual autonomy presupposes "communicative freedom," and such liberties should thus be enabled and enforced by the legal system, rather than to reduce or restrain such possibilities, Barron (2012) writes:

> Intellectual autonomy in turn presupposes communicative freedom: the freedom to articulate one's thoughts in public, subject to principles entailed by the internal logic of communication itself as a mode of interaction between a plurality of (at least potentially) rational persons. It is this *principled* freedom of thought and communication that alone serves humanity's collective project of advancing towards a mature, and therefore fully emancipated, culture.
>
> (Barron, 2012: 39)

Rather than to have intellectual ideas being protected in ways that restrain rather than what enables their circulation and use on the basis of references made to, e.g., moral vocabularies, in Kant's view, intellectual property rights should recognize the *collective resources* that have enabled the expression of such new ideas in the first place. In Kant's view, any legal system, including intellectual property right devices, should thus seek to strike a balance between "authors' rights" and a "free culture" (Barron, 2012: 40). In practice, this means that not every activity that includes the use of available works cannot "properly be regarded as infringing" (Barron, 2012: 36), i.e., to ensure the individual right to freely circulate, reformulate, modify, or further develop intellectual ideas, regardless of their medium and means of expression, should be the purpose of any intellectual property right system, Kant suggests. In turn, such an intellectual property right system not only protects certain interests while "incentivizing expression," but it also contributes to "aggregate welfare" (Barron, 2012: 38). As intellectual work is ultimately based on communal resources, derived from human culture, there is a risk of overprotecting certain ideas as such legal practices and devices restrain rather than secure or expand freedom.

Furthermore, in Barron's (2012) account, this makes Kant a considerably more modern thinker than, e.g., Locke and Mills, inasmuch as he already at the dawn of modernity recognized how intellectual ideas are "mediatized" or "channeled":

> [T]he 1785 Essay on unauthorized reprinting reflects Kant's recognition that communication between speakers in modern conditions is inevitably *channeled*—by technologies and media of communication (print and books in Kant's day; software and networks in ours), by commercial intermediaries (Prussian publishers in Kant's context; global information and entertainment corporations in ours), and by institutional structures (book markets then; information markets generally now)—in ways that

may shape the form and content of communication and so the nature of the communication community itself.

(Barron, 2012: 40)[1]

During the first days of modernity, in the decades between the American and the French revolutions (in 1776 and 1789) marking its inception, intellectuals and creatives were struggling to create markets for their services to escape the patronage of the courts, and the monarchs and aristocrats that historically have acted as their benefactors, financiers, and primary clients. Norbert Elias's ([1991] 1993) biography of Wolfgang Amadeus Mozart, the archetypical musical genius, who left his contemporaries speechless in wonder whenever he displayed his compositional and musical skills, sketches a bleak image of how Mozart was fettered to the court system and the petty tastes of the royals and courtiers with whom he was bounded. In contrast, Ludwig van Beethoven, born only a generation after Mozart, and at par with Mozart's compositional talent and skills, could benefit from the creation of a bourgeoisie-generated "culture market," wherein concert halls and symphonic orchestras were transferred to a public sphere and financed by wealthy donors (a governance model that is still predominant in the US; see e.g., Glynn, 2000). Kant presumably intuitively understood that these changes were underway and addressed them in his philosophical writing, Barron (2012: 42) argues: "Kant's Essay was centrally oriented towards establishing the right of authors to earn a living from their works, thereby fostering the emergence of a class of professional intellectuals released from dependence on courtly and ecclesiastical patronage." The idea of copyrights was thus premised on "the right of public presentation": "An author's exclusive right to address the public, in his or her own words, in the form of a work" (Barron, 2012: 36).

Copyrights and branding

This idea of intellectual ideas as being inextricably entangled with the capacity to participate in public conversations and speeches shifts the focus from

1 Pottage and Biagioli (2023: 606) propose that Kant considered the book as a "medium for the conveyance of thought," not the entity itself to be patented or otherwise legally protected. In this view, a published book is "at once" *opera*, "the action of the author engaging the public through speech," and *opus*, "the 'mute instrument' for this relationship between author and public" (Pottage and Biagioli, 2023: 608). Juridically, it follows that the purchaser of a copy of a book could do anything with their copy as an object of property, but the owner of the book must not exploit what Kant referred to as the "intellectual contents" (*gelehrte Grundstoff*) of the book, say, by reprinting and selling copies of the book (Pottage and Biagioli, 2023: 611). Through this distinction between *opera* and *opus* on the basis of the intellectual content of the work, and by shifting the focus "from the composition of things" to "the agencies and competences of persons" (Pottage and Biagioli, 2023: 615), Kant established the basis for the "modern distinction between tangible property and intellectual property," Pottage and Biagioli (2023: 608) argue.

any intellectual ideas as being solitary and idiosyncratic, to become widely understood as being cut from the cloth of a communal culture whose internal boundaries are fluid and porous. The concern is still that while most market actors who benefit from copyright protection agree on these terms, there is still a need to preserve an elementary right to the work an actor has invested time and effort in developing, and how this is to be done, also after Kant's propositions have been recognized and incorporated into legislation and in legal practices, is a thorny issue to handle. As Biagioli (2022: 471) remarks, speaking about scientific publications, while copyrights construe the author as "the owner" of the intellectual property of the work published, scientific authorship on the other hand construes the author "[a]s the point of origin (but not the owner) of the claims presented in the publication," as well as the person who asserts the integrity of these claims made (see, e.g., Brandom, 2019, on scientific inferences as being based on empirical data presented and the assertion made by the researcher that the data should be understood within the specific theoretical model being chosen). Being legally defined as the "point of origin," rather than being the "owner" of the text does then not carry much legality (but is primarily guided by social norms), and consequently, Biagioli (2022: 471) deduces, the scientific writers' status is "functionally and conceptually comparable to the brand"—scientific authorship acts as a brand that signals certain qualities. Biagioli (2022: 472) thus concludes that authorship as "defined by copyright law" and "by scientific authorship" are two "very different constructs," especially around the issue of responsibility, which is of key importance in academic scholarship and for scientific research work more generally. For instance, when it comes to ghostwriting (which is considerably more common in scientific writing than what is arguably commonly understood; Singh and Jayanti, 2013; Healy, 2006; Mirowski and Van Horn, 2005), these issues matter:

> Those who look at ghostwriting through the lens of work for hire law see a straightforward legal arrangement concerning intellectual property issues, but those who look at it through the lens of scientific authorship see authors listed on the byline who can hardly take any responsibility for a work whose production they may be unconnected to.
>
> (Biagioli, 2022: 472)

Thus, the combination and co-presence of copyright legislation (which is legally justifiable on substantive terms) and ideas about scientific authorship (e.g., the legal status of ghost-written scientific texts, such as in the case of medical journal articles; Mirowski and Van Horn, 2005) makes the question of legality complicated: if the authors are simply understood to obey intellectual property rights, then ghostwriting is legally unproblematic, but if the name on the journal frontpage differs from the actual author of the text, then the social norms of authorship responsibilities in scientific quarters are violated regardless of whether the current legislation vindicates such practices. The point to be made here is that legal rights need to be consistent with social norms and other types of private ordering devices and mechanisms so that there is preferably few, if any, inconsistencies between such governance devices.

In summary, the patent system and the copyright system, two domains of legislations intended to establish intellectual property rights, need to be grounded in some plausible and logically consistent political philosophy framework that both assists the interests of the individual innovator and the more heterogeneous participants active in the market for innovation ideas at large. The Lockean argument pro intellectual property rights either invokes a natural rights discourse (which is inconsistent with the fact that intellectual property rights deal with entities that are socially and culturally embedded), or as a species of *droit morale* (which is inconsistent with the characterization of ideas as non-excludable and non-rival, as in the case of a person who learns to speak, say, Portuguese, this newly acquired skill does not in any way restrain other Portuguese-speaking persons from using the language; in fact, the newly added speaker of the language makes this specific language skill even more attractive to have or to acquire as the number of speakers increases). In contrast, Kant's more pro-social political philosophy is more consistent with how intellectual ideas are developed and circulated in a liberal society, and better values the freedom to act (i.e., "positive freedoms," in Isiah Berlin's, 1958, description) vis-à-vis the more strict protection of intellectual propositions advocated by the "if value, then a right" community. Under all conditions, it does matter on what basis intellectual property rights are justified and that this justification considers a variety of scenarios.

If patents are incomplete legal devices, legally ambiguous in both practice and in court cases such as litigations, then what is their role? A literature review indicates at least four roles:

- To disclose information so it become publicly available.
- To promote enterprising on the basis of the legal protection of intellectual property rights and similar legal devices.
- To signal to actors that society and policy makers who act in the interests of voters and/or citizens value enterprising and innovations as the basis for entrepreneurial activities.
- To signal to the international community of investors that the jurisdiction is governed on the basis of the rule of law, and that nepotism and opportunistic behaviour such as rent-seeking are not tolerated.

The patent legislation does all of these things at the same time, but incompletely so. That is not because of incompetence, or a lack of resources committed to patenting activities, but because in an advanced and dynamic economy, such as that of the economic system of competitive capitalism, the future is uncertain, and there are many things that policy makers, legislators, judges, market actors, etc., do not yet know. Therefore, an incomplete and intentionally rational patent legislation is the best thing to accomplish under such conditions. Furthermore, that accomplishment is consistent with the legal institutionalism view that the rule of law does matter, but that laws are located in an institutional setting wherein social norms, political ideologies and beliefs, and a large number of other conditions need to be taken into account.

The legislative system and the question of public interest

In the legal institutionalism perspective, presented and advocated in Chapter 2 of this volume, the sovereign state is the principal legislator, but the sovereign state also collaborates with transnational governance organizations that establish their own regulatory rules and supports soft law and private ordering standard devices such as the use of contracts. Regardless of the institutional setting that supports the rule of law in the domain of economic affairs, the question remains then to what end legislative practices should be directed? For instance, the patent system should support innovative activities, and such activities are generally considered to be of "public interest," but it is often not sufficiently specified what public interests would mean in either theoretical or practical terms. If there is no solid definition of key terms, especially those that are of principal importance as they justify a series of legal devices, mechanisms, and principles "further downstream," in the legislative and regulatory system, then it is difficult to determine whether, e.g., "public interest" is worth considering in the first place (see, e.g., Dworkin, 1980: 194). Second, and related to the theoretical problem of what public interest would mean in propositional or stipulative terms, an empirical question to be determined on the basis of empirical studies is to what extent the state's legislature and judiciary are *de facto* passing legislation and establish new regulatory standards that are consistent with public interest as this concept was first defined.

The concept of public interest

Political scientists, legal scholars, and several other social science discipline scholars are likely to either explicitly or implicitly assume that what they study, or the legal-administrative reforms they advocate, are determined by public interest. For instance, Schneiberg and Bartley (2001: 102) propose that "a common notion" is that the state regulates industries "in the public interest," in order to protect consumers "against capitalists' self-interest or the excesses of the market." In this view, the state and its various agencies are populated by officials who hold fiduciary duties of care and loyalty vis-à-vis their citizens, and who recognize the risk that enterprising agents (e.g., corporations) may cause harm that befalls citizens, which therefore is a condition that needs to be mediated by legal and regulatory action. Levine and Forrence (1990: 167) refer to this notion as "the 'public interest' theory of regulation." Regardless of the substance of this claim—which intuitively seems plausible, at the same time as the risks of overregulation remains a concern—it remains unclear what "public interest" itself denotes, as Omarova (2012: 669) remarks in her study of finance industry regulation and monitoring:

> What exactly is the 'public interest' in this context, and who defines the substantive meaning of that term? As scholars have long recognized, defining 'public interest' as an independent rationale for economic regulation is inherently vulnerable to criticisms as excessively abstract, vague, and analytically weak.
>
> (Omarova, 2012: 669)

To temporarily pause this inquiry, it is worth noticing that legislative practices are not simply a matter of passing new legislation in a parliament (or similar), but to also ensure that new legislation is being implemented and assessed in terms of its outcomes and consequences. In the case of the US and many other advanced economies, these legal practices can be separated into (1) the legislature, "in principle responsible for making policy"; (2) the judiciary, responsible for interpreting the new policy, and setting legal constraints on it; and (3) the executive branch, which implements policy in a real-world economy setting (Zacka, 2022: 23). In this tripartite model, it is primarily the legislature that is held accountable for being able to monitor (or to construct the image of) public interest. Already at this stage, it is complicated to have good faith in knowing what public interest would be, and Zacka (2022) is agnostic regarding the possibilities for reaching some point of certainty regarding the content and substance of this term: "[T]he legislature remains the final arbiter of the public interest, but the guidance it provides is bound to remain underdeterminate" (Zacka, 2022: 26).

One candidate for qualifying for what is consistent with public interests is what political scientists that study "the quality of governance" have found to be a shared theme in their data, that is, that what the voters and the general public want is substantive improvements in the quality of life, rather than some other symbolic changes, including—perhaps somewhat surprising—the capacity to vote on proposals: "[S]everal studies have shown that when it comes to trust and perceptions of legitimacy, people seem to care more about institutions getting things done (outputs) than about having a say in directing the actions of such institutions (inputs)," Zacka (2022: 30) writes. That is, *grosso modo*, the voters and the general public want the legislature to pass laws that increase the general quality of life in substantive terms. As this is arguably a too-vague reference point or instruction for any policy maker to make any difference in the legislative process, it would be fair to conclude that the concept of public interest is itself a piece of legal fiction, a placeholder term that enables certain action to be taken, but that is being defined in semantic terms only after the fact.

A further complication is, as Zacka (2022: 25) shows, that there is a certain discontinuity between the legislature, the judiciary, and the executive branch inasmuch as in every step from conception to materialization, there are actors who interpret and otherwise shape or even distort original policy ideas when they reach individuals who experience legal reforms first-hand and in a real-world economy setting (for an empirical study see, e.g., Merriman and Pacewicz, 2022). Based on this insight, Zacka (2022: 25) says it is reasonable to introduce new metaphors for how legislation de facto operates in a real-world economy setting:

> Rather than thinking of the legislature as being in the "driver seat," we should think of it as a "taxicab passenger who sets the destination: '620 Main St., please,'" leaving the driver in charge of finding the best route.
>
> (Zacka, 2022: 25)

If public interests are considered a piece of legal fiction, does it then mean that public interests are no longer useful for the legislature? That is arguably not the case as the very idea of legal fiction is to use certain terms as a placeholder in a line of reasoning so that desirable outcomes can be generated, albeit not so much on the basis of a watertight and robust theory of what the public either needs or wants (which does not necessarily converge in all situations), but on the basis of intelligent and accountable policy makers who have the best intentions to pass legislation supporting optimal economic and social welfare. The concern is still that even if such a piece of legal fiction is introduced, the empirical question remains whether the legislature *de facto* passes legislation on the basis of this ideal, or if legislation is passed on the basis of other interests expressed, e.g., in the advocacy of legal reform that business lobbying firms provide during legislative episodes in parliaments, e.g., US Congress?

Does the legislature consider public interest when passing new legislation?

By and large, political scientists tend to hold legislative practices in high esteem, and to regard them as one of the more prominent devices in statecraft. For instance, Dahl (1977: 7) declares that corporate legislation and the incorporated business is "one of the most radical innovations that mankind has ever invented for economic organization, control, and growth." Given the centrality of legislative activities, it is noteworthy that Hacker, Hertel-Fernandez, Pierson, and Thelen (2022: 201) argue that American political science research has primarily been concerned with what happens in the US Congress, whereas studies of "the courts, federalism, local governance, para-state institutions like regulatory commissions, or even the executive branch" are considerably fewer in numbers. This observation indicates how political scientists stipulate that no discontinuities are the case when legislation is passed on from the legislature to the judiciary, and further on to the executive branch. To amend this situation, Hacker, Hertel-Fernandez, Pierson, and Thelen (2022: 198) call for a study program of what they refer to as the American Political Economy (APE), which includes three components. First, the study should include a "substantive focus on the interaction of markets and governance" to better understand how the legislature responds to perceived market demands (Hacker, Hertel-Fernandez, Pierson, and Thelen, 2022: 198). Rather than stipulating that the legislature sets the rules for the markets, the APE framework recognizes that governance practices and markets activities are entangled in ways that are considerably more non-linear than is generally assumed. Second, the study program should examine what is being referred to as "meta-politics," i.e., the "processes of institution shaping, agenda setting, and venue shopping" that unfold "before and alongside the more visible processes of mass politics" that "figure so centrally" in American politics research (Hacker, Hertel-Fernandez, Pierson, and Thelen, 2022: 198). The concept of meta-politics thus indicates that there is more than meets the eye when it comes to how political and legislative bodies interact with, e.g., markets actors and market regulators, and in order to fully understand such polymorphous interactions between governance practices and market activities, a broader view of these concerns needs to be taken. Third and finally, and premised on the first two components of the research program, the APE framework is not only concerned with the "last mile" of the legislative process, but also seeks to examine the various activities that precede the final decision to be made in US congress:

> Mainstream research on American politics is often focused on this crucial but circumscribed last mile. APE, by contrast, shifts the emphasis to the long transit that leads up to the last mile—the many, many previous miles that shape the substance and scope of conflict, the venues where decisive authority over policy resides, the key political actors who operate in these venues, and the balance of power among those actors.
>
> (Hacker, Hertel-Fernandez, Pierson, and Thelen, 2022: 198)

Hacker, Hertel-Fernandez, Pierson, and Thelen (2022: 201) argue that their political science study program matters as the American tradition to let elites and other resourceful groups rule via, e.g., lobbying activities, may result in policies that "citizens might resist." For instance, the ongoing economic decline in the US has "fed a 'politics of resentment'" that has dangerously "upended politics, policy, and even American democracy" (Hacker, Hertel-Fernandez, Pierson, and Thelen, 2022: 208). Although such tendencies have been observed in many democratic countries that host advanced economies, measured by, for instance, the growth of political support for right-wing or left-wing populist parties, the case of the US is unique in this group of countries, Hacker, Hertel-Fernandez, Pierson, and Thelen (2022: 201) propose:

> Far more than in other rich democracies, political contestation in the United States is situated within a multi-venue, multilevel political space in which inequalities across venues and levels are rife and active governance of markets is difficult, contested, biased, and fragile.
>
> (Hacker, Hertel-Fernandez, Pierson, and Thelen, 2022: 201)

More specifically, the idiosyncratic regime of American plutocratic populism "rests on the Republican Party's ability to attract organized interests with conservative economic policies while adopting cultural appeals to mobilize its mass base," Hacker, Hertel-Fernandez, Pierson, and Thelen (2022: 210) add, and call for more studies of why and how this alliance between disgruntled Republican voters and the moneyed plutocracy is preserved, and why there appear to be few alternatives for the voters who believe they have been deprived of their rights and entitlements.

Under all conditions, the question to be examined here is to what extent the legislature passes laws that are consistent with, no matter how vaguely defined the term is, public interests. If the legislature considers what is in the best interests for all citizens, and not only the interest of a minority, or some elite, then there are presumably better chances for improving the overall economic and social welfare for all citizens and stakeholders. To make such an assessment, empirical material related to the work to pass legislation is to be collected, and the results need to be theorized.

Empirical studies of interests considered in policy making

Gilens (2005) examined whether public interests are considered in the policy-making process, and found that it is difficult to say whether that is the case unless public interests are defined with some precision. Still, policy making is commonly more consistent with the preferences of high-income stakeholders (the income deciles ranging from the 10th to the 1st decile) than with those of median-income stakeholders. "[H]igher income respondents' views are more strongly related to government policy," Gilens (2005: 786) writes: "For respondents at the 10th income percentile, the probability of policy change rises from .21 with 10 percent favouring to .42 with 90 percent support" (Gilens, 2005: 786).

Gilens and Page (2014: 568) repeated Gilens (2005) study on the basis of the methodological assumption that "[t]he preferences of 'affluent' Americans at the ninetieth income percentile can usefully be taken as proxies for the opinions of wealthy or very-high-income Americans" (Gilens and Page, 2014: 568). This is not necessarily the case as there may of course be billionaires who advocate, e.g., progressive fiscal schemes, but by and large there is a consistency in preferences among income groups, if not on the basis of deontic values (i.e., the belief that wealthy individuals deserve to be so because they are morally entitled to the wealth they have acquired, all things equal), at least on the basis of the alleged value of consistency in policy making and in market rules more generally. Gilens and Page (2014: 574) found that organized interest groups, dominated by "corporations and business and professional associations," and supporting high-net-worth household preferences, are influential in having policies and legislation passed that are consistent with their own interests; in fact, "interest-group alignments" are "almost totally unrelated" to the preferences of "average citizens," Gilens and Page (2014: 574) report. "Overall, net interest-group alignments are not significantly related to the preferences of average citizens. The net alignments of the most influential, business-oriented groups are negatively related to the average citizen's wishes" (Gilens and Page, 2014: 576).

As Gilens and Page (2014: 576) emphasize, even if the preferences of economic elites have a "far more independent impact upon policy change than the preferences of average citizens do," it does not necessarily follow that the average citizen does not get his or her interests considered in new policy or legislation, but such outcomes are only the case when this average citizen group expresses preferences that are already consistent with the preferences of the economic elites that "wield the actual influence." Furthermore, as economic elites invest considerable resources in shaping the public opinion and the public's preferences, it may be that the average citizen group by default have their preferences considered, as they have already been able to change their opinions on the basis of such sponsored communication, Gilens and Page (2014: 576) write: "We know that interest groups and policy makers themselves often devote considerable effort to shaping opinion. If they are successful, this might help explain the high correlation we find between elite and mass preferences."

Based on these results, Gilens and Page (2014: 576) propose that the average citizens' influence on policy making "is near zero," which is a result, when expressed in theoretical terms, supporting so-called *biased pluralism theory* in political science (Gilens and Page, 2014: 574). Hertel-Fernandez's (2014) study of the role of the American Legislative Exchange Council (ALEC), a "business-backed, conservative group" that actively works with state lawmakers to shape the legislative practices to benefit its members' interests, sheds some light on how the policy-making process actually occurs (see also Hertel-Fernandez, 2019). ALEC provides companies, representing a broad variety of industries including "Amazon, UPS, pharmaceutical firms, private prison operators, Enron, insurance companies, and tobacco manufacturers" (Hertel-Fernandez, 2014: 582–583), with the opportunity to work with state lawmakers "to draft model bills that are distributed to state legislatures across the country—often with great success for the companies" (Hertel-Fernandez, 2014: 582). The structure of ALEC is "relatively unusual" inasmuch as it offers a case of lobbying that is "distinct from other business associations or labor groups," as ALEC "does not give political contributions or engage in electoral politics" (Hertel-Fernandez, 2014: 583). When serving this role, Hertel-Fernandez (2014: 583) continues, ALEC offers "a chance to look beyond political campaigning and donations to other mechanisms that businesses use to influence the policymaking process."

In his analytical model, Hertel-Fernandez (2014: 586) formulates a "third way" between "pluralist" and "elitist" perspectives on business power, and thus hypothesizes that corporations can influence the policy-making process by providing "policy inputs to legislators who would otherwise lack such resources." In this view, the underfinancing of the state policy-making process provides business-funded consortia such as ALEC with the possibility to influence the policy-making process:

> Corporate interests, in essence, are lowering the cost of passing business-friendly bills relative to the cost of passing non-business friendly bills. Provided with cheaper business-friendly bills, we ought to see resource-constrained legislators enact more of those bills.
>
> (Hertel-Fernandez, 2014: 586)

The empirical results show that "on average," about 15% of legislators' sponsored bills "matched ALEC legislation" in the ten states being examined (Hertel-Fernandez, 2014: 591). Furthermore and largely consistent with conventional wisdom, "conservative legislators" relied on ALEC model bills for "a greater share of their total legislation," as did Republicans (Hertel-Fernandez, 2014: 591). Importantly, Hertel-Fernandez (2014: 591) also shows that "[a] non-trivial number of Democrats and Independents" in the sample "introduced and sponsored ALEC bills," i.e., the reliance on ALEC model bills "appears to be more of an ideological, rather than a partisan, affair" (Hertel-Fernandez, 2014: 591). In summary, Hertel-Fernandez

(2014: 591) writes that "business influence," exercised through ALEC in this case, is "high when legislators lack policy resources," and especially so when legislators are "more receptive to businesses' interests." In the end, this finding is more consistent with an "elitist" than a "pluralist" perspective on business power:

> "Citizen" legislatures thus appear much more likely to rely on business-drafted bills compared with more professionalized legislatures. ALEC bills were also much more likely to be enacted when legislators viewed business, rather than labor, as their political constituency and when states were governed by conservative lawmakers.
>
> (Hertel-Fernandez, 2014: 583)

State policy making and the legislation that follows therefrom are shaped by the social actors who hold the resources needed to influence the political process, Hertel-Fernandez (2014: 594) concludes: "[T]he financial resources of ALEC are important to provide the trips, conferences, and resources that bring legislators together with corporate representatives." Consequently, labour interests appear to be secondary to business interests.

Theories of biased pluralism generally assume that "both the thrust of interest-group conflict and the public policies that result" tend to tilt toward "the wishes of corporations and business and professional associations" (Gilens and Page, 2014: 567). Many, if not most, American political scientists are prone to believe, either by training or by conviction or preferences, that the policy preferences of "the median voter" tend to drive policy outputs from the US political system, Gilens and Page (2014: 565) propose, but such beliefs are not supported by the empirical data that Gilens (2005) and Gilens and Page (2014) present. In sharp contrast to this belief in the accuracy of majoritarian pluralism theories, wherein median voter interests are effectively considered, "most middle-income Americans think that public officials do not care much about the preferences of 'people like me,'" Gilens (2005: 794) writes: "Sadly, the results presented," he continues, "suggest they may be right": "[i]nfluence over actual policy outcomes appears to be reserved almost exclusively for those at the top at the income distribution" (Gilens, 2005: 794).[2] Gilens's claims may be daunting for proponents of

2 It is important to notice that the scholarly literature includes studies that provide evidence of less democratic deficit in the policy-making cycle (e.g., Branham, Soroka, and Wlezien, 2017). They write that it has been assumed in the scholarly literature that "[t]he rich advocate and win on conservative policies that give them economic advantages, such as tax cuts, over the objections of the middle (and poor)." In contrast, Branham, Soroka, and Wlezien (2017: 46) argue that they "[f]ind very little evidence to support such an inference." Instead, the results indicate that "[t]he poor do slightly worse than the other income groups, although even they occasionally win over the preferences of the middle or rich"

the political system of representative democracy, and several scholars have pointed to the sharp decline in faith in the US Congress to have the capacity to accomplish any factual changes and improvements in the everyday lives of Americans. "Many have ceased to believe in the possibility of legislation to address societal issues such as climate change, redistribution, stagnant wages, etc.," Rock (2021: 367) writes. Such "democratic backsliding" and growth in populist beliefs (Berman, 2021: 21) are hardly surprising given the aggressive critique of any kind of policy or reform that actively seeks to improve the quality of life of millions of Americans, including the Patient Protection and Affordable Care Act, also referred to as the Obamacare reform, passed by the US Congress during the first term of the Obama presidency (Merriman and Pacewicz, 2022; Crouch, 2011: 67).

Anyway, the key learning here is that economic elites, for various reasons and on the basis of a variety of mechanisms and devices (including, e.g., campaign donations and business lobbying, two of the most salient activities that interfere with the policy-making process), have the authority to make their interests considered in the policy-making process. Again, it is important to recognize that this does not mean that elite interests would not be consistent with "median voter interest" (or the interests of any other social strata or community), as it may be, somehow, that elites have the capacity to know what is best for all citizens. If that would have been the case, the economic interests of elites would express some kind of market-based rationality of the kind that free-market theorists are prone to believe in, i.e., that self-interest, instrumental rationality, and minimal property rights legislation are all that is needed for a society to optimize its welfare, essentially on the basis of honouring the singular parameter of efficiency in all decisions being made and the activities that follows. However, such a "one-sentence theory" (Ayres and Gertner, 1989: 89) of economic and social welfare is not only implausible in the eyes of more moderate commentators, but such a theory would disqualify the very idea of social norms as being a legitimate component in any governance system that would effectively monitor and regulate an advanced economy. In other words, as was considered in the section about the role of deontic vocabulary to justify the copyright system, a governance model that shuns social norms in favour of a singular efficiency criterion is inoperable as it undermines the authority of legislation that is introduced to achieve a singular objective, not objectives or policy goals considered in broader terms.

In order to formulate a legal theory of innovations, it is thus important to recognize that even if laws and regulations are institutionally embedded

---

(Branham, Soroka, and Wlezien, 2017: 46). Still, when all things are considered, this research finding runs counter to what several other studies cited in this section show.

(as was proposed and substantiated in Chapters 2 and 3), it does not necessarily follow that these laws and regulations are fair, or even reasonable, but they remain institutional creations of the legislative state just the same. That is, there is a straightforward analytical thread from political science and the field of politics and policy making (i.e., the legislature) to the legal affairs that pertain to, e.g., the patent system (monitored by the judiciary), and further on to the domain of practical innovation work in industry and organizational fields, unified and theoretically consistent on the basis of the legal institutionalism perspective. Furthermore, legal institutionalist theory recognizes that law is necessarily incomplete, which means that while the legislation passed may be unduly shaped by elite interests, its implementation and medium- to long-term consequences may still be consistent with non-elite interests, i.e., there is a perhaps small but noticeable divergence between laws in books and laws in real-world economies (Merriman and Pacewicz, 2022). Whether the outcomes would be in the interest of the many rather than a few remains an empirical question, which then calls for more research that explores what the immediate and unintended consequences of legislative reforms would be.

Summary and conclusion

In a democratic liberal society, characterized by the formulation and introduction of new ideas and new concepts, the question of justice as fairness needs to be considered in dynamic rather than static terms. As new ideas are introduced, social changes may occur, and such changes may to a varying degree affect the everyday lives of social actors. To fully understand legal devices such as the patent system, part of the governance of such a society, it is important to consider the ethical and legal principles that can justify the legal protection of new ideas, commonly described as intellectual property. The patent system is introduced to accomplish two mutually exclusive goals: to provide legal stability on the basis of enforceable rights in a milieu characterized by the continuous production of new know-how and new ideas (such as in a vibrant scientific field, say, the research and production of antibodies), and to create possibilities for enterprising activities under the protection of patent law, and similar intellectual protection legislation. The patent system as a legal-institutional creation does not exist independent of moral, ethical, or political ideas that pertain to and that may justify such legal devices, and consequently it is important to consider on what legal principles and traditions that intellectual property rights can be justified to ensure that both freedom and a dynamic economic system and society are preserved even as the benefits of intellectual property rights are established. In the democratic liberal society, the Lockean idea to regard intellectual property rights as being premised on one's own personal labour, which do have some intuitive benefits, become inoperable as legal statutes premised on these ideas would possibly restrict the freedom of expression of other social actors (as in the case of biographers, who can no longer freely use other authors' work without being accused of stealing original ideas and text passages, thus inaccurately being portrayed as "thieves" rather than as "creators"; Waldron, 1992). To handle such concerns, scholars recognize a Kantian view of intellectual property rights as being more open towards the free use of ideas as being the most reasonable basis for intellectual property rights protection.

In both the Lockean and Kantian justification of intellectual property rights, the basis for the patent system, the question of public interest is foregrounded. Unfortunately, the questions of what public interest consists of, and how it can be determined, are often vaguely formulated. This makes public interest some kind of revered reference point in public debates, what is held in esteem as a legal and regulatory principle, and yet being difficult to pin down in stipulative terms. A political science literature that examines primarily American legislative practices and policy making demonstrates that the public interest is an ideal that is inconsistent with empirical data, which indicates that the interests of specific groups are primarily attended to in the policy-making process. This does not necessarily mean that policy making in the US diverges from what the majority wants, but such expressed preferences may only be honoured by default as the majority's interest coincides with that of specific interest groups, such as corporations that invest considerable sums in lobbying activities. By the end of the day, the sole praise of public interest in policy-making quarters does not necessarily counteract a democratic deficit in US policy making.

In the end, when considering all the moral, ethical, political, and practical aspects that are part of the patent system and that have been developed and refined over time, it is plausible to assume that the legal protection of innovation ideas (being a piece of intellectual property) has occurred in a stepwise and not fully transparent manner; new legal ideas have been introduced (following, e.g., new technological developments; see, e.g., Luther, 2020; Brummer and Yadav, 2019; Magnuson, 2018), and consequently new pieces of legislation have been passed to amend the situation, but the consequences of such a continuous legislative process are difficult to fully anticipate from the vantage point of the present, and new possibilities for legal arbitrage and similar behaviour emerge. In this manner, legal devices such as the patent system, intentionally serving a variety of interests, become a patchwork of legal doctrines, principles, rules, and devices, not always in full harmony or rid of inconsistencies. However, the legal system is intended to optimize justice as fairness, not to be considered from some design perspective and valued in terms of its sleekness, and therefore also legal devices that reveal some shortcomings may nonetheless serve their economic and social purposes as intended.

6 Law makes markets and establishes market rules, and markets generate innovation

Legal institutionalism and its analytical benefits

Introduction

A major concern in an institutional theory view of economic affairs is that the economic system and its rules and practices need to be regarded as legitimate in the eyes of the majority, and preferably by all participants. As the English Lord Chief Justice Gordon Hewart once remarked, "Not only must Justice be done; it must be *seen to been done*" (cited in Tucker, 2018: 52). Baccaro, Blyth, and Pontusson (2022) address the question of how the economic system of competitive capitalism can preserve its legitimacy during, e.g., periods of economic stagnation. "[W]e see capitalism as a social order whose stability depends on its capacity to satisfy expectations of materials improvements," Baccaro, Blyth, and Pontusson (2022: 1) write. If the main mechanism for securing the "legitimacy of democratic capitalism" resides in the ability to generate (and widely diffuse) economic growth, periods of limited economic growth may create a loss of faith in this economic system's capacity to benefit all participants (Baccaro, Blyth, and Pontusson, 2022: 1). Baccaro, Blyth, and Pontusson (2022: 2) report that they identify "a broad stagnationist tendency" in advanced capitalism, "harking back to the crisis of 'wage-led growth.'" Such tendencies are not only of interest for policy makers and academic researchers with an interest in the fine-tuned mechanism of the economic system as the consequences of economic stagnation have been proved to strongly affect social and economic welfare on the household and individual levels (Case and Deaton, 2020, 2021; Deaton, 2013). For instance, in Russia, during the collapse of the corrupt and inefficient communist economic system between 1988 and 1994 only to eventually be replaced by an equally corrupt and inefficient, but more aggressive authoritative kleptocracy, male life expectancy "fell from 64.6 to 57.6 years" (Scheiring and King, 2023: 146). Similar figures were reported from de-industrialized parts of Hungary: "[d]eindustrialization could have been a major cause of the deaths of despair in the 1990s in Russia and Hungary" (Scheiring and King, 2023: 146). Also in the US,

DOI: 10.4324/9781003460220-6

one of the richest per capita countries in the world, similar tendencies are observed, Case and Deaton (2021) argue: "We see the increasing mortality and declining adult life expectancy of less-educated Americans not only as a catastrophe in its own right but also as a powerful indicator that American society is not working for the majority of its population" (Case and Deaton, 2021: 3). A vital, dynamic, and not the least fair (or, perceived as fair) economic system is the basis for a society characterized by high levels of economic and social welfare, and consequently the rule of law and transparent and understandable legal rules and regulatory frameworks are the keys to such a society.

More widely speaking, concerns such as the stagnationist tendency in the economic system of competitive capitalism have been addressed by, e.g., management studies scholars as one of the "Grand Challenges" that needs to be handled on the basis of, e.g., scholarly research activities. "[I]t is only through education and self-governance that capitalism stands a chance of reforming itself from within and promoting both economic wealth and societal well-being," Aguilera, Aragón-Correa, and Marano (2022: 644) declare. At the same time, such statements that point at matters of joint concern do not necessarily specify in detail on what basis such grand challenges are to be examined or solved. For instance, Arend (2022: 332) emphasizes that the field of management studies is characterized by diversity and competing theories and perspectives, rather than by some consensus regarding what problems to examine, or what theories or methods to use when addressing such problems:

> We have no widely agreed upon standards for what theory is and is not, for what better theory is, for when bad theory should be rejected, for what are acceptable critiques of published theory, for how to hold editors and reviewers responsible for rejecting good or accepting bad theory, and so on.
>
> (Arend, 2022: 332)

A further complication is that even as there is no scholarly consensus regarding how to address matters of joint concern, there is also no shared view of how this scholarly work should influence managerial practices, i.e., how managers working in industry and public administration should be informed about how to perceive actual problems or how to solve them. As Arend (2022: 332) remarks, management studies scholars are not primarily animated by the idea to provide detailed rules to practicing managers. Instead, qualified and intelligent managers and decision makers should be provided with "deeper insights and critical tools" that support good managerial practices (Arend, 2022: 332). That is, Arend (2022) advises against being too sure about how to "fix capitalism" on the basis of some bookish learning and empirical studies; on the other hand, theory and empirical material may be a very useful resource when trying to figure out how the economic system of capitalism can preserve its vitality and dynamics, so scholarly activities and know-how should not be discounted either.

This volume has emphasized that the rule of law, expressed within the analytical framework of legal institutionalism, acts as the basis for any dynamic economic system. That is because laws not only express rules and provide a mechanism for having actual disputes examined in a court of law if needed, but law both expresses social norms that prevail in society and shapes social norms as rules regarding illegal behaviours are established (as stipulated by the so-called expressive theory of law). Still, such legislation and regulatory frameworks are human creations, which means that they are incomplete, far from infallible, and always open to contest, which is also happening on a day-to-day basis as both corporations, other organizations, and individuals put the accuracy of law to the test of actual practices. In fact, as Pollman (2019a: 748) says, speaking about the platform economy, "corporate disobedience has been an important engine for transforming various areas of law." Such corporate disobedience is consistent with what Zhang, Mohliver, and King (2022: 231) refer to as ***deviant practices***, defined as "[t]he act of knowingly breaking with societal norms or laws in ways that carry punishment for those caught doing so." Corporate disobedience and deviant practices are thus the mechanisms that call attention to certain facets of the legislation, and therefore either contribute to reforming the law or the legal rules, or to serve to establish the law or the rule as being substantiated on the basis of legal decisions and court ruling. Pollman (2019a: 764) notices that corporate disobedience "paradoxically undermines the integrity of the legal system while at the same time plays an important role in shaping it." This paradox is at the very heart of the legal institutionalism framework inasmuch as the economic system of competitive capitalism that the legal system is both constitutive of (as has been argued in this volume) and that the legal system dynamically responds to (as, e.g., Pollman, 2019a, claims is the case) are co-created and dependent on each other to upheld operative and functional rules that preserve and propel economic activities and transactions.

In an institutional theory view, society is constituted on the basis of the institutions and the institutionalized beliefs that are expressed by the participants, but institutions are always possible to question and are open for modification, albeit not all of them at the same time. In this view, corporate disobedience and deviant practices in the realm of corporate affairs do not in any way undermine or marginalize law or the rule of law, but rather serve to put pressure on the legislation to adjust itself to new market conditions and new social norms, etc., so that the principle that economic activities and transactions remain what are determined by the rule of law. Legal institutionalism thus provides a dynamic, yet theoretically embedded analytical framework that helps, e.g., scholars to understand how and why, e.g., the patent system and the patent law it rests on supports innovation activities of the kind that economists have proved to be the primus motor of the economic system of competitive capitalism.

In this last chapter, some of the implications from the analysis presented in the previous chapters will be examined. A theory of the legal embedding of innovation activities will be presented, not intended to fully apprehend all of the complexity of the relations between legislative and judiciary affairs and corporate innovative output, but to provide a basis for further scholarly research in the area. Ultimately, such a theory addresses the question of why corporate actors are motivated to participate in time- and resource-consuming and uncertain innovative activities. As G.E.M. Anscombe ([1957] 1976: 19) points out, "motives may explain actions to us; but that is not to say that they 'determine,' in the sense of causing, actions." Motives are thus reasonable under some description, Anscombe ([1957] 1976) proposes (a proposition that is also shared by, e.g., Davidson, 1963), but to understand such a description, the broader institutional context wherein the motive is expressed needs to be examined. That is, what reasonable behaviour or expectations would be is a matter of how consistent such behaviours or expectations are with the social norms that are recognized in a community. As social norms are both constitutive of institutional beliefs and are shaped by institutions, motives are thus inherently collective inasmuch as they express beliefs, ambitions, or desires that are shared with others. Law and regulatory rules that are premised on institutional conditions therefore have a role to play when shaping the motives of self-interested and intelligent human beings who have the skills and the capacities to make contributions to the shared economic and social welfare. In this view, laws are not only things to be found in books, or what passes the lips of the functionaries of the judiciary when they speak of law and legality, but are what fundamentally shape beliefs, aspirations, and desires on the level of day-to-day practices. Consequently, a legal institutional view of patent law and the patent system has immediate and direct consequences for everyday life in the contemporary economy. Such academic sophistications taken aside, the rule of law is conducive of a dynamic and changeable society as it provides the greatest possible opportunity for the greatest possible number of people, but not so much on the basis of some once-and-for-all fixed governance model that mustn't be questioned (either justified by the authority of some political party, some religious doctrine, or some other mythical entity, e.g., "the grandiosity of the nation, "the innate rationality of the market," etc.) but on the basis of a legal-political model that is open to modifications as changes occur. This rule of law, grounded in democratic procedures, is the mark of the liberal, enlightened society.

A summary of the argument

In Chapter 1 of this volume, innovations were portrayed as "new combinations" or "new inventions" that have not previously been introduced on the market; innovations (new technology, new services, new business models, new asset classes in financial trade, etc.) propel economic activity and are conducive to economic and social welfare. Furthermore, the economic theory idea that the market, appearing *ex nihilo*, singlehandedly provides all the resources needed to innovate was rejected on the basis of the inability of such a theory to explain both the origin and the regulation of markets.

In Chapter 2, it was argued that the market does not pre-date the legislative state, or even being its antecedent, as the sovereign state and (eventually, but only at a later stage) transnational governance organizations create possibilities for markets to be formed and created and to become operable. Markets are generated on the basis of a variety of legislations, including, e.g., corporate law, and more specific functional laws such as contract law, fiduciary law, patent law, etc., that jointly create possibilities for venturing under the legal protection of the sovereign state. This legal institutional framework portrays patents as intellectual property rights, provided by the state to accomplish certain policy goals that policy makers have defined as desirable (e.g., to reward ingenuity by protecting intellectual property rights and to create a market for innovation ideas as an auxiliary benefit).

In Chapters 3 and 4, it was demonstrated that when reviewing the literature on patent law, one exemplary case of legislation that supports increased innovation work activities, it is clear that patent law is far from perfected and complete. In its formulation, patent law divides the patent into one descriptive component that explains what the new innovation consists of and a justificatory component that underlines how the innovation, if materializing, would serve to benefit human interests "in the arts." Critics of the patent system recognize the first component as being a *sine qua non* of the patent system, but are often more skeptical regarding the justificatory component. The justificatory component contains thought experiments and even mere speculations regarding presumptive possibilities for practical use of the innovation under consideration, and studies show that this information has little value for, e.g., practicing researchers, who tend to look elsewhere for direction or inspiration regarding how to formulate and develop innovation ideas. Unfortunately, the current patent system provides the possibility to acquire patents that are broad-ranging and indiscrete, and this generosity paves the way for opportunistic behaviour, critics contend, including the litigations initiated by Patent Assertion Entities (PAEs) and so-called patent trolls. Less skeptical commentators are not so concerned with such legal activities as they believe that the value of a market for innovation ideas, enabled by the patent system, has, on balance, greater value than the cost to handle cases of opportunistic behaviour. In the end, the patent system represents a paternalist legislation that reduces the freedom of certain actors to benefit the overall efficiency in how innovation ideas are handled in the public domain.

In Chapter 5, the basis for the justification of paternalist legislation was sought for in the domain of political philosophy. In this literature, several scholars have argued that John Locke's idea to consider intellectual property protection, in the contemporary meaning of the term, as being derived from natural or moral rights, is theoretically and legally inconsistent. As the patent system deals with ideas that are fundamentally social in nature, it does not follow that natural or moral rights would be able to justify a paternalist legislation in this domain. Consequently, leaving John Locke's ideas behind—originally developed to defend entirely different rights—paves the way for alternative theories that justify legislation that pertains to intellectual property rights, such as Immanuel Kant's claim that copyrights can be permitted only insofar as the right to freely use and to further develop ideas is granted to all social actors being part of a social conversation regarding matters of joint concern. In the end, this scholarly literature indicates that legislative activities are ultimately grounded in politics, and that politics de facto is a matter of how power is distributed in society, and to what extent specific actors bestowed with power can and have the ambition to pass legislation that is in the interests of the majority of citizens. This question is further examined in the last section of the volume.

In the last sections of Chapter 5, the question whether policy makers, who are involved with the state's legislature and who instruct the judiciary on how to act and rule on the basis of legal issues being subject to dispute, are in fact capable of fulfilling ambitious democratic goals (or, in the absence of democratic mechanisms that hold policy makers accountable for their decisions and the laws being passed, other policy goals) so that policies and legislation are passed that are consistent with the interests (and possibly also the preferences) of a majority of the citizens. The political science literature indicates on the basis of empirical studies that this is possibly not the case, but that power differentials in society (measured in terms of, e.g., economic power and political influence) are mirrored in what legislation is being passed. Such empirical research findings indicate that there is democratic deficit in the legislative process, but such studies also show that such biased legislation may be counterweighted in both the judiciary and in the executive branch of the administrative state (Merriman and Pacewicz, 2022). Under all conditions, legislative practices are shaped by elite interests—which does not of necessity result in or indicate a divergence between elite and popular interests (which then remains an empirical question to examine in more detail)—which makes this condition a policy challenge as the long-term effect of elite rule may result in a gradual decline in economic and social welfare. This means that paternalist legislation, such as patent law, is likely to not primarily reflect public and popular interests, but is instead premised on elite interests and preferences. Whether such divergences matter de facto is, to repeat, an empirical question that demands more research work as outcomes cannot be assessed in the absence of such data.

A legal-institutional theory of innovation

Innovations are premised on economic conditions (e.g., the supply of finance capital that can support development work in entrepreneurial activities), but such economic conditions are only established if legislation that is supportive of and protects economic interests is in place. Markets, such as the market for innovation ideas and for finance capital investment, do therefore not precede the legislative activities that enable markets to differentiate. That is, markets are not simply naturally emerging from some mystical price theory component, intuitively understood by everyone, but are rather the outcome of human activities and, prior to that, legislative activities. At the bottom of the market, legal rules and social norms provide the incentives for the individual market actor to use and to trust market mechanisms. This legal institutionalism framework applies to the case of market making. Elementary neoclassical economic theory thus has the causality backward: rather than starting with markets, legislation (or, in pre-modern societies, social norms that pertain to fairness, justice, honour, etc.) serves as the basis of any market-based transaction. Markets are thus productive human accomplishments that provide many of the transactional and allocative benefits that economists are fond of documenting and theorizing, but they are in place only on the basis of the original legislation (or the social norms) that render such markets functional and worthy of being trusted.

The proposition that humans make laws, and laws make markets, but also establish the private ordering activities (say, the use of contracts) that a faith in the market may generate, is itself trivial. The legal institutionalism framework is premised on the assumption that economic and social actors act on rational grounds (which expresses the principle of charity), at the same time as what qualifies as rational behaviour within a particular culture or within a horizon of meaning is not immediately given. This condition thus applies to legislation, which denotes human-made rules intended to create clarity regarding what practices are tolerable or not. In the legal institutionalism framework, law is always of necessity incomplete as it needs to be able to apprehend a wide set of contingencies and conditions, and the legislators cannot anticipate every condition or situation from the vantage point of the present. This means that no legislation is complete or infallible, but laws do still play the key institutional role to express the authority of certain rules, norms, and beliefs in ways that makes the legislation practically useful.

To apply this general framework to the patent system and its underlying patent law, the scholarly literature on patenting activities and the logical consistency of patent law indicates that the law is far from complete, and that there are many areas wherein amendments can be made. However, in a legal institutional framework, the shortcomings, inconsistencies, and glitches in a piece of legislation are worthy of exploring further, and hopefully changes in the law or in its application can be made to make the current legislation more efficient, more fair, more comprehensive, etc., but as patent law always of necessity operates and is enforced in the shadow of the future, it still provides many benefits regardless of its documented and alleged limitations. Expressed differently, it is better to have an incomplete patent law with the potential to be gradually improved than to not have any patent law at all: the absence of such a law would result in social and economic costs such as the loss of incentives to innovate, the loss of a legal vocabulary that defines and expresses the activities and components involved when producing innovations, and a loss of a sense of legality that pertains to the innovation work, a signal that society does not fully value the ingenuity and creativity of would-be innovators, regardless of who they are, where they come from, and in what domain "of the arts" they are active. The legal institutionalism framework thus recognizes both the current patent system as it is and the critique addressed regarding its consequences, but the larger question from an economic welfare perspective is if the world would be a better place in the absence of this legislation. The answer to this question is then no: the world would not be a better place as innovations would then need to be produced outside of the legal protection of the legislative state and its allied transnational governance organizations.

A legal theory of innovation thus recognizes that the legal system generates markets for, e.g., innovation ideas, and signals to all market participants that society values and appreciate innovation work, even in the absence of any evidence of progress for the time being, as in the case of a bioscience start-up that fails as it encounters insurmountable difficulties when, e.g., raising new financial capital funds to finance its development work. A legal theory of innovation still recognizes that most of the work conducted to produce innovations has little to do with legal affairs, but is instead the outcome from the hard and persistent work to combine intellectual and analytical capacities with material resources, often within a team production framework, such as an R&D project, wherein new innovations can be generated. That is, there is no such thing as a "legal fundamentalism" in a legal theory of innovation as the legislation is only what exists prior to such activities taking place and what reduces the uncertainty regarding the ownership of the work conducted; the work done thereafter is perfectly well suitable to be examined on the basis of, e.g., innovation management theories and models. The issue is just that to assume that the market and the actors populate markets that generate innovations, regardless of the legislation that has been passed, is an implausible proposition as it neglects the role of clear "rules of the game" when it comes to time- and finance capital-consuming activities such as innovation work. Therefore, it is more consistent with good philosophical conscience to stipulate that laws make markets, and markets attracts market actors, whereof some may have the capacity to generate innovations that add to the economic and social welfare, than to obscure the intricacies of the innovation process by claiming that such markets were somehow already available. The reliance on law implies the rule of humans who pass the law they regard as necessary, not being subject to some pre-social structures that would precede any legislative action. The objection to this claim would be that economic transactions took place in what Marshall Sahlins (1972) refers to as "stone age economies," i.e., in archaic economic systems, but such transactions arguably took place under the influence of social norms that regulated such transactions. As social norms are both the antecedents of legislation, and what laws passed should preferably express, this means that social norms played the same role in pre-modern societies as laws do today in highly differentiated societies and economies.

In the end, a legal theory of innovation is comparably "weak" (which is not to be confused with "ineffective") inasmuch as it recognizes the incompleteness of law and the significant variety in the expertise needed to generate innovation in, say, the pharmaceutical industry, software engineering, or the finance industry. Although weakness may be associated with unattractive features that are far from optimal, it is important that in theoretical domains, weakness does not necessarily carry such pejorative associations (see, e.g., Granovetter, 1973). A value-neutral concept of weakness has been positively associated with robust outcomes and resilience in, e.g., studies of legislative activities (Lucas, Grimes, and Gehman, 2022; Pedriana and Stryker, 2004), regulatory affairs (Hirsh, 2009), and labour markets (Granovetter, 1973). More specifically, Perrow and Guillén (1990: 40) have examined organizations as being "imperfected and refractory tools" that are "always failing to some degree." That is, simply because policy makers may regard the world as being unilinear, rational, and predictable in their ideal image, it does not follow that the co-workers in frontline organizations who are subject to policies, enacted on the presumption that such ideal conditions would be possible to obtain, would share such beliefs. That is, weakness in the sense described by Perrow and Guillén (1990), in the sense of accomplishing less than in an ideal word description but considerably more than nothing at all, poorly qualifies as a pejorative term in everyday semantics. A legal theory of innovation being weak does then not indicate that the theory is poorly formulated or otherwise deficient, but that it is expressed in terms that defies the Nirvana fallacy that ideal theories succumb to, i.e., the fallacy to compare an actual real-world economy activity with an ideal fictive state where there are no transaction costs, no opportunistic behaviour, and all actors behave in accordance with the same instrumental rationality that lends itself to precise formal descriptions (as in the case of the agent making choices on the basis of endogenous preferences that are structured on an ordinal scale and that are stable and thus predictable over time), etc. When an analyst can release him or herself from the idea that weakness denotes some imputed deficiency, then more and more useful theories may be expressed, simply because such theories are no longer claimed to be fully inclusive, comprehensive, and thus authoritative. In its place, several theories may explain matters of joint concern, including a legal theory of how and why innovations are generated *at all*, when rational apathy would be the more plausible attitude towards these issues.

Theoretical implications: on the question, how do firms and markets generate innovations?

A legal theory of innovation has some theoretical implication that should be discussed in relation to mainstream economic theory, i.e., neoclassical economic theory. For management studies scholars, companies act as the primary source of innovation activities, i.e., corporate actors formulate innovation ideas and develop them accordingly. For economists, the market prices all commodities and therefore enables transactions that serve as the basis for innovation activities. In the management studies scholar's perspective, companies for the most part follow the rule of law and adhere to regulations in their day-to-day work (even though rule-breaking occurs unintentionally or as a component of an entrepreneurial strategy, as in the case of the ride-sharing company Uber; Rosenblat, 2018; Thelen, 2018). Corporate activities are thus institutionally embedded, yet embedded in ways that support their autonomy, i.e., companies are autonomously embedded (Evans, 1995; Styhre, 2020). For economists, the concept of embedding is already to start with too sociological to be accepted out of hand, but if this term would be approved, the transactions and innovations, which are assumed to exist as an autonomous order, rather than the institutions (say, legislation, social norms) generate the market, which expresses a proposition that needs to be examined. A theoretical question is then if it is possible to find some kind of "third way" that aligns the institutional theory view and economic theory.

In the first chapter of this volume, Godechot (2019: 89) was cited, saying that the rents that corporations generate are the outcome from a number of mechanisms that limit competition, including regulations, property rights, and transaction costs derived from such market devices. Consequently, as

Boyd (2020: 756) remarks (also cited in Chapter 1), the prices that are set by market actors who recognize and act on the basis of such mechanisms and devices, including not the least corporations, enable transactions and push down transaction costs so that markets can be developed and established over time. Economists are thus mistaken in believing that markets precede prices and the market actors; markets are on the contrary the product of institutional conditions that are historically complex and difficult to disentangle *ex post*, and they are rather the *effect* of price-setting activities than the *cause* of such price-setting. In this institutional view, Boyd (2020: 823) says, prices are not simply "pieces of information," but are essentially "objects of struggle" inasmuch as they are embedded in thick institutional conditions. The rule of law as an institutional fact is then not some mere afterthought that are ambiguously related to markets and market formation activities, but law is a social technology (in Reyes's, 2021: 983, formulation) constitutive of markets.

In order to redress this perceived rift between the institutional view of market making and the neoclassical economic theory view, a classic encounter between legal scholars and economists is revisited. The seminal work of Adolf Berle and Gardiner Means, *The Modern Corporation & Private Property* (1934), published in the New Deal era, addressed how the "corporate system" is both the pathway to economic welfare and also at risk to be dominated by specific interests, represented by the emerging managerial class, in turn representing the finance capital-owning class, constituted as a professional class of its own, with its own interests and agenda. Thorstein Veblen, one of the most prominent institutional economists by the turn of the twentieth century, had already addressed this issue in the 1910s (see, e.g., Veblen, 1916), but after the Wall Street crash of 1929, there were more concerns in policy-making quarters regarding whether growing corporations would assist general economic welfare or result in economic inequality and the proletarization of the working population. For Adolf Berle, one of President Roosevelt's entrusted advisors on economic affairs, the corporate system and the market system are both embedded in institutional rules, enshrined by the laws that apply to specific economic activities. Furthermore, economic growth and the economic welfare that the corporate system generates is "almost entirely" the result of corporations' "internal capital accumulation," Berle (1962: 440) adds. That is, the corporate entity is the single most important economic entity in the market economy, the type of economy that both institutionalists and neoclassicists agree remains in the superior market system from an efficiency perspective (albeit the question what type of efficiency measure that should be prioritized remains debated). This superior, potentially even unsurpassable efficiency is accomplished on the basis of "the most active, decisive, and determinative of all capital funds," what

Berle (1962: 440) refers to as "risk capital" being managed by "competent men"—"the corporate managers in fact" (Berle, 1962: 440).[1]

While Berle's work published with Gardiner Means in the 1930s has been consistently read as an argument against unbridled managerial authority (and by implication, for some commentators, at least in principle, supporting the shareholder value governance model advocated by agency theorists in the 1970s and thereafter), Berle (1962) argues that the corporate system is premised on the work of competent mangers who have the capacity to use business judgment, not to "rove the market seeking the highest profit or the most useful allocation available on the economic scene," but to optimize the long-term value, and not the least survival of the corporate entity. Importantly, Berle (1962: 442) proposes that this managerial control of the corporation is "scarcely in accord with the full free-market theory of capital allocation." In the end, Berle formulates a praise of the "American industrial system," but without overstating the role of the market as being the sole basis for the accomplishment to raise economic welfare to unprecedented levels:

> The American industrial system, under guidance and control, has done more for more people, has made possible a higher standard of living for the vast majority of a huge population in a huge country, has preserved more liberty for individual self-development, and now affords more tools (however unused or badly used) from which a good society can be forged so far as economics can do so, than any system in recorded history. It is eons from perfection.
>
> (Berle, 1962: 437)

For Berle, the corporate entity is "not simply a collection of individual freedoms," but is more accurately portrayed as an institution "born out of relations of power," Gane (2023: 77) proposes. At the same time as the corporate entity has extraordinary economic power, not the least on the basis of its historical track record to consistently reduce transaction costs as part of internal team-production activities, coordinated within a hierarchical structure, its legitimacy is closely bound up with its capacity to both generate economic welfare and to comply with the various institutional rules that pertain to its activities (Gane, 2023: 77).

1 As late as 1962, it did not occur to Berle that managers would also be female, which explains the sexism in this quote. In the 1960s and thereafter, the women's "liberation" movement would render claims of this kind antiquated, but still to this date, men are consistently overrepresented in senior managerial positions in major corporations (see, e.g., Snellman and Solal, 2023; Rivera and Tilcsik, 2016; Ridgeway et al., 2009; Philips, 2005).

New economic doctrines in the 1970s

In the 1970s, the institutional view of the corporate entity was discounted as it was associated with the Keynesian economic doctrine that lost some of its credibility in the 1970s' economic recession, characterized by stagflation (reduced economic growth in combination with persistent inflation). For the new generation of economists advocating a supply-side view of the economic system, economic incentives and not institutional rules regulated economic affairs: "It was no longer the mass purchasing power of well-paid workers that assured economic growth and stability; supply-side factors did that. Business ingenuity and innovation produced wealth and distributed it through job creation," Reddy (2023: 1424) writes. "In the supply-side view," Reddy (2023: 1426) continues, "employers were 'job creators,' and workers could not survive without them." The new supply-side economics doctrine thus suggested that employment was "a public service," rather than a site of "political and economic subjugation" (Reddy, 2023: 1426). This new doctrine also affected policy making and economic policy implementation activities. In 1982, all Keynesian economists "[w]ere abruptly fired from the World Bank and the International Monetary Fund" to be replaced by economists "with supply-side views" (Reddy, 2023: 1423).

Despite a new doctrinal era beginning, there were still mainstream and pro-market economists such as Harold Demsetz who honoured the thinking that legal scholars such as Adolf Berle represented. For Demsetz (1988), the new economic theory, which he was part of, tends to overstate economic mechanisms and devices, such as the highly praised price system and transaction costs, at the expense of other legal-political conditions and devices:

> The role of transaction costs in explaining the manner in which organizations responds to these problems [corporate decisions] is like the role of gravity in explaining chemical reaction; gravity influences chemical reactions, but seldom is it the key variable whose behavior importantly explains the variations in the reactions observed.
>
> (Demsetz, 1988: 151)

More importantly, in Demsetz's (1983: 377) account, the new breed of economists make the category mistake to "confuse the firm of economic theory with its real-world namesake." For Demsetz (1983: 377), the "chief mission of neoclassical economics" is to understand how the price system "coordinates the use of resources" on an aggregated level, not to "understand the inner workings of the real firm," which is part of the jurisdictional authority of management scholars, including not the least accounting researchers. That is, it is a complicated epistemological leap to extrapolate from some macroeconomic model that pertains to the price system how executive decisions should be conducted in corporate entities that are part of the market examined on the basis of such theoretical terms, Demsetz (1983) proposes. This fallacy has resulted in an unjustifiably negative view of the corporate entity among economists, Demsetz argued already in the late 1960s, years prior to the formulation of agency theory and its much-debated shareholder value governance model:

> To say that private enterprise is inefficient because indivisibilities and imperfect knowledge are part of life, or because people are susceptible to the human weaknesses subsumed in the term moral hazards, or because marketing commodity-options is not costless, or because persons are risk-averse, is to say little more than that the competitive equilibrium would be different if these were not the facts of life. But, if they are the facts of life, if, that is, they cannot be erased from life at zero cost, then truly efficient institutions will yield different long-run equilibrium conditions than those now used to describe the ideal norm.
>
> (Demsetz, 1969: 19)

Therefore, similar to Berle in the 1930s and in the 1960s, by the end of his career, Demsetz argues that rather than idealizing the market system, economists and other scholars should address and examine what Demsetz (1969: 20) refers to as "the basic problem facing public and private policy," namely how to design the "institutional arrangements" that provide incentives to "encourage experimentation (including the development of new products, new knowledge, new reputations, and new ways of organizing activities)," but without "overly insulating these experiments from the ultimate test of survival." Similar to Berle (1962: 437), who claimed that the "American industrial system" had many benefits, yet being "eons from perfection," Demsetz (1969) calls for an equally pragmatic view of the corporate entity:

> No known institutional arrangement can simultaneously maximize the degree to which each of these [efficiency] objectives is achieved. A difficult-to-achieve balance is sought between the returns that can be earned by additional experimentation, by giving directional guidance to investment in experimentation, and by reducing the cost of producing goods through the use of existing knowledge. The concepts of perfect competition and Pareto optimality simply are unable at present to give much help in achieving this balance.
>
> (Demsetz, 1969: 20)

Demsetz (1969) thus grants some analytical integrity to the corporate entity more than most other free-market theory economists would possibly care to do. It is not the market that makes corporations, or that serves to optimize the use of their resources, but a corporate entity is the elementary analytical unit that renders markets both functional and efficient in day-to-day activities. From Berle (1962, 1963) and Demsetz (1969, 1983, 1988), we learn that an institutional view of markets does not necessarily prioritize corporate efficiency or market efficiency goals, but that an institutional view, which deals with the corporate entity in a real-life economic setting, considers a broader set of conditions, and regards efficiency as a condition that can be achieved, but only after other features have been examined. For scholars such as Berle and Demsetz, the real-world economy is something different from the highly schematic and idealized models that economists tend to develop and to work with as part of their pursuit to understand the complexities and intricacies of the market system and the economy at large (see, e.g., Hirschman, 2021). To confuse the map and the territory is an elementary cognitive fallacy, and in Berle and Demsetz's views, it is more rewarding to appreciate what the corporate system has accomplished to date, rather than to seek to identify every single source of suboptimal allocation of resources, as the wider view, and the wider view only, enables an understanding of the corporate and market systems and their institutional embedding.

In theoretical terms, this means that both the legal-institutionalist and the neoclassical views of the corporate entity can be aligned by the question of how economic and social welfare are to be optimized on the basis of available resources and mechanisms. Furthermore, to address a more contemporary governance issue, under this description, the question "Do companies have social responsibilities?" is vacuous as the corporate entity is already from its inception a socio-legal creation, and any such creations do have, by their very legal constitution (which in turn is derived from social norms and ethical and moral beliefs), social rights and responsibilities (as to obey by the law, etc.). The corporate entity is necessarily a piece of legal fiction (as agency theorists remark), but such legal fiction is prevalent in the legal-institutional order and the governance practices that are premised on legislation, and the legal status of the corporate entity does not in any way undermine its institutional embedding—its embedded autonomy.

Furthermore, all advanced economies are premised on sapience, higher-order cognition that includes the intelligible use of contentful concepts that express thoughts and ideas that are abstract to a varying degree (Brandom, 1994), and such contentful concepts also include legal fiction terms. This means that it is virtually impossible to fully understand an advanced economic system in the absence of contentful concepts that have the capacity to both communicate ideas that pertain to economic affairs but that also are the vehicle of thought that expresses new economic ideas, including economic objectives, goals, etc. Thus, Berle and Demsetz call for economic theories that recognize accomplishments made in the economy and not only compare such achievements with some ideal theory model, is consistent with the legal-institutional theory that this volume has examined and has applied to ground the patent system in a meta-theoretical model that apprehends practical economic affairs, such as innovation activities and, on the aggregated level, innovation management practices. There are no legal rules on the one hand, and economic affairs on the other, but these activities are entangled in ways that are fully recognized by the legal-institutional framework.

Summary and conclusion

Burk and Lemley (2003) recognize the duality of the patent system and the legislation and regulatory rules and principles that it rests on, on the one hand plausibly one of the most significant governance tools available, while on the other hand being only indirectly or even weakly connected to incentives to innovate. "Patent law is our primary policy tool to promote innovation, encourage the development of new technologies, and increase the fund of human knowledge," Burk and Lemley (2003: 1576) write. In order to accomplish such goals, the patent system is premised on "a general set of legal rules" that govern a wide variety of activities. At the same time, there is "no simple or universal correlation" between the availability of patents and "the incentive to innovate," Burk and Lemley (2003: 1589) conclude. Stiglitz (2008) expresses this idea accordingly:

> Our innovation system rests on foundations of basic research, and most basic research occurs within academia and government-sponsored research laboratories. Monetary returns are only a small part of what motivates these researchers. Thus, the basic framework of what induces people to engage in research is really not reflected in the intellectual property regime.
>
> (Stiglitz, 2008: 1697)

Also Ohlhausen (2016: 127) stresses the dissociation of R&D expenditure, innovation, and patents, but points at the consistency in the evidence that patents and innovations do correlate, at least in developed countries that host advanced economies. At the same time, Ohlhausen (2016: 125) continues, "[e]ven if studies consistently revealed a statistically significant correlation between patents and innovation, that observation would not necessarily mean that patents and innovation have any causal relationship." Instead, it is plausible that the patent system serves an intermediary role when venture capital investors decide how to allocate their funds, as indicated in a 2008 survey that found that 76% of venture-backed start-up managers reported that "venture-capital investors consider patents important to funding decisions" (Ohlhausen, 2016: 140). Despite being concerned with what Ohlhausen (2016: 150) regards as a climate of "intellectual property right skepticism," she argues that the "US innovation experience," based on a combination of a variety of legal and regulatory tools and devices such as patent law, still provides "a powerful argument against abandoning or compromising the patent system." The conclusion is thus that the patent system does play a role in supporting innovation output, but the causal links between laws and regulatory rules and innovation output may be more complex than the proxies used by econometricians to calculate the economic effects of legal reforms suggests:[2]

> In crafting the most beneficial patent policy, we should not overlook or minimize the strong theoretical and evidentiary justifications for property rights in technology, although this does not mean that granting ever-stronger patent protection will inevitably lead to ever-greater innovation.
> (Ohlhausen, 2016: 104)

In fact, this difficulty to establish robust linear connections between, e.g., patent law and innovation output is not a specific feature of advanced economies. The economic historian Richard J. Sullivan disputes the hypothesis that the English industrial revolution was propelled exclusively by more strict patent legislation. First, the increased growth of productivity accounts for "approximately 30 percent of increased growth of total output during the English industrial revolution," Sullivan (1990: 349) suggests, and second, during the early period of the industrial revolution (1760–1780), there was considerable inventive activity in sectors "not normally associated with advancing technology" in the English economy (Sullivan, 1990: 350). Third, many inventions being implemented and spread are not patentable, as in the case of farming, wherein many "biological and organizational advances" that increased productivity were neither patentable nor attempted to be patented (Sullivan, 1990: 350). Based on these empirical observations, Sullivan (1990: 358–359) proposes that the widespread increase in patenting after 1760, which many economic historians have treated as the primus motor of increased economic activity and growth in the period, is in fact

2 For instance, Katz and Veel (2013) argue that intellectual property right (IPR) legislation shapes antitrust law, and that there is a difference between the US and the European Union in how the protection of IPRs and market competition is preserved on the basis of the balancing of the two types of legislation. On the one hand, "conventional wisdom holds that EU competition law is far more willing than US antitrust law to override firms' unilateral decisions whether to license their intellectual property rights (IPRs) in the interest of promoting competition," Katz and Veel (2013: 140) write; on the other hand, decisions made by, e.g., the European Union "[e]xemplify a more activist antitrust approach" (Katz and Vee, 2013: 151–152). IPR and antitrust legislations thus appear to be complementary when policy makers wish to both create incentives to innovate and to preserve market competition.

dependent on broader institutional conditions rather than being traceable to some specific and discrete legal reform: "Perceived profits from invention increased over the entire spectrum of industry in a relatively short period of time . . . suggests the work of a macroeconomic 'trigger' mechanism," Sullivan (1990: 358–359) contends:

> By the early eighteenth century England had a number of characteristics in place (a market-oriented economy, a good standard of living, a significant mercantile class) that would have been required for accelerating invention. Several forces came together in the mid-eighteenth century to trigger an acceleration of invention. Important elements of these forces include an increasing willingness consciously to search for solutions to technical problems and an upturn in the growth of population.
>
> (Sullivan, 1990: 361)

This view is consistent with the legal institutionalism view that has served to structure the analysis of the legal literature on patents and other intellectual property rights inasmuch as it points at broader changes and more deep-seated shifts in society. "Intellectual Property Rights are important," Stiglitz (2008: 1711) writes, "but the importance of IPR has been exaggerated, as they form only one part of our innovation system. IPR should be seen as part of a portfolio of instruments." Patent law certainly played a key role in protecting would-be innovators' rights and investments in R&D, but such legal reforms matter only when the surrounding society has the capacity to recognize the value of innovation activities. For instance, as Sullivan (1990: 359) notices, writers active in the seventeenth century, in the earliest period of the emerging industrial revolution, saw invention as "bestowed by providence," as an act of God, but by the end of the eighteenth century, many writers regard invention as what arises "from human effort" (Sullivan, 1990: 359). Furthermore, political reforms and increased trade, following, *inter alia*, the end of religious wars ravaging Europe until the end of the seventeenth century, created a new social order and an economic system wherein patent legislation both made sense and mattered, further lubricating the wheels of commerce that was under quick development and expansion (Braudel, 1992), further evolving into the colonial economies of the eighteenth and nineteenth centuries (Stern, 2023), and what was increasingly referred to as globalization by the end of the twentieth century and in the new millennium.

Under all conditions, as Lemley (2016b: 38) says, R&D "shouldn't translate immediately into patents," as R&D expenditure may only generate inventions "some years later," patent applications "later still," and issued patents "several years later after that." "Perhaps," Lemley (2016b: 40) muses, "patents are like lottery tickets, obtained for inventions that are mostly worthless in the hopes of hitting it big with an invention that does take off." From a legal institutionalism perspective, economic and social welfare should preferably not be considered in entirely stochastic terms, but is on the contrary what is generated on the basis of conscious and intentionally rational concerted action to promote an enterprising spirit at the same time as liberal freedoms are preserved and protected. Given the complexity of the patent system and its intricate relationship to actual, hands-on and material innovations, a legal institutionalism perspective is arguably of great analytical value when seeking to understand the relations between legal rights and legal reforms on the one hand, and economic and social welfare on the other, and with new innovation acting as the intermediary factor between law as it is written and enforced and the socio-economic changes that it purportedly supports. In this view, law matters, but it matters in ways that may be considerably more complex than the first glance or the intuitive hunch may suggest.

Bibliography

Abbott, Kenneth W., and Snidal, Duncan, (2000), Hard and soft law in international governance, *International Organization*, 54(3): 421–456.

Abi-Rached, Joelle M., and Rose, Nikolas, (2010), The birth of the neuromolecular gaze, *History of the Human Sciences*, 23(1): 11–36.

Abrams, David S., and Wagner, R. Polk, (2013), Poisoning the next apple: The America invents act and individual inventors, *Stanford Law Review*, 65(3): 517–564.

Aghion, Philippe, and Bolton, Patrick, (1992), An incomplete contracts approach to financial contracting, *Review of Economic Studies*, 59(3): 473–494.

Aguilera, Ruth V., Aragón-Correa, J. Alberto, and Marano, Valentina, (2022), Rethinking corporate power to tackle grand societal challenges: Lessons from political philosophy, *Academy of Management Review*, 47(4): 637–645.

Akerlof, George A., and Shiller, Robert J., (2009), *Animal spirits: How human psychology drives the economy, and why it matters for global capitalism*, Princeton & London: Princeton University Press.

Allison, John R., and Ouellette, Lisa Larrimore, (2016), How courts adjudicate patent definiteness and disclosure, *Duke Law Journal*, 65(4): 609–696.

Almeling, Rene, (2011), *Sex cells: The medical market for eggs and sperm*, Berkeley, Los Angeles & London: University of California Press.

Alp, Aysun, (2013), Structural shifts in credit rating standards, *The Journal of Finance*, 68(6): 2435–2470.

Alstadsæter, Annette, Johannesen, Niels, and Zucman, Gabriel, (2019), Tax evasion and inequality, *American Economic Review*, 109(6): 2073–2103.

Anderson, J. Jonas, (2011), Secret inventions, *Berkeley Technology Law Journal*, 26(2): 917–978.

Anscombe, G. E. M., ([1957] 1976), *Intention*, 2nd ed., Oxford: Blackwell.

Arend, Richard J., (2020), On the irony of being certain on how to deal with uncertainty, *Academy of Management Review*, 45(3): 702–704.

Arend, Richard J., (2022), We are crisis: Runtime errors in programmatic theory, *Academy of Management Review*, 47(2): 331–333.

Asay, Clark D., (2017), Patenting elasticities, *Southern California Law Review*, 91(1): 1–64.

Autor, David, Dorn, David, Katz, Lawrence F., Patterson, Christina, and Van Reenen, John, (2017), Concentrating on the fall of the labor share, *American Economic Review*, 107(5): 180–185.

Awrey, Dan, (2013), Toward a supply-side theory of financial innovation, *Journal of Comparative Economics*, 41(2): 401–419.

Ayres, Ian, and Gertner, Robert, (1989), Filling gaps in incomplete contracts: An economic theory of default rules, *Yale Law Journal*, 99(1): 87–130.

Baccaro, Lucio, Blyth, Mark, and Pontusson, Jonas, (2022), Introduction. Rethinking comparative capitalism, in Baccaro, Lucio, Blyth, Mark, and Pontusson, Jonas, (eds.) *Diminishing returns: The new politics of growth and stagnation*, New York & Oxford: Oxford University Press, pp. 1–50.

Bagchi, Aditi, (2019), Interpreting contracts in regulatory state, *University of San Francisco Law Review*, 54(1): 35–86.

Barnett, Jonathan M., (2021), The great patent grab, in Haber, Stephen H., and Lamoreaux, Naomi R., (eds.) *The battle over patents: History and politics of innovation*, New York & Oxford: Oxford University Press, pp. 208–277.

Barron, Anne, (2012), Kant, copyright and communicative freedom, *Law and Philosophy*, 31(1): 1–48.

Baumol, William J., (2002), *The free-market innovation machine: Analyzing the growth miracle of capitalism*, Princeton: Princeton University Press.

Beckert, Jens, (2022), Durable wealth: Institutions, mechanisms, and practices of wealth perpetuation, *Annual Review of Sociology*, 48: 233–255.

Beckett, Katherine, and Western, Bruce, (2001), Governing social marginality: Welfare, incarceration, and the transformation of state policy, *Punishment & Society*, 3(1): 43–59.

Bekiempis, Victoria, (2023), Sam Bankman-Fried found guilty of defrauding FTX customers out of billions, *The Guardian*, November 3, 2023, (URL: https://www.theguardian.com/business/2023/nov/02/sam-bankman-guilty-ftx-alameda) Accessed Nov. 7, 2023.

Benigno, Gianluca, and Fornaro, Luca, (2017), Stagnation traps, *Review of Economic Studies*, 85(3): 1425–1470.

Berg, Tobias, Fuster, Andreas, and Puri, Manju, (2022), FinTech lending, *Annual Review of Financial Economics*, 14: 187–207.

Berle, Adolf A., (1931), Corporate powers as powers in trust, *Harvard Law Review*, 44(7): 1049–1074.

Berle, Adolf A., (1932), For whom corporate managers are trustees: A note, *Harvard Law Review*, 45(8): 1365–1372.

Berle, Adolf A., (1962), Modern functions of the corporate system, *Columbia Law Review*, 62: 433–449.

Berle, Adolf A., (1963), *The American economic republic*, New York: Harcourt, Brace & World.

Berle, Adolf A., and Means, Gardiner C., ([1934] 1991), *The modern corporation & private property*, New Brunswick: Transaction Publishers.

Berlin, Isaiah, (1958), *Two concepts of liberty: An inaugural lecture, delivered before the University of Oxford on 31 October 1958*, Oxford: Clarendon Press.

Berman, Elizabeth Popp, (2008), Why did universities start patenting: Institution-building and the road to the Bayh-Dohl act, *Social Studies of Science*, 38(6): 835–871.

Berman, Elizabeth Popp, (2012), *Creating the market university: How academic science became an economic engine*, Princeton & Oxford: Princeton University Press.

Berman, Sheri, (2021), The causes of populism in the West, *Annual Review of Political Science*, 24: 71–88.

Berman, Elizabeth Popp, and Pagnucco, Nicholas, (2010), Economic ideas and the political process: Debating tax cuts in the U.S. House of Representatives, 1962–1981, *Politics and Society*, 38(3): 347–372.

Bernanke, Ben S., (2023), Nobel lecture: Banking, credit, and economic fluctuations, *American Economic Review*, 113(5): 1143–1169.

Bernstein, Lisa, (1992), Opting out of the legal system: Extralegal contractual relations in the diamond industry, *Journal of Legal Studies*, 21(1): 115–157.

Bernstein, Shai, (2015), Does going public affect innovation? *Journal of Finance*, 70(4): 1365–1403.

Besedovsky, Natalia, (2018), Financialization as calculative practice: The rise of structured finance and the cultural and calculative transformation of credit rating agencies, *Socio-Economic Review*, 16(1): 61–84.

Best, Jacqueline, (2022), Uncomfortable knowledge in central banking: Economic expertise confronts the visibility dilemma, *Economy and Society*, 51(4): 559–583.

Beunza, Daniel, and Stark, David, (2004), Tools of the trade: The socio-technology of arbitrage in a Wall Street trading room, *Industrial and Corporate Change*, 13(2): 369–400.

Bhaskarabhatla, Ajay, and Hegde, Deepak, (2014), An organizational perspective on patenting and open innovation, *Organization Science*, 25(6): 1744–1763.

Biagioli, Mario, (1999), Aporias of scientific authorship: Credit and responsibility in contemporary medicine, in Biagioli, Mario, (ed.) *The science studies reader*, London & New York: Routledge, pp. 12–30.

Biagioli, Mario, (2022), Ghosts, brands, and influencers: Emergent trends in scientific authorship, *Social Studies of Science*, 52(3): 463–487.

Biagioli, Mario, and Pottage, Alain, (2021), Patenting personalized medicine: Molecules, information, and the body, *Osiris*, 36(1): 221–240.

Birch, Kean, (2017), Rethinking value in the bio-economy: Finance, assetization, and the management of value, *Science, Technology, & Human Values*, 42(3): 460–490.

Blix, Mårten, and Jordahl, Henrik, (2020), *Privatizing welfare services: Lessons from the Swedish experiment*, Oxford & New York: Oxford University Press.

Bloomberg News, FTX Group Bankruptcy Filing Shows Cash Balance of $1.24 Billion, November 21, 2022, (URL: https://www.bloomberg.com/news/articles/2022-11-22/ftx-group-bankruptcy-filing-shows-cash-balance-of-1-24-billion) Accessed Dec. 1, 2022.

Blyth, Mark, (2002), *Great Transformations: Economic ideas and institutional change in the twentieth century*, New York: Cambridge University Press.

Bourgeron, Théo, and Geiger, Susi, (2022), (De-)assetizing pharmaceutical patents: Patent contestations behind a blockbuster drug, *Economy and Society*, 51(1): 23–45.

Boyd, William, (2020), Ways of price making and the challenge of market governance in U.S. energy law, *Minnesota Law Review*, 105(2): 739–830.

Boyle, James, (2003), The second enclosure movement and the construction of the public domain, *Law and Contemporary Problems*, 66(1/2): 33–74.

Brandom, Robert, (1994), *Making it explicit: Reasoning, representing, and discursive commitment*, Cambridge: Harvard University Press.

Brandom, Robert, (2007), Inferentialism and some of its challenges, *Philosophy and Phenomenological Research*, 74(3): 651–676.

Brandom, Robert, (2019), *A spirit of trust: A reading of Hegel's Phenomenology*, Cambridge: Belknap Press.

Branham, Alexander, Soroka, Stuart N. and Wlezien, Christopher, C. (2017), When do the rich win? *Political Science Quarterly*, 132(1): 43–62.

Braudel, Fernand, (1992), *The wheels of commerce: Civilization & capitalism 15th–18th century*, Vol. 2, Berkeley & Los Angeles: The University of California Press.

Brown, Darryl K., (2014), The perverse effects of efficiency in criminal process, *Virginia Law Review*, 100(1): 183–223.

Brummer, Chris, and Yadav, Yesha, (2019), Fintech and the innovation trilemma, *Georgetown Law Journal*, 107: 235–307.
Bud, Robert, (1983), *The uses of life: A history of biotechnology*, Cambridge: Cambridge University Press.
Budish, Eric, Roin, Benjamin N., and Williams, Heidi, (2015), Do firms underinvest in long-term research? Evidence from cancer clinical trials, *American Economic Review*, 105(7): 2044–2085.
Burk, Dan L., (2016), On the sociology of patenting, *Minnesota Law Review*, 101(2): 421–452.
Burk, Dan L., and Lemley, Mark A., (2003), Policy levers in patent law, *Virginia Law Review*, 89(7): 1575–1696.
Burke, Peter, (1994), *Venice and Amsterdam: A study of seventeenth-century elites*, 2nd ed., Oxford: Polity Press.
Büthe, Tim, and Mattli, Walter, (2011), *The new global rulers: The privatization of regulation in the world economy*, Princeton: Princeton University Press.
Campbell, John L., and Pedersen, Ove K., (2015), Policy ideas, knowledge regimes and comparative political economy, *Socio-Economic Review*, 13(4): 679–701.
Carnes, Nicholas, (2013), *White-collar government: The hidden role of class in economic policy making*, Chicago & London: The University of Chicago Press.
Carolan, Michael S., (2010), The mutability of biotechnology patents: From unwieldy products of nature to independent 'objects/s', *Theory, Culture & Society*, 27(1): 110–129.
Carreyrou, John, (2018), *Bad blood: Secrets and lies in a silicon valley startup*, New York: Knopf.
Case, Anne, and Deaton, Angus, (2020), *Deaths of despair and the future of capitalism*, Princeton: Princeton University Press.
Case, Anne, and Deaton, Angus, (2021), The great divide: Education, despair, and death, *Annual Review of Economics*, 14: 1–21.
Casey, Anthony J., and Macey, Joshua C., (2020), The Hertz maneuver (and the limits of bankruptcy law), *University of Chicago Law Review Online*: 1–22.
Cech, Erin, Rubineau, Brian, Silbey, Susan, and Seron, Caroll, (2011), Professional role confidence and gendered persistence in engineering, *American Sociological Review*, 76(5): 641–666.
Cherry, Mark J., (2005), *Kidney for sale by owner: Transplantation and the market*, Washington: Georgetown University Press.
Chien, Colleen V., (2016), Contextualizing patent disclosure, *Vanderbilt Law Review*, 69(6): 1849–1892.
Chwieroth, Jeffrey M., and Walter, Andrew, (2022), Financialization, wealth and the changing political aftermaths of banking crises, *Socio-Economic Review*, 20(1): 55–84.
Claessens, Stijn, Feijen, Erik, and Laeven, Luc, (2008), Political connections and preferential access to finance: The role of campaign contributions, *Journal of Financial Economics*, 88(3): 554–580.
Clark, Robert C., (1989), Contracts, elites, and traditions in the making of corporate law, *Columbia Law Review*, 89(7): 1703–1747.
Coen, David, Katsaitis, Alexander, and Vannoni, Matia, (2021), *Business lobbying in the European union*, Oxford & New York: Oxford University Press.
Cohen, Felix S., (1935), Transcendental nonsense and the functional approach, *Columbia Law Review*, 35(6): 809–849.
Cohen, Lauren, Gurun, Umit G., and Kominers, Scott Duke, (2019), Patent trolls: Evidence from targeted firms, *Management Science*, 65(12): 5461–5486.

Cohen, Michael D., March, James G., and Olsen, Johan P., (1972), A garbage can model of organizational choice, *Administrative Science Quarterly*, 17: 1–25.
Cole, Simon A., and Bertenthal, Alyse, (2017), Science, technology, society, and law, *Annual Review of Law and Social Science*, 13: 351–371.
Collier, Ruth Berins, Dubal, V. B., and Carter, Christopher, (2018), Disrupting regulation, regulation disruption: The politics of Uber in the United States, *Perspectives on Politics*, 16(4): 919–937.
Colyvas, Jeannette A., and Powell, Walter W., (2007), From vulnerable to venerated: The institutionalization of academic entrepreneurship in the life sciences, *Research in the Sociology of Organizations*, 25: 219–259.
Cong, Lin William, and He, Zhiguo, (2019), Blockchain disruption and smart contracts, *Review of Financial Studies*, 32: 1754–1797.
Conley, Diane, (1990), Author, user, scholar, theif: Fair use and unpublished works, *Cardozo Arts & Entertainment Law Journal*, 9(1): 15–60.
Cooter, Robert, (1998), Expressive law and economics, *Journal of Legal Studies*, 27(S2): 585–607.
Cordelli, Chiara, (2020), *The privatized state*, Princeton: Princeton University Press.
Cotropia, Christopher A., (2012), What is the 'invention'? *William and Mary Law Review*, 53(6): 1855–1914.
Cotropia, Christopher A., Kesan, Jay P., and Schwartz, David L., (2014), Unpacking patent assertion entities (PAEs), *Minnesota Law Review*, 99(2): 649–704.
Covarrubias, Matias, Gutiérrez, Germán, and Philippon, Thomas, (2020), From good to bad concentration? US industries over the past 30 years, *NBER Macroeconomics Annual*, 34(1): 1–46.
Craig, Carys J., (2002), Locke, labour and limiting the author's right: Warning against Lockean approach to copyright law, *Queen's Law Journal*, 28(1): 1–60.
Cramer, Tobias, (2015), Building the 'world's pharmacy': The rise of the German pharmaceutical industry, 1871–1914, *Business History Review*, 89(1): 43–73.
Crouch, Colin, (2011), *The strange non-death of neo-liberalism*, Cambridge: Polity Press.
Cunningham, Colleen, Ederer, Florian, and Ma, Song, (2021), Killer acquisitions, *Journal of Political Economy*, 129(3): 649–702.
Dahl, Robert, (1977), On removing certain impediments to democracy in the United States, *Political Science Quarterly*, 92(1): 1–20.
Davidson, Donald, (1963), Actions, reasons, and causes, *The Journal of Philosophy*, 60(23): 685–700.
De Araujo, M., (2009), Hugo Grotius, contractualism, and the concept of private property: An institutionalist interpretation, *History of Philosophy Quarterly*, 26(4): 353–371.
De Figueiredo, Rui J. Jr, and Edwards, Geoff, (2007), Does private money buy public policy? Campaign contributions and regulatory outcomes in telecommunications, *Journal of Economics & Management Strategy*, 16(3): 547–576.
De Fontenay, Elisabeth, (2017), The deregulation of private capital and the decline of the public company, *Hastings Law Journal*, 68(3): 445–502.
de Goede, M., (2005), *Virtue, fortune, and faith: A genealogy of finance*, Minneapolis & London: Minnesota University Press.
de Saussure, Ferdinand, (1959), *Course in general linguistics*, London: Peter Owen.
Deakin, Simon, Gindis, David, Hodgson, Geoffrey M., Huang, Kainan, and Pistor, Katharina, (2017), Legal institutionalism: Capitalism and the constitutive role of law, *Journal of Comparative Economics*, 45(1): 188–200.
Deaton, Angus, (2013), *The great escape: Health, wealth and the origins of inequality*, Princeton: Princeton University Press.

Decker, Ryan A., Haltiwanger, John, Jarmin, Ron S., and Miranda, Javier, (2014), The role of entrepreneurship in US job creation and economic dynamism, *The Journal of Economic Perspectives*, 28(3): 3–24.

Decker, Ryan A., Haltiwanger, John, Jarmin, Ron S., and Miranda, Javier, (2017), Declining dynamism, allocative efficiency, and the productivity slowdown, *American Economic Review*, 107(5): 322–326.

Demaine, Linda J., and Fellmeth, Aaron Xavier, (2002), Reinventing the double helix: A novel and nonobvious reconceptualization of the biotechnology patent, *Stanford Law Review*: 303–462.

Demsetz, Harold, (1969), Information and efficiency: Another viewpoint, *Journal of Law and Economics*, 12(1): 1–22.

Demsetz, Harold, (1983), Structure of ownership and the theory of the firm, *Journal of Law and Economics*, 26: 375.

Demsetz, Harold, (1988), The theory of the firm revisited, *Journal of Law, Economics and Organization*, 4(1): 141–161.

Devlin, Alan, (2010), The misunderstood function of disclosure in patent law, *Harvard Journal of Law & Technology*, 23(2): 401–446.

Dick, Diane Lourde, (2021), Hostile restructurings, *Washington Law Review*, 96(4): 1333–1388.

DiMaggio, Marco, and Yao, Vincent, (2021), Fintech borrowers: Lax screening or cream-skimming? *The Review of Financial Studies*, 34(10): 4565–4618.

DiMaggio, Paul, and Powell, Walter W., (1983), The iron cage revisited: Institutional isomorphism and collective rationality in organizational fields, *American Sociological Review*, 48(2): 147–160.

Dobbin, Frank, and Kalev, Alexandra, (2021), The civil rights revolution at work: What went wrong, *Annual Review of Sociology*, 47: 281–303.

Dobbin, Frank, Schrage, Daniel, and Kalev, Alexandra, (2015), Rage against the iron cage: The varied effects of bureaucratic personnel reforms on diversity, *American Sociological Review*, 80(5): 1014–1044.

Dodd, E. Merrick Jr, (1932), For whom are corporate managers trustees? *Harvard Law Review*, 45(7): 1145–1163.

Drutman, Lee, (2015), *The business of America is lobbying: How corporations became politicized and politics became more corporate*, Oxford: Oxford University Press.

Dworkin, Ronald M., (1975), Hard cases, *Harvard Law Review*, 88: 1057–1109.

Dworkin, Ronald M., (1980), Is wealth a value? *Journal of Legal Studies*, 9(2): 191–226.

Edelman, Lauren B., Fuller, Sally Riggs, and Mara-Drita, Iona, (2001), Diversity rhetoric and the managerialization of law, *American Journal of Sociology*, 106(6): 1589–1641.

Edelman, Lauren B., and Suchman, Mark C., (1997), The legal environment of organizations, *Annual Review of Sociology*, 23: 479–515.

Eichenseht, Kristen E., (2019), Digital Switzerland's, *University of Pennsylvania Law Review*, 167(3): 665–732.

Eisenstein, Elizabeth, (1983), *The printing revolution in early modern Europe*, Cambridge: Cambridge University Press.

Eisenberg, Melvin Aron, (1989), The structures of corporate law, *Columbia Law Review*, 89: 1461–1526.

Eisenberg, Rebecca S., (2007), The role of the FDA in innovation policy, *Michigan Telecommunications and Technology Law Review*, 13: 345–388.

Elias, Norbert, ([1991] 1993), *Mozart: Portrait of a genius*, Trans. by Edmund Jephcott, Cambridge: Polity Press.

Ellias, Jared A., (2023), Bankruptcy law's knowns and unknowns, *Annual Review of Law and Social Science*, 19: 319–335.

Elkin-Koren, Niva, (2005), What contracts cannot do: The limits of private ordering in facilitating a creative commons, *Fordham Law Review*, 74: 375–422.

Elster, Nanette R., (2010), Egg donation for research and reproduction: The compensation conundrum, in Goodwin, Michele Bratcher, (ed.) *Baby markets: Money and the new politics of creating families*, Cambridge & New York: Cambridge University Press, pp. 226–236.

Engelen, Ewald, (2017), Shadow banking after the crisis: The Dutch case, *Theory, Culture & Society*, 34(5–6): 53–75.

Enriquez-Sarano, Louis, (2020), Data-rich and knowledge-poor: How privacy law firms privatized medical data and what to do about it, *Columbia Law Review*, 120(8): 2319–2357.

Evans, Peter, (1995), *Embedded autonomy*, Princeton & London: Princeton University Press.

Feinberg, Joel, (1973), Duty and obligation in the nonideal world, *Journal of Philosophy*, 70(9): 263–275.

Feinman, Jay M., (1990), The significance of contract theory, *University of Cincinnati Law Review*, 58(4): 1283–1318.

Fennell, Lee Anne, and McAdams, Richard H., (2016), The distributive deficit in law and economics, *Minnesota Law Review*, 100(3): 1051–1130.

Fligstein, Neil, (2021), *The banks did it: An anatomy of the financial crisis*, Cambridge & London: Harvard University Press.

Fontaine, Laurence, (2014), *The moral economy: Poverty, credit, and trust in early modern Europe*, New York & Cambridge: Cambridge University Press.

Foucault, Michel, (1980), *Power/knowledge*, New York: Harvester Wheatsheaf.

Fourcade, Marion, Ollion, Etienne, and Algan, Yann, (2015), The superiority of economists, *The Journal of Economic Perspectives*, 29(1): 89–113.

Freilich, Janet, (2019), Prophetic patents, *University of California, Davis Law Review*, 53: 663–731.

Freilich, Janet, (2020), The replicability crisis in patent law, *Indiana Law Journal*, 95(2): 431–484.

Fromer, Jeanne C., (2016), Dynamic patent disclosure, *Vanderbilt Law Review*, 69(6): 1715–1738.

Funke, Manuel, Schularick, Moritz, and Trebesch, Christoph, (2023), Populist leaders and the economy, *American Economic Review*, 113(12): 3249–3288.

Gane, Nicholas, (2023), Neoliberalism and the defence of the corporation, *Theory, Culture & Society*, 40(3): 63–80.

Giere, Ronald N., and Moffatt, Barton, (2003), Distributed cognition: Where the cognitive and the social merge, *Social Studies of Science*, 233: 301–310.

Gilens, Martin, (2005), Inequality and democratic responsiveness, *Public Opinion Quarterly*, 69(5): 778–796.

Gilens, Martin, and Page, Benjamin I., (2014), Testing theories of American politics: Elites, interest groups, and average citizens, *Perspectives on Politics*, 12(3): 564–581.

Gittelman, Michelle, (2016), The revolution re-visited: Clinical and genetics research paradigms and the productivity paradox in drug discovery, *Research Policy*, 45: 1570–1585.

Gittelman, Michelle, and Kogut, Bruce, (2003), Does good science lead to valuable knowledge? Biotechnology firms and the evolutionary logic of citation patterns, *Management Science*, 49(4): 366–382.

Glaeser, Edward L., (2006), Psychology and paternalism, *University of Chicago Law Review*, 73: 133–156.

Glynn, Mary Ann, (2000), When cymbals become symbols: Conflict over organizational isomorphism and organizational names, *Organization Science*, 45: 267–280.

Godechot, Olivier, (2019), *Wages, bonuses and appropriation of profit in the financial industry*, London & New York: Routledge.

Godi, Matteo, (2019), Beyond nudging: Debiasing consumers through mixed framing, *Yale Law Journal*, 126(7): 2034–2086.

Golka, Philipp, (2023), The allure of finance: Social impact investing and the challenges of assetization in financialized capitalism, *Economy and Society*, 52(1): 62–86.

Gorton, Gary, (2018), Financial crises, *Annual Review of Financial Economics*, 15: 43–58.

Granovetter, Mark S., (1973), The strength of weak ties, *American Journal of Sociology*, 78(6): 1360–1380.

Grewal, David Singh, (2014), The laws of capitalism, *Harvard Law Review*, 128(2): 626–668.

Grullon, Gustavo, Larkin, Yelena, and Michaely, Roni, (2019), Are US industries becoming more concentrated? *Review of Finance*, 23(4): 697–743.

Gugliuzza, Paul R., (2016), Early filing and functional claiming, *Boston University Law Review*, 96: 1223–1243.

Haber, Stephen H., and Lamoreaux, Naomi R., (2021), Introduction: The battle over the surplus from innovation, in Haber, Stephen H., and Lamoreaux, Naomi R., (eds.) *The battle over patents: History and politics of innovation*, New York & Oxford: Oxford University Press, pp. 1–26.

Hacker, Jacob S., (2004), Privatizing risk without privatizing the welfare state: The hidden politics of social policy retrenchment in the United States, *American Political Science Review*, 98(2): 243–260.

Hacker, Jacob S., Hertel-Fernandez, Alexander, Pierson, Paul, and Thelen, Kathleen, (2022), The American political economy: Markets, power, and the meta politics of US economic governance, *Annual Review of Political Science*, 25: 197–217.

Hall, Rodney Bruce, and Biersteker, Thomas J. (eds.), (2002), *The emergence of private authority in global governance*, New York & Cambridge: Cambridge University Press.

Hamm, Patrick, King, Lawrence P., and Stuckler, David, (2012), Mass privatization, state capacity, and economic growth in post-communist countries, *American Sociological Review*, 77: 295–324.

Hara, Takuji, (2003), *Innovation in the pharmaceutical industry: The process of drug discovery development*, Cheltenham & Northampton: Edward Elgar.

Hardin, Garrett, (1968), The tragedy of the commons, *Science*, 162: 1343–1348.

Harrington, Brooke, (2016), *Capital without borders: Wealth managers and the one percent*, Cambridge: Harvard University Press.

Haskel, Jonathan, and Westlake, Stian, (2017), *Capitalism without capital: The rise of the intangible economy*, Princeton: Princeton University Press.

Healy, David, (2006), The new medical oikumene, in Petryna, Adriana, Lakoff, Andrew, and Kleinman, Arthur, (eds.) *Global pharmaceuticals: Ethics, markets, practices*, Durham & London: Duke University Press, pp. 61–84.

Helmore, Edward, (2022), FTX founder Sam Bankman-Fried says he 'screwed up' but didn't commit fraud, *The Guardian*, December 1, 2022, (URL: https://www.theguardian.com/technology/2022/nov/30/ftx-sam-bankman-fried-i-screwed-up) Accessed Dec. 1, 2022.

Hertel-Fernandez, Alexander, (2014), Who passes business's 'model bills'? Policy capacity and corporate influence in US state politics, *Perspectives on Politics*, 12(3): 582–602.

Hertel-Fernandez, Alexander, (2019), *State capture: How conservative activists, big businesses, and wealthy donors reshaped the American states–and the nation*, New York: Oxford University Press.
Hinton, Elizabeth, (2016), *From the war on poverty to the war on crime: The making of mass incarceration in America*, Cambridge: Harvard University Press.
Hirschman, Daniel, (2021), Rediscovering the 1%: Knowledge infrastructures and the stylized facts of inequality, *American Journal of Sociology*, 27(3): 739–778.
Hirsh, C. Elizabeth, (2009), The strength of weak enforcement: The impact of discrimination charges, legal environments, and organizational conditions on workplace segregation, *American Sociological Review*, 74(2): 245–271.
Hockett, Robert C., and Omarova, Saule T., (2016), Special, vestigial, or visionary: What bank regulation tell us about the corporation—*and vice versa*, *Seattle University Law Review*, 39(2): 453–500.
Hughes, Sally Smith, (2001), Making dollars out of DNA: The first major patent in biotechnology and the commercialization of molecular biology, 1974–1980, *Isis*, 92(3): 541–575.
Ikemoto, Lisa C., (2009), Eggs as capital: Human egg procurement in the fertility industry and the stem cell research enterprise, *Signs*, 34(4): 763–781.
Ingram, Paul, Vue, Lori Qingyuan, and Rao, Hayagreeva, (2010), Trouble in store. Probes, protests, and store openings by Wal-Mart, 1988–2007, *American Journal of Sociology*, 116(1): 53–92.
Jolls, Christine, Sunstein, Cass R., and Thaler, Richard R., (1998), A behavioral approach to law and economics, *Stanford Law Review*, 50: 1471–1550.
Jones, Owen, (2011), *Chavs: The demonization of the working class*, London: Verso.
Judge, Brian, (2021), The impossibility of a Rawlsian liberal, *Cambridge Journal of Economics*, 45(1): 195–208.
Kadens, Emily, (2019), Cheating pays, *Columbia Law Review*, 119(2): 527–589.
Kahan, Marcel, and Kamar, Ehud, (2002), The myth of state competition in corporate law, *Stanford Law Review*, 55(3): 679–749.
Katz, Ariel, and Veel, Paul-Erik, (2013), Beyond refusal to deal: Cross-Atlantic view of copyright, competition, and innovation policies, *Antitrust Law Journal*, 79(1): 139–184.
Katz, Avery, (1996), Taking private ordering seriously, *University of Pennsylvania Law Review*, 144: 1745–1763.
Kelly, Erin, and Dobbin, Frank, (1999), Civil rights law at work: Sex discrimination and the rise of maternity leave policies, *American Journal of Sociology*, 105(2): 455–492.
Kertum, Samuel, and Lerner, Josh, (2000), Assessing the contribution of venture capital to innovation, *RAND Journal of Economics*, 31: 674–692.
Khan, Lina M., (2020), The end of antitrust history revisited, *Harvard Law Review*, 133(5): 1655–1683.
Kiebzak, Stephen, Rafert, Greg, and Tucker, Catherine E., (2016), The effect of patent litigation and patent assertion entities on entrepreneurial activity, *Research Policy*, 45(1): 218–231.
Kitch, Edmund W., (1977), The nature and function of the patent system, *Journal of Law and Economics*, 20(2): 265–290.
Kleinman, Daniel Lee, and Vallas, Steven P., (2001), Science, capitalism, and the rise of the 'knowledge worker': The changing structure of knowledge production in the United States, *Theory and Society*, 30(4): 451–492.
Klick, Jonathan, and Mitchell, Gregory, (2006), Government regulation of irrationality: Moral and cognitive hazards, *Minnesota Law Review*, 90: 1620–1664.

Kline, Patrick, Petkova, Neviana, Williams, Heidi, and Zidar, Owen, (2019), Who profits from patents? Rent-sharing at innovative firms, *Quarterly Journal of Economics,* 134(3): 1343–1404.

Knight, Carly, Dobbin, Frank, and Kalev, Alexandra, (2022), Under the radar: Visibility and the effects of discrimination lawsuits in small and large firms, *American Sociological Review*, 87(2): 175–201.

Kogan, Leonid, Papanikolaou, Dimitris, Seru, Amit, and Stoffman, Noah, (2017), Technological innovation, resource allocation, and growth, *Quarterly Journal of Economics*, 132(2): 665–712.

Kogut, Bruce, and Muir, Macpherson, J., (2011), The mobility of economists and the diffusion of policy ideas: The influence of economics on national policies, *Research Policy*, 40: 1307–1320.

Kovvali, Aneil, (2023), Stark choices for corporate reform, *Columbia Law Review*, 123(3): 693–760.

Krawiec, Kimberly D., (2013), Don't 'screw Joe the Plummer': The sausage-making of financial reform, *Arizona Law Review*, 55: 53–103.

Kronman, Anthony T., (1983), Paternalism and the law of contracts, *The Yale Law Journal*, 92(5): 763–798.

Lambert, Thomas E., (2019), Monopoly capital and entrepreneurship: Whither small business? *Cambridge Journal of Economics*, 43(6): 1577–1595.

Lane, Tom, Nosenzo, Daniele, and Sonderegger, Silvia, (2023), Law and norms: Empirical evidence, *American Economic Review*, 113(5): 1255–1293.

Lazonick, William, and Mazzucato, Mariana, (2013), The risk-reward nexus in the innovation-inequality relationship: Who takes the risks? Who gets the rewards? *Industrial and Corporate Change*, 22(4): 1093–1128.

Lemley, Mark A., (2004), Ex ante versus ex post justifications for intellectual property, *University of Chicago Law Review*, 71(1): 129–150.

Lemley, Mark A., (2015), Faith-based intellectual property, *UCLA Law Review*, 62(5): 1328–1347.

Lemley, Mark A., (2016a), Ready for patenting, *Boston University law Review*, 96: 1171–1195.

Lemley, Mark A., (2016b), The surprising resilience of the patent system, *Texas Law Review*, 95(1): 1–58.

Lemley, Mark A., and Melamed, A. Douglas, (2013), Missing the forest for the trolls, *Columbia Law Review*, 113(8): 2117–2190.

Lemley, Mark A., and Sherkow, Jacob S., (2023), The antibody patent paradox, *Yale Law Journal*, 132(4): 994–1064.

Lépinay, Vincent Antonin, (2011), *Codes of finance: Engineering derivatives in a global bank*, Princeton: Princeton University Press.

Levine, Michael E., and Forrence, Jennifer L., (1990), Regulatory capture, public interest, and the public agenda: Toward a synthesis, *Journal of Law, Economics, & Organization*, 6: 167–198.

Levitin, Adam J., (2011), In defense of bailouts, *Georgetown University Law Review*, 99: 435–514.

Levy, Jay, and Jakobsson, Pye, (2014), Sweden's abolitionist discourse and law: Effects on the dynamics of Swedish sex work and on the lives of Sweden's sex workers, *Criminology & Criminal Justice*, 14(5): 593–607.

Lexchin, Joel, (2006), The pharmaceutical industry and the pursuit of profit, in Cohen, Jillian Clare, Illingworth, Patricia, and Schüklenk, Udo, (eds.) *The power of pill: Social, ethical and legal issues in drugs development, marketing, pricing*, London & Ann Arbor: Pluto, pp. 11–24.

Lifshitz, Shafar, and Finkelstein, Elad, (2017), A hermeneutic perspective on the interpretation of contracts, *American Business Law Journal*, 54(3): 519–579.
Light, Donald W., and Warburton, Rebecca, (2011), Demythologizing the high costs of pharmaceutical research, *BioSocieties*, 6(1): 34–50.
Liscow, Zachary, (2014), Reducing inequality on the cheap: When legal rule design should incorporate equity as well as efficiency, *Yale Law Journal*, 123: 2478–2511.
Listokin, Yair, and Murphy, Daniel, (2019), Macroeconomics and the law, *Annual Review of Law and Social Science*, 15: 377–396.
Liu, Glory M., (2022), *Adam's Smith America: How Scottish philosopher became an icon of American capitalism*, Princeton: Princeton University Press.
Lock, Margaret, (2002), *Twice dead: Organ transplants and the reinvention of death*, Berkeley, Los Angeles & London: University of California Press.
LoPucki, Lynn M., (1996), The death of liability, *Yale Law Journal*, 106(1): 1–92.
LoPucki, Lynn M., (1997), The systems approach to law, *Cornell Law Review*, 82(3): 479–522.
LoPucki, Lynn M., (2022), Chapter 11's descent into lawlessness, *American Bankruptcy Law Journal*, 96(2): 247–310.
Lucas, David S., Grimes, Matthew G., and Gehman, Joel, (2022), Remaking capitalism: The strength of weak legislation in mobilizing B corporation certification, *Academy of Management Journal*, 65(3): 958–987.
Lund, Dorothy S., (2022), Asset managers as regulators, *University of Pennsylvania Law Review*, 171(1): 77–146.
Lund, Dorothy S., and Pollman, Elizabeth, (2021), The corporate governance machine, *Columbia Law Review*, 121(8): 2563–2634.
Luther, Jeffrey, (2020), Twenty-first century financial regulation: P2P lending, fintech, and the argument for a special purpose fintech charter approach, *University of Pennsylvania Law Review*, 168(4): 1013–1059.
Ma, Song, Tong, Joy Tianjiao, and Wang, Wei, (2022), Bankrupt innovative firms, *Management Science*, 68(9): 6971–6992.
Machlup, Fritz, and Penrose, Edith, (1950), The patent controversy in the nineteenth century, *The Journal of Economic History*, 10(1): 1–29.
Mackie, John L., (1978), Can there be a right-based moral theory? *Midwest Studies in Philosophy*, 3(1): 350–359.
Mackie, John L., (2013), The subjectivity of values, in Shafer-Landau, Russ, (ed.) *Ethical theory: An anthology*, New York: Wiley, pp. 22–30.
MacLeod, Christine, (2002), *Inventing the industrial revolution: The English patent system, 1660–1800*, Cambridge: Cambridge University Press.
Magnuson, William, (2018), Regulating fintech, *Vanderbilt Law Review*, 71: 1167–1126.
Mann, William, (2018), Creditor rights and innovation: Evidence from patent collateral, *Journal of Financial Economics*, 130(1): 25–47.
Marwell, Nicole P., (2004), Privatizing the welfare state: Nonprofit community-based organizations as political actors, *American Sociological Review*, 69(2): 265–291.
Masterman, Clayton J., (2016), The customer is not always right: Balancing worker and customer welfare in antitrust law, *Vanderbilt Law Review*, 69: 1387–1422.
Mayer, Kyle J., and Argyres, Nicholas S., (2004), Learning to contract: Evidence from the personal computer industry, *Organization Science*, 15: 394–410.
McGoey, Linsey, (2021), Philanthrocapitalism and the separation of powers, *Annual Review of Law and Social Science*, 17: 391–409.
Mehrpouya, Afshin, and Salles-Djelic, Marie-Laure, (2019), Seeing like the market; exploring the mutual rise of transparency and accounting in transnational

economic and market governance, *Accounting, Organizations, and Society*, 76: 12–31.

Merriman, Ben, and Pacewicz, Josh, (2022), The great interstate divergence: Partisan bureaucracies in the contemporary United States, *American Journal of Sociology*, 127(4): 1221–1266.

Merton, Robert C., (1987), A simple model of capital market equilibrium with incomplete information, *Journal of Finance*, 42(3): 483–510.

Merton, Robert K., (1957), *Social theory and social structure*, Glencoe: Free Press.

Meyer, John W., and Rowan, Brian, (1977), Institutionalizing organizations: Formal structure as myth and ceremony, *American Journal of Sociology*, 83(2): 340–363.

Mirowski, Philip, and Van Horn, Robert, (2005), The contract research organization and the commercialization of scientific research, *Social Studies of Science*, 35(4): 503–548.

Montesquieu, Charles-Louis de Secondat, (1788a), *De l'espirit des loix: Oeuvres de Montesquieu*, Tome Deuxième, Paris: Jean-Françoise Bastien.

Montesquieu, Charles-Louis de Secondat, (1788b), *De l'epsirit des loix: Oeuvres de Montesquieu*, Tome Troisième, Paris: Jean-Françoise Bastien.

Moore, Kimberly A., (2005), Worthless patents. *Berkeley Technology Law Journal*, 20(4): 1521–1552.

Morten, Christopher J., (2023), Publicizing corporate secrets, *University of Pennsylvania Law Review*, 177(5): 1319–1404.

Moser, Petra, (2016), Patents and innovation in economic history, *Annual Review of Economics*, 8: 241–258.

Mowery, David C., (2009), *Plus ça change*: Industrial R&D in the 'third industrial revolution', *Industrial and Corporate Change*, 18(1): 1–50.

Muniesa, Fabian, (2017), On the political vernaculars of value creation, *Science as Culture*, 26(4): 445–454.

Muniesa, Fabian, (2022), Paranoid finance, *Social Research: An International Quarterly*, 89(3): 731–756.

Naczyk, Marek, (2013), Agents of privatization? Business groups and the rise of pension funds in continental Europe, *Socio-Economic Review*, 11(3): 441–469.

Naidu, Suresh, Posner, Eric A., and Weyl, Glen, (2018), Antitrust remedies for labor market power, *Harvard Law Review*, 132: 536–601.

Naudé, Wim, (2022), From the entrepreneurial to the ossified economy, *Cambridge Journal of Economics*, 46(1): 105–131.

Nelson, Richard R., (2022), The economic system question revisited, *Industrial and Corporate Change*, 31(3): 591–609.

Nguyen, Xuan-Thao, (2021), Promoting corporate irresponsibility? Delaware as the intellectual property holding state, *Journal of Corporation Law*, 46(3): 717–750.

Nyarko, Julian, (2021), Stickiness and incomplete contracts, *University of Chicago Law Review*, 88(1): 1–80.

Nye, David E., (2006), *Technology matters: Questions to live with*, Cambridge & London: The MIT Press.

Oberman, Michelle, Wolf, Leslie, and Zettler, Patti, (2010), Where stem cell research meets abortion politics: Limits on buying and selling human oocytes, in Goodwin, Michele Bratcher, (ed.) *Baby markets: Money and the new politics of creating families*, Cambridge & New York: Cambridge University Press, pp. 251–264.

Ohlhausen, Maureen K., (2016), Patent rights in a climate of intellectual property rights skepticism, *Harvard Journal of Law & Technology*, 30(1): 103–152.

Olson, Mancur, (1965), *The logic of collective action*, Cambridge: Harvard university Press.

Omarova, Saule T., (2012), Bankers, bureaucrats, and guardians: Toward tripartism in financial services regulation. *Journal of Corporation Law*, 37(3): 621–674.
Omarova, Saule T., (2019), New tech v. new deal: Fintech as systemic phenomenon, *Yale Journal on Regulation*, 36(2): 735–794.
Omarova, Saule T., (2020), Technology v technocracy: Fintech as a regulatory challenge, *Journal of Financial Regulation*, 6(1): 75–124.
Ortiz, Horacio, (2014), The limits of financial imagination: Free investors, efficient markets and crisis, *American Anthropologist*, 116(1): 38–50.
Ouellette, Lisa Larrimore, (2012), Do patents disclose useful information, *Harvard Journal of Law & Technology*, 25(2): 545–608.
Pagano, Udo, (2014), The crisis of intellectual monopoly capitalism, *Cambridge Journal of Economics*, 38(6): 1409–1429.
Pagano, Ugo, and Rossi, Maria Alessandra, (2009), The crash of the knowledge economy, *Cambridge Journal of Economics*, 33(4): 665–683.
Palan, Ronen, Murphy, Richard, and Chavagneux, Christian, (2010), *Tax havens: How globalization really works*, Ithaca: Cornell University Press.
Palmer, Tom G., (1990), Are patents and copyrights morally justified the philosophy of property rights and ideal objects, *Harvard Journal of Law & Public Policy*, 13(3): 817–866.
Pansera, Mario, and Fressoli, Mariano, (2021), Innovation without growth: Frameworks for understanding technological change in a post-growth era, *Organization*, 28(3): 380–404.
Pargendler, Mariana, (2021), Veil peeking: The corporation as a nexus for regulation, *University of Pennsylvania Law Review*, 169(3): 717–782.
Parikh, Samir D., (2023), Financial disequilibrium, *University of Pennsylvania Law Review*, 177(7): 1925–1973.
Patterson, Mark R., (2016), *Antitrust law in the new economy: Google, Yelp, LIBOR, and the control of information*, Cambridge & London: Harvard University Press.
Paul, Kari, (2022), Theranos founder Elizabeth Holmes sentenced to more than 11 years for defrauding investors, *The Guardian*, November 18, 2022, (URL: https://www.theguardian.com/us-news/2022/nov/18/elizabeth-holmes-theranos-trial-sentencing) Accessed Dec. 1, 2022.
Paul, Sanjukta, (2021), Recovering the moral economy foundations of the Sherman Act, *Yale Law Journal*, 131(1): 175–255.
Pedriana, Nicholas, and Stryker, Robin, (2004), The strength of a weak agency: Enforcement of title VII of the 1964 civil rights act and the expansion of state capacity, 1965–1971, *American Journal of Sociology*, 110(3): 709–760.
Perrow, Charles, and Guillén, Mauro F., (1990), *The AIDS disaster: The failure of organizations in New York and the nation*, New Haven: Yale University Press.
Philippon, Thomas, (2019), *The great reversal: How America gave up on free markets*, Cambridge: Belknap Press.
Philips, Damon J., (2005), Organizational genealogies and the persistence of gender inequality: The case of Silicon Valley law firms, *Administrative Science Quarterly*, 50: 440–472.
Pinzur, David, (2021), Infrastructure, ontology and meaning: The endogenous development of economic ideas, *Social Studies of Science*, 51(6): 914–937.
Pistor, Katharina, (2019), *The code of capital. How the law creates wealth and inequality*, Princeton: Princeton University Press.
Pistor, Katharina, (2020), The value of law, *Theory and Society*, 49(1): 165–186.

Pistor, Katharina, (2022), Legal coding beyond capital? *European Law Open*, 1(2): 344–350.
Pollman, Elizabeth, (2019a), Corporate disobedience, *Duke Law Journal*, 68(4): 709–766.
Pollman, Elizabeth, (2019b), Startup governance, *University of Pennsylvania Law Review*, 168(1): 155–221.
Pollman, Elizabeth, and Barry, Jordan M., (2017), Regulatory entrepreneurship, *Southern California Law Review*, 90: 383–448.
Posner, Eric A., (1996), Law, economics, and inefficient norms, *University of Pennsylvania Law Review*, 144(5): 1697–1744.
Pottage, Alain, and Biagioli, Mario, (2023), What is a book? Kant and the law of the letter, *Critical Inquiry*, 49(1): 605–625.
Pound, Roscoe, (1910), Law in books and law in action, *American Law Review*, 44: 22–36.
Powell, Walter W., and Snellman, Kaisa, (2004), The knowledge economy, *Annual Review of Sociology*, 30: 199–220.
Price, W. Nicholson II, and Rai, Arti K., (2016), Manufacturing barriers to biologics competition and innovation, *Iowa Law Review*, 101(3): 1023–1064.
Quack, Sigrid, (2007), Legal professionals and transnational law-making: A case of distributed agency, *Organization*, 14(5): 643–666.
Ramanna, Karthik, (2020), Friedman at 50: Is it still the social responsibility of business to increase profits? *California Management Review*, 62(3): 28–41.
Rawls, John, (1958), Justice as fairness, *Philosophical Review*, 67(2): 164–194.
Rawls, John, ([1971] 1999), *A theory of justice*, Oxford & New York: Oxford University Press.
Rawls, John, (1985), Justice as fairness: Political not metaphysical, *Philosophy and Public Affairs*, 14(3): 223–251.
Reddy, Diana S., (2023), After the law of apolitical economy: Reclaiming the normative stakes of labor unions, *Yale Law Journal*, 132(5): 1391–1461.
Regan, Milton, and Hall, Kath, (2016), Lawyers in the shadow of the regulatory state: Transnational governance on business and human rights, *Fordham Law Review*, 84: 2001–2037.
Reinecke, Juliane, (2010), Beyond a subjective theory of value and towards a 'fair price': An organizational perspective on Fairtrade minimum price setting, *Organization*, 17(5): 563–581.
Reinhart, Carmen M., and Rogoff, Kenneth S., (2009), *This time is different: Eight centuries of financial folly*, Princeton & Oxford: Princeton University Press.
Reyes, Carla L., (2021), A unified theory of code-connected contracts, *Journal of Corporation Law*, 46(4): 981–1001.
Richard, R. John, and Phillips-Fein, Kim, (2017), *Capital gains: Business and politics in twentieth-century America*, Philadelphia: University of Pennsylvania Press.
Richard, R. John, and Smith, Jason Scott, (2017), Beyond the new deal: Thomas McCraw and the political economy of capitalism, in Richard, R. John, and Phillips-Fein, Kim, (eds.) *Capital gains: Business and politics in twentieth-century America*, Philadelphia, PA: University of Pennsylvania Press, pp. 94–116.
Ricks, Morgan, (2011), Regulating money creation after the crisis, *Harvard Business Law Review*, 1: 75–143.
Ridgeway, Cecilia L., Li, Yan E., Erickson, Kristan G., Backor, Kristen, and Tinkler, Justine E., (2009), How easily does a social difference become a status distinction? Gender matters, *American Sociological Review*, 74(1): 44–62.

Riles, Annelise, (2011), *Collateral knowledge: Legal reasoning in the global financial markets*, Chicago: The University of Chicago Press.
Rivera, Lauren A., and Tilcsik, András, (2016), Class advantage, commitment penalty: The gendered effect of social class signals in an elite labor market, *American Sociological Review*, 81(6): 1097–1131.
Robins-Early, Nick, (2024), 'He knew it was wrong': Sam Bankman-Fried sentenced to 25 years in prison over FTX fraud, *The Guardian*, March 28, 2024 (URL: https://www.theguardian.com/business/2024/mar/28/sam-bankman-fried-sentenced-prison-ftx-fraud). Accessed April 29, 2024.
Rock, Edward B., (2021), For whom is the corporation managed in 2020? The debate over corporate purpose, *Business Lawyer*, 76(2): 363–395.
Rodrik, Dani, Subramanian, Arvind, and Trebbi, Francesco, (2004), Institutions rule: The primacy of institutions over geography and integration in economic development, *Journal of Economic Growth*, 9(2): 131–165.
Roe, Mark J., and Roy, Shapira, (2021), The power of the narrative in corporate lawmaking, *Harvard Business Law Review*, 11(2): 233–278.
Rogal, Lauren, (2021), Secrets, lies, and lessons from the Theranos scandal, *Hastings Law Journal*, 72(6): 1663–1702.
Romano, Roberta, (2005), The Sarbanes-Oxley act and the making of quack corporate governance, *Yale Law Journal*, 114: 1521–1611.
Romer, Paul M., (1990), Endogenous technological change, *Journal of Political Economy*, 98(5): S71–102.
Rorty, Richard, (1980), *Philosophy and the mirror of nature*, Cambridge: Cambridge University Press.
Rosa, Hartmut, Dörre, Klaus, and Lessenich, Stephan, (2017), Appropriation, activation, and acceleration: The escalatory logics of capitalist modernity and the crises of dynamic stabilization, *Theory, Culture, and Society*, 34(1): 53–73.
Rosenblat, Alex, (2018), *Uberland: How algorithms are rewriting the rules of work*, Oakland: University of California Press.
Rushe, Dominic, (2022a), New FTX boss, who worked on Enron bankruptcy, condemns 'unprecedented failure', *The Guardian*, November 17, 2022, (URL: https://www.theguardian.com/technology/2022/nov/17/ftx-enron-crypto-collapse-john-ray-unprecedented) Accessed Dec. 1, 2022.
Rushe, Dominic, (2022b), FTX was run as 'personal fiefdom' of Sam Bankman-Fried, court hears, *The Guardian*, November 22, 2022, (URL: https://www.theguardian.com/technology/2022/nov/22/ftx-delaware-bankruptcy-court-cryptocurrency-sam-bankman-fried) Accessed Dec. 1, 2022.
Safari, Arsalan, (2017), Worldwide venture capital, intellectual property rights, and innovation, *Industrial and Corporate Change*, 26(3): 485–515.
Sahlins, Marshall, (1972), *Stone age economics*, Chicago & New York: Aldine-Atherton.
Schaefer, Alexander, (2023), Is justice a fixed point? *American Journal of Political Science*, 67(2): 277–290.
Scheiring, Gábor, and King, Lawrence, (2023), Deindustrialization, social disintegration, and health: A neoclassical sociological approach, *Theory and Society*, 52(1): 145–178.
Schneiberg, Marc, and Bartley, Tim, (2001), Regulating American industries: Markets, politics, and the institutional determinants of fire insurance regulation, *American Journal of Sociology*, 107(1): 101–146.
Schumpeter, Joseph A., (1928), The instability of capitalism, *Economic Journal*, 38: 361–386.
Schumpeter, J. A., (1939), *Business cycles*, Vol. 1, New York: McGraw-Hill.

Schwarcz, Steven L. L., (2002), Private ordering, *Northwestern University Law Review*, 97(1): 319–349.
Schwartz, Herman Mark, (2016), Wealth and secular stagnation: The role of industrial organization and intellectual property rights, *RSF: The Russell Sage Foundation Journal of the Social Sciences*, 2(6): 226–249.
Sellars, Wilfrid, (1956), Empiricism and the philosophy of mind, *Minnesota Studies in the Philosophy of Science*, 1(19): 253–329.
Selznick, Philip, (1948), Foundations of the theory of organization, *American Sociological Review*, 13(1): 25–35.
Selznick, Philip, (1949), *TVA and the grassroots*, Berkeley: University of California Press.
Seymour, Jonathan M., (2022), Against bankruptcy exceptionalism, *University of Chicago Law Review*, 89(8): 1925–2012.
Shaffer, Gregory, (2009), How business shapes law: A socio-legal framework, *Connecticut Law Review*, 42(1): 147–183.
Sharp, Lesley A., (2003), *Strange harvest: Organ transplants, denatured bodies, and the transformed self*, Berkeley, Los Angeles & Oxford: University of California Press.
Shrestha, Sannu K., (2010), Trolls or market-makers: An empirical analysis of non-practicing entities, *Columbia Law Review*, 110(1): 114–160.
Simon, Lindsey D., (2022), Bankruptcy grifters, *Yale Law Journal*, 131(4): 1154–1216.
Singh, Jagdip, and Jayanti, Rama K., (2013), When institutional work backfires: Organizational control of professional work in the pharmaceutical industry, *Journal of Management Studies*, 50(5): 900–929.
Skaggs, Sheryl, (2009), Legal-political pressures and African American access to managerial jobs, *American Sociological Review*, 74(2): 225–244.
Skeel, David A., (2020), Distorted choice in corporate bankruptcy, *Yale Law Journal*, 130(2): 366–426.
Skeel, David A., (2023), Bankruptcy's identity crisis, *University of Pennsylvania Law Review*, 177(7): 2097–2128.
Slaughter, Sheila, and Leslie, Larry L., (1997), *Academic capitalism: Politics, policies, and the entrepreneurial university*, Baltimore & London: The Johns Hopkins University Press.
Smith, Edward Bishop, and Gai, Shelby L., (2017), Institutional interruption: A relational account of the growth and decline of product heterogeneity in the global hedge fund industry, *Industrial and Corporate Change*, 26(6): 1039–1066.
Snellman, Kaisa, and Solal, Isabelle, (2023), Does investor gender matter for the success of female entrepreneurs? Gender homophily and the stigma of incompetence in entrepreneurial finance, *Organization Science*, 34(2): 680–699.
Soener, Matthew, and Nau, Michael, (2019), Citadels of privilege: The rise of LLCs, LPs and the perpetuation of elite power in America, *Economy and Society*, 48(3): 399–425.
Somaya, Deepak, (2012), Patent strategy and management: An integrative review and research agenda, *Journal of Management*, 38(4): 1084–1114.
Sørensen, Morten, (2007), How smart is smart money? A two-sided matching model of venture capital, *Journal of Finance*, 62(6): 2725–2762.
Spears, Taylor, (2019), Discounting collateral: Quants, derivatives and the reconstruction of the 'risk-free rate' after the financial crisis, *Economy and Society*, 48(3): 342–370. DOI: 10.1080/03085147.2018.1525153
Stern, Philip J., (2023), *Empire, incorporated: The corporations that built British colonialism*, Cambridge: The Belknap Press of Harvard University Press.

Stiglitz, Joseph E., (2008), Economic foundations of intellectual property rights, *Duke Law Journal*, 57(6): 1693–1724.

Strathern, Marilyn, (2004), Losing (out on) intellectual resources, in Pottage, Alain, and Mundy, Martha, (eds.) *Law, anthropology and the constitution of the social*, Cambridge: Cambridge University Press, pp. 201–233.

Styhre, Alexander, (2020), *The institutional theory of the firm: Embedded autonomy*, New York & London: Routledge.

Styhre, Alexander, and Arman, Rebecka, (2016), *Institutionalizing assisted reproductive technologies: The role of science, professionalism, and regulatory control*, New York & London: Routledge.

Sullivan, Richard J., (1990), The revolution of ideas: Widespread patenting and invention during the English industrial revolution, *The Journal of Economic History*, 50(2): 349–362.

Sunder Rajan, Kaushik, (2012), Introduction. The capitalization of life and the liveliness of capital, in Sunder Rajan, Kaushik, (ed.) *Lively capital*, Durham & London: Duke University Press, pp. 1–41.

Sunstein, Cass R., (1996), On the expressive function of law, *University of Pennsylvania Law Review*, 144(5): 2021–2053.

Sutton, John R., and Dobbin, Frank, (1996), Two faces of governance: Responses to legal uncertainty in U.S. firms, 1955–1985, *American Sociological Review*, 61(5): 794–811.

Tait, Allison Anna, (2019), The law of high-wealth exceptionalism, *Alabama Law Review*, 71: 981–1038.

Tantri, Prasanna, (2021), Fintech for the poor: Financial intermediation without discrimination, *Review of Finance*, 25(2): 561–593.

Thelen, Kathleen, (2018), Regulating Uber: The politics of the platform economy in Europe and the United States, *Perspectives on Politics*, 16(4): 938–953.

Thörn, Catharina, and Thörn, Håkan, (2017), Swedish cities now belong to the most segregated in Europe, *Sociologisk Forskning*, 54(4): 293–296.

Thrift, Nigel, (2005), *Knowing capitalism*, London, Thousand Oaks & New Delhi: Sage.

Tingle, Bryce C., (2023), Returning markets to the center of corporate law, *Journal of Corporation Law*, 48(4): 663–718.

Topol, Eric, (2018), Blood, sweat and tears in biotech—the Theranos story, *Nature*, 557(7706): 306–308.

Travis, Adam, (2019), The organization of neglect: Limited liability companies and housing disinvestment, *American Sociological Review*, 84(1): 142–170.

Tucker, Paul, (2018), *Unelected power: The quest for legitimacy in central banking and the regulatory state*, Princeton: Princeton University Press.

Tyler, Charles, and Gerken, Heather, (2022), The myth of the laboratories of democracy, *Columbia Law Review*, 122(8): 2187–2240.

Vaheesan, Sandeep, (2018), Accommodating capital and policing labor: Antitrust in the two gilded ages, *Maryland Law Review*, 78(4): 766–827.

Vallas, Steven Peter, and Kleinman, Daniel L., (2008), Contradiction, convergence and the knowledge economy: The confluence of academic and industrial biotechnology, *Socio-Economic Review*, 6(2): 283–311.

Van Loo, Rory, (2020), The new gatekeepers: Private firms as public enforcers, *Virginia Law Review*, 106(2): 467–522.

Veblen, Thorstein, (1916), *The industry systems and the captains of industry*, New York: Oriole Chapbooks.

Vertommen, Sigrid, Pavone, Vincenzo, and Nahman, Michal, (2022), Global fertility chains: An integrative political economy approach to understanding the reproductive bioeconomy, *Science, Technology, & Human Values*, 47(1): 112–145.

Wacquant, Loïc J. D., (2009), *Punishing the poor: The neoliberal government of social insecurity*, Durham & London: Duke University Press.

Waldron, Jeremy, (1992), From authors to copiers: Individual rights and social values in intellectual property, *Chicago-Kent Law Review*, 68: 841–887.

Wu, Tim, (2018), *The curse of bigness: Antitrust in the new Gilded Age*, New York: Columbia Global Reports.

Weick, Karl E., (1976), Educational organizations as loosely coupled systems, *Administrative Science Quarterly*, 21: 1–19.

White, Lawrence J., (2013), Credit rating agencies: An overview, *Annual Review in Financial Economics*, 5: 93–122.

Wolfson, Martin H., and Epstein, Gerald, A. (eds.), (2013), *Handbook of the political economy of financial crises*, New York & Oxford: Oxford University Press.

Young, Charlotte R., (2018), A lawyer's divorce: Will decentralized ledgers and smart contracts succeed in cutting out the middleman, *Washington University Law Review*, 96: 649–679.

Zacka, Bernardo, (2022), Political theory rediscovers public administration, *Annual Review of Political Science*, 25: 25–42.

Zhang, Letian, (2022), Regulatory spillover and workplace racial inequality, *Administrative Science Quarterly*, 67(3): 595–629.

Zhang, Victoria, Mohliver, Aharon Cohen, and King, Marissa, (2022), Where is all the deviance? Liminal prescribing and the social networks underlying the prescription drug crisis, *Administrative Science Quarterly*, 68(1): 228–269.

Index